Books by Co

M000205926

The
⊷ **BOOKS** ⊶
in My Life

Colin Wilson

HAMPTON ROADS
PUBLISHING COMPANY, INC.

Cover design by Mayapria Long
Cover art by Frank Riccio

For information write:
Hampton Roads Publishing Company, Inc.
134 Burgess Lane
Charlottesville, VA 22902

Or call: 804-296-2772
FAX: 804-296-5096
e-mail: hrpc@hrpub.com
www.hrpub.com

If you are unable to order this book from your local
bookseller, you may order directly from the publisher.
Quantity discounts for organizations are available.
Call 1-800-766-8009, toll-free.

Library of Congress Catalog Card Number: 98-71595

ISBN 1-57174-111-9

10 9 8 7 6 5 4 3 2 1

Printed on acid-free paper Canada

DEDICATION

To Frank DeMarco, with affection

CONTENTS

1

How Many Books is Too Many?

In 1950, at the suggestion of a librarian from Los Angeles, Henry Miller began to make a list of the hundred books that had influenced him most. As usual, he got carried away, and ended by writing a 300-page volume, *The Books in My Life*. Moreover, in his preface, he explained that "this book will run to several volumes in the course of the next few years." (In fact, the rest never got written.)

I can understand why he felt that it would take several volumes. When I began to make a list of the books that had influenced me most, I expected it to run to twenty or so—on each of which I intended to write an essay of perhaps a dozen pages. In fact, before I could pause for breath, my list had already reached fifty. And it was obvious that without much effort, I could add another fifty. That would make a book of twelve hundred pages. Clearly, I shall have to exercise the utmost self-discipline.

I have always been something of an obsessive about books—which is why the house in which I live contains between twenty and thirty thousand of them. Every room is lined with bookshelves, so that there is no more space for more. There are roughly the same number of long-playing records, as well as a few hundred compact discs—even videotapes are now posing a major storage problem. When we ran out of wall space, we began to erect sheds in the garden—three so far.

1

When I show visitors around my books, they never fail to ask me, "Have you read them all?" and I explain that many of them are bought for reference purposes, since I live so far from a public library, and that others have been bought with the intention of reading them when I have time (like the set of Sir Walter Scott, which still remains unread). But the truth is that I have read most of them.

Which means that, in theory, a work about the books in my life could easily run to several volumes.

Let me explain how this absurd situation came about.

Forty years ago, my wife—Joy—and I were living in a tiny cottage near the sea. We had fled to Cornwall from London, and from the notoriety that had followed the success of my first book, *The Outsider*. The poet from whom we rented it worked for a publisher in London, and dreamed of returning one day to his beloved Cornwall. He agreed to let the cottage to us on a two year lease, and if, at the end of two years, he was still unable to return, then we could rent it for another two years.

It was an Elizabethan cottage, whose walls were made of cob—a kind of mud—and were two feet thick. A stream ran close to its front door, filling the air with a continual sound of running water. Cows grazed in the field on the opposite hillside, and beyond them were the cliffs and the sea, looking across towards France.

I immediately built a large bookshelf in the sitting room, and filled it with the books I had brought from London.

I also had about two hundred gramophone records. The long-playing record had been invented less than a decade earlier, and one of the first things I did with the first royalties on *The Outsider* was to buy myself a gramophone, and records of my favorite music—the symphonies of Brahms, Bruckner and Mahler; Beethoven quartets and piano sonatas; Wagner's *Valkyrie* and *Götterdammerung*. Our cottage had no electricity supply—being more than a mile from the main road—but we installed a dozen car batteries, a "converter" to turn direct current into alternating current, and a dynamo to charge the batteries.

It was a relief to live in the country. After the initial success of *The Outsider*, the atmosphere had soured. The book had been reviewed on the same day as John Osborne's first play *Look Back in Anger*, and the popular press had decided to label us "Angry Young Men." As far as I was concerned, the term was absurdly inappropriate. I had nothing in common with Osborne, or with novelists like Kingsley Amis and

John Wain. I regarded myself as a writer of ideas, working in the same European tradition as Sartre and Camus. But in England there is no tradition of interest in ideas. The success of *The Outsider* had been a kind of fluke, and by the time we moved to Cornwall, nine months later, I had already become aware that—as far as my own country was concerned—I was working in a vacuum. Forty years later, I still feel that nothing has changed—in England I seem doomed to remain an "outsider."

We had been in the cottage for two years when, in the spring of 1959, we heard rumors that our landlord wanted to return there. We wrote and asked him if this was true. Being a poet, he was too lazy to reply. I was writing my novel *Ritual in the Dark*, about a sex killer based on Jack the Ripper. So Joy went off to see if she could find us another place to live.

She returned in the late afternoon, and said that she had been looking at a house in the next village. She had seen a "For Sale" notice at the end of a small private lane, and had decided to walk up. Looking through the gate, she concluded that the house was too big for us. But just as she was about to turn away, she realized that someone was looking at her out of the window. She felt that it would be impolite to walk away, and went and knocked on the door. The owners invited her in for tea—an elderly couple from Brighton, who had retired to spend their declining years in the country, then found it too lonely, and decided to return to civilization.

Joy found them charming. But she still felt that the house was too big—and that it cost rather more than we could afford. (It cost £4,500—about $7,500—but this was about twice as much as most of the houses for sale at the local estate agent.)

When she told me it was too big, I said, "Good—lots of room for books." That evening we both went to see the house. It stood in a two-acre field, with no other houses in sight. Below us there were sloping fields, and beyond them, the sea. It was not an attractive house, having been built only six years earlier out of grey concrete blocks, and then painted a dull green. But, as Joy had said, it had plenty of space for books.

We had very little money—a year earlier, my second book, *Religion and the Rebel*, had been violently attacked by the critics, and had not reached a second printing. But we could probably raise a mortgage. I decided immediately that I would like to buy it.

So we did. We raised a mortgage, and moved in—together with my parents, whom I had invited to come and live with us. And I began to build bookshelves. Whenever we drove through some small town, we would find the secondhand bookshops, and drive away with the car packed with books. At first, there seemed to be so much wall space that the thought of filling the house seemed impossible. And when all the rooms filled up with bookcases, we built more shelves along the corridors, a few inches above the height of our heads. We even had a small porch built outside the front door, and filled it with bookshelves. Until one day we realized that there was simply no more room, not even in the kitchen, and that we would have to build a shed.

What kind of books did I buy? Anything on subjects that interested me. For example, I had always been interested in crime—ever since, as a child, I had read a book called *The Fifty Most Amazing Crimes in the Last Hundred Years*. Secondhand books were cheap—often as little as 2/6d (15¢) each. So I soon had shelves full of books on famous murder cases. I had always loved poetry—now I bought hundreds of volumes, from Chaucer and Milton to T. S. Eliot. I bought books on music, philosophy, biography, history, literary criticism, science, even mathematics. And, of course, fiction. In the nineteenth century, they loved to issue "complete sets"—Dickens, Sir Walter Scott, Landor, George Eliot, Trollope, Disraeli, Pater. And since modern houses do not have room for complete sets, they could be bought for as little as a single modern novel. Soon I had complete sets of all my favorite authors—like Dostoevsky and Tolstoy, Bernard Shaw and H. G. Wells—and also sets of authors I intended to read one day, like Carlyle and Ruskin.

Ever since I had been a child, I had loved to buy secondhand books. Now it was like the fulfillment of a dream. I bought as if I intended to live forever—not only books, but gramophone records of every kind of music from Beethoven to jazz. I think I had reached my mid-forties before I suddenly realized that I would never have time to read all the books or play all the records. I worked out that if I played records for ten hours a day, it would take ten years to play all of them. And yet whenever I read some critic praise the latest issue of Beethoven's Ninth Symphony or Strauss' Rosenkavalier, I was unable to resist the temptation to add it to my collection. I suppose this kind of enthusiasm counts as a mild form of insanity.

And so it came about that we live in a house with piles of books in corners and in the corridors, and huge piles of videotapes in the room we call the suntrap. Now I no longer read book reviews, because the temptation would be too great.

2

THE TRUTH
ABOUT WILSON

Although this obsession with books began fairly early, I was
not one of those children who learns to read at the age of
three or four. I have always had a tendency to devote effort
only to those things that arouse my enthusiasm. And as a child, these
were cakes, toys and comics—particularly the kind that featured
Mickey Mouse and Donald Duck. So although I learned the alphabet
in my first two years at school, I felt no impulse to decipher the words
in our spelling books. But I progressed to the point where I could read
the balloons that came out of the mouths of comic characters. Then I
tried deciphering a story with an interesting picture, and discovered to
my surprise that I could read all the words. I turned to another comic
weekly where the print was even smaller, and realized that I could read
this too. By the time I was about seven, I was reading the weekly
magazines intended for twelve year olds.

Two years later, by the age of nine or ten, in the early years of the
Second World War, I was an enthusiastic reader of a "boys'" paper
called the *Wizard*. It was one of five such magazines, each published
on a different day of the week—*Adventure* on Monday, the *Wizard* on
Tuesday, the *Rover* on Wednesday, *Hotspur* on Thursday, and *Skipper*
on Friday. But among schoolboys, the *Wizard* was the most highly
regarded. And this was due almost entirely to a series of stories called
The Truth about Wilson, followed a year or so later by a sequel. Every

6

Tuesday evening after school, I rushed to the local newsagent, paid my 2d (two pence), and began reading immediately as I walked home, raising my eyes only to look both ways at the street corner, to make sure I was not knocked down by a bus.

"At last," began the first episode, "I am able to tell *The Truth about Wilson*. No more sensational figure has appeared in sporting history. His name was on the lips of those who ordinarily had not the least interest in athletics. The photographs of this amazing man were published all over the world. Films in which he appeared flashed on the screens of cinemas from Melbourne to Valparaiso."

That first paragraph helps to explain why the story had such an appeal for its schoolboy readers: it assumed they were intelligent enough to have heard of Melbourne and Valparaiso. In fact, the whole serial was on an amazingly high intellectual level for a boys' paper—the apparent omniscience about sports meetings in different parts of the globe conveyed a powerful impression of authenticity. *The Truth about Wilson* addressed schoolboys as if they were adults.

But the real attraction of the story was, of course, the hero himself. It opens at an international sports meeting in which Britain has been losing most of the events. The loudspeakers announce the one-mile flat race. And just as the runners are crouching for the start, a strange figure climbs over the barrier and joins them. He has a thin face with deep-set eyes, and is wearing an old black running costume made of wool which stretches to his ankles; only his feet are bare. And as the officials are wondering whether to halt the race, the newcomer surges forward with a tremendous burst of speed, and quickly passes the rest of the competitors. Everyone waits breathlessly for him to collapse, convinced that no one could sustain this speed for more than a hundred yards. But he continues to run like a racehorse for lap after lap, completing the mile in three minutes and forty-eight seconds. As the crowd cheers itself hoarse, the black-clad runner collapses. The narrator, a sports reporter named Webb, is the first to reach him. The stranger opens his eyes and asks, "Did I run it in less than four minutes?" Webb says yes, and the stranger sighs with relief. He does not seem to care that he has won the race, only that he has broken the record.

In answer to questions he admits that his name is Wilson, but refuses to say any more. (In fact, we never learn his first name.) At this point, Wilson declares that he has to leave, and Webb offers him a lift. But when Webb stops the car to telephone his editor, Wilson disappears.

Fortunately, Webb finds Wilson's notebook in the car—it has fallen out of his pocket. It contains an address at a village called Stayling, in Yorkshire, and Webb drives up to see him. When he arrives, he learns that Wilson lives out on the moors—no one is certain where. And when Webb finally locates him, he discovers that Wilson has walked back to Yorkshire—over two hundred miles.

Now Webb learns why Wilson was so pleased to beat the world record. Nearly two hundred years earlier, a man named Nutsford, who lived in Stayling, had run the mile in three minutes and forty-eight seconds. This is the record Wilson was trying to beat.

In each of the episodes that follows, Wilson beats some new record—the long jump, the high jump, the pole vault, the hundred yards. He even beats the champion gypsy contender in a bare-fist boxing match. But in each case, we learn that he is doing it simply to break some past record that no one seems to know about. In one episode, he even beats the record running up the Great Pyramid.

In one of the final episodes, Wilson scales a tremendous cliff face in Switzerland—a climb that only one man has ever accomplished before: a mysterious Englishman in the nineteenth century. And when he learns that this man's name was also Wilson, Webb has a wild suspicion. "How old are you?" he asks Wilson. But before Wilson can answer, they are interrupted.

And in the final episode, Wilson tells his amazing story. He is nearly two hundred years old. When, in the early nineteenth century, some epidemic disease killed nearly everyone in Stayling, he began to brood on the problem of death, and the imperfection of the human body. "I became convinced that the body, if developed and treated properly, is a practically indestructible mechanism," he says. And so Wilson went to universities on the Continent and studied medicine and biology in an attempt to learn how to cheat death. Finally he discovered the secret—slowing down the body's metabolism by sheer willpower. His heartbeat is so slow that there is a pause between each pulse.

The story ends when Wilson joins the Royal Air Force, and is reported missing in action. But of course, every schoolboy knew that he was indestructible, and would be back again. In fact, he reappeared in at least one sequel, although I can no longer remember much about it.

The Truth about Wilson influenced me deeply. It seemed to me that Wilson was perfectly correct. There is no good reason why human beings should not learn to cheat death. And when, at the age of fifteen, I came across Bernard Shaw's *Man and Superman* and *Back to Methuselah*, I recognized immediately that Shaw was raising the same question. Among all the gloom and defeat that seems so typical of twentieth-century writing, Shaw alone had the courage to assert that man is potentially a god.

In 1958, two years after my first book, *The Outsider*, was published, I began to write a book about the pessimism that permeates modern literature. Of course, I understood precisely how this had come about. The great Romantics of the early nineteenth century had experienced moods of ecstasy in which they became convinced that man is potentially a god. Yet they were unable to sustain this ecstasy; it disappeared, leaving them feeling miserable and tired of life. This is why so many of these Romantics committed suicide, or died of discouragement. Writers of the early twentieth century—like T. S. Eliot and D. H. Lawrence—inherited this problem, but were unable to find any solution. And in due course their heirs—Sartre, Camus, Samuel Beckett, Graham Greene—came to take it for granted that human life is meaningless, and that (as Sartre said) "Man is a useless passion." And now, nearly half a century later, the pessimists still dominate modern literature—it would not be unfair to say that if a writer hopes to get the Nobel Prize, he must believe that human life is futile and tragic.

My book, *The Age of Defeat*, was an attack on this whole attitude. (In America it was called *The Stature of Man*, because my American publisher wanted an "upbeat" title.) And in the course of this book, I mentioned *The Truth about Wilson* as a powerful influence on my ideas. The result was a letter from someone who had worked for the publisher of the *Wizard*, enclosing several paperbacks, including *The Truth about Wilson*. He explained that all these stories had been the work of a team of writers, which included himself, and that he was delighted and flattered to read my complimentary reference to *The Truth about Wilson*.

I began rereading the book with some misgivings, convinced that I would find it disappointing. In fact, I was surprised to discover how good it was. Unlike the other stories written by the same team (with titles like *Killer Slade of the Pony Express* and *The Goalmaker*), it had pace, suspense and imagination.

I hasten to add that the style was atrocious. No one ever merely "says" something; instead it is "I gasped," "he groaned," "Wilson stated," "the boy declared eagerly." Yet in spite of all this, it has a quality of sheer inventiveness that I found very impressive.

Of course, the book also has its absurdities. When Wilson collapses, after running the mile in less than four minutes, is it likely that the assembled journalists would allow him to escape? He would be followed all the way back to Yorkshire by a cavalcade of cars. *The Truth about Wilson* operates on the same basic conventions as Superman or Batman: the superhero emerges from his anonymity whenever he feels like it, and is allowed to return to his mysterious hideout as soon as he has accomplished some amazing feat.

When I compare *The Truth about Wilson* with *Killer Slade of the Pony Express* and the other similar titles, I am reminded of Bram Stoker, who produced one single masterpiece—*Dracula*—and then followed it with several novels which are so bad that it is impossible to believe that they are by the same author. It seems almost as if the theme of vampirism inspired Stoker to produce a masterpiece, and that his flash of genius then simply deserted him.

Jung would certainly declare that the vampire is one of the "archetypes of the collective unconscious," and that the collective unconscious played some part in the inspiration of Dracula. But then, is not the superhero also one of the archetypes of the collective unconscious? And in that case, is it not also possible that the collective unconscious could "possess" a team of hack writers on a boys' paper, and produce a kind of masterpiece about an archetypal "superman"?

3

TOM SAWYER

When I was eleven, our literature class was issued copies of *Tom Sawyer*. Since I read anything I could lay my hands on, I took it home with me that same day, and began to read it on the bus. From the first page, where Aunt Polly catches Tom in the larder stealing jam, I was gripped. (My brother and I never missed an opportunity to raid the larder, although we were less interested in jam than in a sticky sweet substance called condensed milk.)

Even so, the first two chapters were like any normal boys' story. It was not until chapter 3, where Becky Thatcher is introduced, that I realized that this was far from the ordinary boys' story. The *Magnet* and the *Gem* never mentioned girls; and yet, ever since I had been in nursery school, girls had been a major fascination. I had no sisters, and I found them creatures of mystery. At the age of six, I sat next to a little girl called Hazel, and regarded her as delicious. Of course, I never betrayed any sign of my interest, for I had not the slightest idea of how to go about it. But in subsequent years I "fell in love" with a whole series of girls—I once compared lists with a friend of mine, and we discovered that each of us was in love with at least ten of our classmates.

When I went to see romantic films, I envied grown-ups, in whose world love and romance had their accepted place. I would have been quite prepared to get engaged at the age of seven, and frequently daydreamed of rescuing the object of my adoration from marauding

11

Red Indians. But although I fell in love at least once a week, I was not to have any kind of a girlfriend until I was about ten or eleven years old, and learned that I myself was admired from afar by a pretty little girl called Betty Kemp, who was a year my junior. We never did anything but play games together with other children, and exchange an occasional kiss behind a hedge; after awhile I realized that she was too young for me, and gave her up.

Mark Twain was the first writer I came across who made allowance for the intense romanticism that is inherent in all boys (and probably girls too).

"As he was passing by the house where Jeff Thatcher lived he saw a new girl in the garden—a lovely little blue-eyed creature with yellow hair plaited into two long tails, white summer frock and embroidered pantalettes. The fresh-crowned hero fell without firing a shot. A certain Amy Lawrence vanished out of his heart and left not even a memory of herself behind. He had thought he loved her to distraction, (he had regarded his passion as adoration); and behold it was only a poor little evanescent partiality. He had been months winning her; she had confessed hardly a week ago; he had been the happiest and the proudest boy in the world only seven short days, and here in one instant of time she had gone out of his heart like a casual stranger whose visit is done."

The only thing I could not understand about this was that Becky Thatcher displaced Amy Lawrence. I had room in my heart for a dozen little girls at a time, and my friends seemed much the same. I suspect all schoolboys are polygamous.

"He worshiped this new angel with a furtive eye till he saw that she had discovered him; then he pretended he did not know she was present, and began to 'show off' in all sorts of absurd boyish ways, in order to win her admiration. He kept up this grotesque foolishness for some time; but by and by, while he was in the midst of some dangerous gymnastic performance, he glanced aside and saw that the little girl was wending her way towards the house. . . But his face lit up, right away; for she tossed a pansy over the fence a moment before she disappeared."

The psychology was amazingly accurate—particularly the way that Tom edges towards the pansy until he can pick it up between his toes, then buttons it inside his jacket, next to his heart.

The same was true of the scene in which Tom's half-brother Sid breaks a sugar bowl, and Aunt Polly slaps Tom. When he shouts "Sid broke it" she stops, conscience stricken, and yearns to apologize—but feels that this would be losing face. So she says nothing, and Tom sits there, wallowing in self-pity, and imagines that he is dying, and that Aunt Polly is begging him for forgiveness, but he turns his face to the wall and dies without speaking. "How her tears would rain down on the poor little sufferer whose griefs were now at an end." Then, as he continues this delicious revery on a raft on the river, he thinks of how Becky Thatcher would feel to learn that he was dead. In the dark, he sneaks into her garden and lies under her window—until the maid servant empties a bucket of water over him.

No one, it seemed to me, had ever understood the mind of a boy so amazingly well, with his heroic fantasies and his daydreams in which the whole world glows with a soft melancholy.

In fact, the secret of the appeal of *Tom Sawyer* is that it is Tom's daydream; the kind of adventures that befall Tom are the kind that Mark Twain had once imagined for himself. When Becky accidentally tears the schoolmaster's book, and Tom takes the blame, and observes the gratitude and adoration in Becky's eyes, every small boy identifies with Tom, and drifts into a romantic daydream in which a pretty girl with blonde pigtails looks at him with adoring eyes. Moreover, Twain is quite ready to satisfy this daydream too, and when Becky whispers "I . . . love . . .you" in Tom's ear, and then allows him to kiss her lips, the climax is as satisfying as anything in the great romantic novelists.

But the schoolboy reader feels equally glad to cast himself as the hero of the episode where Tom releases a "pinchbug" in church during a boring sermon, and a small dog sits on it, and rushes, yelping with agony, up one aisle and down the other, while the members of the congregation do their best to hide tears of laughter behind handkerchiefs.

Twain loves these moments of slapstick—although they might cause an animal lover to wince—and the episode of the cat and the pain killer must have caused more shrieks of hysterical merriment than anything else in Twain's work. The pain killer, which Aunt Polly buys to treat Tom's melancholy when Becky stops coming to school, is "fire in liquid form," and when the cat begins to purr and beg for a taste, Tom finally pours a drop down its throat.

"Peter sprang a couple of yards in the air, and then delivered a war-whoop and set off round and round the room, banging against furniture, upsetting flower pots, and making general havoc. Aunt Polly entered to see him throw a few double somersaults, deliver a mighty final hurrah, and sail through the open window, carrying the rest of the flower pots with him."

But undoubtedly the most satisfying episode in the book is where Tom, deeply wounded by Becky's rejection, decides to run away with Joe Harper and Huck Finn and become a pirate on Jackson's Island. I dread to think how many boys have been inspired to run away from home by these three or four chapters—but then, fortunately, most boys do not live next to the Mississippi, or have rafts at their disposal.

The next morning, after taking a swim in the first sunlight and exploring the island, they hear the boom of a cannon being fired over the water, and realize that it is intended to bring a drowned corpse to the surface. Then Tom is struck by inspiration. "Boys, I know who's drownded—it's us!"

They spend several ecstatic days living on the island and catching fish for dinner, until Joe and Huck become homesick. Then Tom gets his greatest idea—they should attend their own funeral. And after the clergyman has delivered a discourse on the sweet and generous nature of the drowned boys, and the whole congregation is in tears, there is a creak from the church door, and the whole congregation stands up and stares as the dead boys march up the aisle. As Tom listens to the congregation singing a hymn of thanksgiving, he "confessed in his heart that this was the proudest moment of his life."

Equally satisfying is the murder trial of the village drunk, Muff Potter. Tom and Huck had been hiding in the graveyard when the doctor had arrived with Muff Potter and Injun Joe to practice a little grave robbing; a quarrel ensues, and Injun Joe kills the doctor, leaving the inebriated Muff to believe that he struck the blow. At the trial, Muff seems practically condemned until Tom is called as a witness, and tells his story. Before he has finished, Injun Joe has leapt out of the window. "Tom was a glittering hero once more—the pet of the old, the envy of the young . . . There were some that believed he would be President, yet, if he escaped hanging."

Fame—that was what the whole daydream was about. Only local fame, of course—but what did that matter when there were little girls like Becky Thatcher to gaze with adoring eyes.

The climax of the book is the episode in McDougal's Cave, where Tom and Becky get lost after a picnic, wandering around underground passages and finally losing themselves in its depths. For days they wander, and Becky gives up hope, and assumes she is going to die. At one point they encounter Injun Joe, who is fortunately more terrified than they are, and runs away. And finally, using a length of kite string as his guide, Tom explores various passages, and sees a tiny gleam of daylight. He goes back to Becky, who at first refuses to believe him; then they push their way out of the hole, and find themselves looking down on the Mississippi. Once again the town celebrates, and once again Tom is the hero.

Becky's father, Judge Thatcher, has the cave closed up with a massive door. And when, more than two weeks later, Tom remembers Injun Joe, the half-breed is found dead on the floor, his broken knife lying nearby.

I cannot remember how long I took to read *Tom Sawyer*, but it can scarcely have been more than twenty-four hours. It seemed to me far and away the best book I had ever read. Oddly enough, no one else in the class read it. And for some unknown reason, they decided to cancel it as a class book, and gave us *A Midsummer Night's Dream* instead, whose interest seemed to me minimal by comparison. I suspect that our literature teacher, Mr. Graves, read the book, and decided that it would be far too embarrassing to read aloud in class. On the whole, I am inclined to agree. *Tom Sawyer* is a book for a boy to read alone, in the privacy of his bedroom, or on the lawn on a summer afternoon.

When I learned there was a sequel called *Huckleberry Finn*, I inquired at the local library. Eventually, I found a copy by chance in another library, and found it thoroughly disappointing. "You don't know about me without you have read a book by the name of *The Adventures of Tom Sawyer*," it began, "but that ain't no matter." This was not what I wanted. Half the pleasure of *Tom Sawyer* lies in Mark Twain's literary style, and in the distance that style establishes between the reader and the events. I read a few chapters of *Huckleberry Finn*, and gave up in disgust. In later years, upon learning that it was supposed to be Twain's masterpiece, I read it again, and found it as unreadable as before. I once sat in on a class about it at an American college where I was lecturing, and ended by having an argument with the teacher, who tried to convince us that it was a great work of literature. Like the second part of Goethe's *Faust*, it seems to me an aberration.

When I learned that there had been a film of *Tom Sawyer*, I was much aggrieved at having missed it. And when, perhaps two years later, it returned to a local cinema, I could hardly believe my luck, and after a week of eager anticipation, hurried to see it one day after school. It was an even greater disappointment than *Huckleberry Finn*. To begin with, I had somehow assumed that Tom was supposed to be about the same age as myself when I first read it—eleven or twelve. But the part was played by a horrible, freckle-faced brat of about seven, with a missing front tooth (which the Americans seem to feel increases a child's charm) and the kind of squeaky, irritating voice affected by child film stars. It was Hollywood at its abysmal worst.

But although I outgrew *Tom Sawyer*—after reading it perhaps three or four times—there was one chapter that stuck in my mind down the years, and has increasingly assumed importance—I mean the second chapter, "The Glorious Whitewasher." It describes how Tom is forced to spend a Saturday morning whitewashing a fence; his friends gather round to jeer. But Tom whistles as he paints, and looks as if he is enjoying it so much that his friends begin to ask if they can take a turn. He refuses, but allows himself to be bribed with such valuable objects as a half-eaten apple, a kite, and a dead rat on a string. Finally, he is able to sit back and watch them paint the fence. Twain draws the moral: "Work is that which one is obliged to do; play is that which one is not obliged to do."

But the real moral, as Twain recognizes, is that "in order to make a man or boy covet a thing, it is only necessary to make the thing difficult to attain." In other words, anything on which we concentrate our full attention becomes desirable. And anything that is difficult to attain becomes twice as desirable.

I came to call this "the Tom Sawyer effect." It was many years before I came across the philosopher Husserl, and discovered that he called it "intentionality." When I perceive a thing, I throw my attention at it like a spear, and if I look at something idly and absent-mindedly, I often fail to see it because I am not paying attention. When we go on holiday, we think we are happy because we are in a strange and interesting place. Not so. We are happy because our belief that we are in a strange and interesting place makes us throw the spear of perception twice as hard.

Tom is not really deceiving his friends when he lures them into painting the fence by pretending he is enjoying it. They are enjoying it—because they have got rid of their assumption that painting a fence is a boring activity, and are directing their full enthusiasm into it. Life

16

is full of things that we assume to be boring and unpleasant, and which are really no more boring and unpleasant than things we pay money for. Everything depends on our attitude. Life is not boring or exciting; it is we who are bored or excited.

So *Tom Sawyer* taught me a lesson in philosophy that still seems to me as important as the day I learned it.

4

HOW TO BECOME A ROMANTIC

My mother was also a reader, unlike my father, who worked in a factory making shoes, and who probably never read a book in his life. My mother was a romantic, like Flaubert's Madame Bovary, and her heroes were film stars like Clark Gable, Ronald Coleman and George Raft—the latter a "tough guy" who played in gangster films. She had married my father because she was pregnant with me, and although my father preferred to spend his evenings in the local pub, they got along well enough—at least my father was a hard worker, who never failed to bring home his weekly pay packet. My mother escaped from the boredom of her life as a working-class housewife by reading a type of magazine called True Romance, as well as a publication called *Woman's Weekly*. But she also enjoyed True Detective magazines, which began to appear in America in the 1920s, and were imported into England. These contained accounts of murder cases, and I found them gruesomely fascinating—although I remember being nauseated by an account of a caretaker who sexually assaulted a small girl, and then threw her alive into the basement furnace.

I cannot remember how old I was when my father brought home from work a popular compilation called *The Fifty Most Amazing Crimes in the Last Hundred Years*. He warned me that I was not to read it—an odd prohibition, since he made no attempt to stop me reading *True Detective*—and I naturally read it every time my parents left the house. It contained accounts of murders like the Crippen case, and the "Brides in the Bath" murderer Smith, and the "Burning Car" murderer Rouse, whom my mother had known when she was a factory girl and Rouse was a commercial traveler. (It is a strange thought that if he had pursued my mother as determinedly as he pursued other women, he might have become my father.)

There was a drawing of each criminal at the head of the article—but there was one exception. At the head of the articles entitled, *The Mystery of Jack the Ripper*, there was only a huge black question mark. No doubt that is why the case came to fascinate me—a fascination that increased when my grandfather told me that he had been a child in London at the time of the murders (1888), and had been warned by his parents not to go out in the evening in case Jack the Ripper got him.

It was *The Fifty Most Amazing Crimes*, rather than *True Detective*, that stimulated an interest in crime and criminals. That led to *An Encyclopedia of Murder* and my first novel, *Ritual in the Dark*, which in turn led me, as I shall later explain, to write *The Outsider*.

When I was eight or nine, I joined the local junior library—I can still remember its smell of leather-bound books and floor polish. A friend of my father had recommended that I read a book called *The Coral Island*, but I found it dull; instead, I read volumes of fairy stories and folktales—I remember particularly a book called *Fairies and Enchanters*, which I read several times.

Then, one day, I discovered Poe's *Tales of Mystery and Imagination*, and found it the most fascinating book I had read so far. Admittedly, Poe's style was rather "grown up," but the pictures—of a gigantic whirlpool, and of an ape climbing in through a window—were so intriguing that I soon overcame this obstacle.

The first full-length novel I read was a paperback called *This Way Out*, whose author I can no longer recall. It was about a man with a nagging wife who decides to kill her by pushing her down stairs. He had met a sweet, gentle girl on a park bench, and decided he preferred her to his domineering wife. I entirely sympathized; my mother struck me as very sweet and good-tempered, compared to the mothers of most of my friends (she inherited her gentle disposition from her own mother), and I knew that, in due course, I would like to marry the same kind of girl. (When I first saw Joy, about twelve years later, I had an immediate inner conviction that she was the girl I had been waiting for, although I was momentarily deterred to learn that she was already engaged to be married.)

By the time I reached the age of ten, it was established that I was a "bookworm." My father, who had always loved outdoor sports, was disgusted, and swore that I would ruin my eyes. But, like my mother, I found the world of books an escape from the boredom of working-class life. Living in a large industrial city, there was simply nothing to do. I have to admit that I would probably have found it just as boring to live in the country, for I had no interest in nature.

Of course, I also found many books rather boring. But when, occasionally, I found a novel that interested me deeply, it was a revelation. I recall borrowing from the public library a volume of extracts from famous novels by Dickens, Thackeray, Dumas and others. When I read a chapter from *The Count of Monte Christo*, about the hero's escape from the fortress called the Chateau D'If, I was almost sick with excitement. And when I read some extracts from *The Old Curiosity Shop*, ending with the death of Little Nell, I experienced a deep but delicious melancholy that made all life seem like a dream.

It was in the world of Poe that I found justification for my romanticism. For his August Dupin—the first detective in fiction—is, like the great Wilson, also a kind of superman. He is certainly a romantic. "It was a freak of fancy in my friend . . . to be enamored of the night for her own sake; and into this bizzarerie, as into all his others, I quietly fell, giving myself up to his wild whims with a perfect abandon." And it is as Dupin and his friend are strolling along a street at night that Dupin gives his first illustration of his deductive powers. He breaks in upon his friend's thoughts with the comment, "He is a very little fellow, that's true, and would do better for the Theatre de Varietés." His friend assents absentmindedly before becoming suddenly aware that Dupin has read his thoughts.

The explanation turns out to be simple. A few minutes before, at the corner of the street, the narrator has been made to stumble on the cracked pavement by a man carrying a basket of apples on his head. After that, Dupin observes his friend staring with disgust at the pavement. Soon they pass an alleyway that has been paved with overlapping blocks, and Dupin observes his friend's face become brighter, and hears him murmur the word "stereotomy"—the name of this type of tiling. Since they have recently been discussing Epicurus, and his theory that the soul is composed of atoms, Dupin reasons that his friend will not be able to think of any kind of "otomy" or "atomy" without thinking of Epicurus. And in discussing Epicurus recently, Dupin has remarked that Epicurus' theories have been confirmed in the nebular hypothesis of Lapace. When his friend glances up at the Orion nebula, Dupin knows that he has been following his thoughts correctly. Now in the previous day's newspaper, there has been a bitter attack on a little cobbler called Chantilly, who has decided to go on the stage and act a tragic role. This critic has quoted a Latin line that refers to Orion, and so Dupin is reasonably certain that his friend will now think about the cobbler. His friend smiles, and Dupin knows he is correct. Then, when his friend draws himself up to his full height, Dupin knows that he is thinking about the cobbler's small stature, and that he would be better suited to comedy than tragedy. At which point, Dupin interrupts his friend's reflections with the comment that indeed, Chantilly would do better to act in a variety theater.

After this, the narrator goes on to tell the story of how Dupin solved the murder of two women in a locked apartment in the Rue Morgue. A mother's throat has been cut so violently that it has almost decapitated her; her daughter has been strangled and thrust up the chimney. Incredibly, it seems that the murderer has escaped through the window, which is high above the street. Shortly before the murders, the voice of a man has been heard shouting angrily, but this is also unexplained. Dupin gets permission from the prefect of police (who owes him a favor) to visit the scene of the crime. There he finds, clutched in the hand of one of the victims, a tuft of tawny hair.

Accordingly, Dupin places an advertisement in a newspaper, in which he claims that an orangutan has been caught in a park, and that its owner—a Maltese sailor—can have it back if he cares to call at a certain address.

How, asks the narrator, can you be sure that it was a Maltese sailor? Because, says Dupin, he has found a piece of greasy ribbon, of the type used by sailors to tie their hair, and has noticed that the ribbon is tied in a knot that is peculiar to Malta.

In due course, a Maltese sailor calls at Dupin's apartment, and admits that Dupin is correct. He had brought an orangutan back from India, with the intention of selling it. Returning to his room in the early hours of the morning, he had found the animal trying to shave itself with a razor, in imitation of its master. When he seized a whip, the animal jumped out of an open window. Its owner followed it, and saw it climbing a lightning conductor and disappearing through an open window. The sailor followed it, and saw that it was trying to "shave" one of the women, while the other had fainted. The woman's struggles enraged it and it slashed her throat, then strangled the other woman and pushed her up the chimney. Then it saw its master and made off through the window, and the sailor followed it.

The narrator tells us that the sailor later recaptures the animal, and sells it to a zoo. And an innocent man who has been arrested for the murders is released.

And so Poe had invented the first detective in 1840, although it would be another dozen years before Dickens invented the word "detective" in *Bleak House*.

What impressed me so much about Dupin was that he lived in a world of books and imagination—just as I did—yet that his powers of reason enabled him to solve an intricate murder case. In due course, he became the inspiration for the most famous detective of all, Sherlock Holmes.

I borrowed the *Memoirs of Sherlock Holmes* from the library when I was about eleven or twelve, and read them avidly—I seem to remember—over the course of two days. And when I came to the last story, describing Holmes' death over the Reichenbach Falls, I was horrified. It seemed incomprehensible that Doyle should kill off his most famous creation.

When, soon after, I came upon a volume containing the complete Sherlock Holmes short stories, I was delighted to find that Doyle had decided to bring his detective back to life. I read it from beginning to end, then succeeded in getting hold of the volume containing the four Sherlock Holmes novels, and read that just as eagerly.

Holmes fascinated me because he seemed even more an intellectual superman than Dupin. He was a scientist, a philosopher, an artist and a man of action—the kind of person that every intelligent schoolboy dreams of becoming.

Many years later, I tried to summarize my feelings about Holmes in an essay that appeared in a book compiled by a friend, Michael Harrison, *Beyond Baker Street*. I had intended to use an edited and shortened version in this book. But rereading it recently, I realized that it is not only a concise summary of my attitude towards Sherlock Holmes, but of some of my central ideas. That is why I offer no apologies for reprinting it here.

5

SHERLOCK HOLMES—THE FLAWED SUPERMAN

When Dr. Conan Doyle moved to Southsea, a suburb of Portsmouth, in July 1882, he was twenty-three years old and had no hard-and-fast plans for the future. He rented a house for £40 a year, screwed his brass plate to the door, and sat back to wait for patients. For many weeks none appeared, so he whiled away the time writing stories. In fact, he had already had a few published—at about three guineas (then worth about fifteen dollars) each—and many more rejected. His penchant was for tales of bizarre adventures set in Africa or the Arctic (he had visited both places as a ship's doctor); the style was influenced by Bret Harte, and had a touch of facetiousness. And sometime that autumn he began a story: "In the month of December 1873, the British ship *Dei Gratia* steered into Gilbraltar, having in tow a derelict brigantine *Marie Celeste*, which had been picked up in latitude 38° 15' W."

For a short sentence, this contains a remarkable number of inaccuracies. The year was actually 1872, the *Dei Gratia* did not tow the *Marie Celeste*—the latter came in under its own sail, and arrived a day later than the *Dei Gratia*; the latitude and longitude are wrong; and the ship was called the plain English Mary, not Marie. Still, "J. Habakuk Jephson's Statement" is, after all, intended to be fiction. This was not made clear to the readers of the *Cornhill Magazine*, when it appeared in January 1884, for the *Cornhill* had a policy of publishing stories anonymously. J. Habakuk Jephson's statement, to the effect that the

Mary Celeste had been taken over by a kind of Black Power leader with a hatred of whites, was accepted as fact by most readers. And, most notably, by Her Majesty's Advocate-General at Gibraltar, Mr. Solly Flood, who had been chief investigator in the *Mary Celeste* case: the indignant Mr. Flood launched a telegram to the Central News Agency denouncing J. Habakuk Jephson as a fraud and a liar. The statement was given wide publicity, and the incident set Doyle's feet on the road to fame; at least, the *Cornhill* was now willing to publish most of his stories at thirty guineas a time.

Doyle took note of the lesson of the *Mary Celeste* case; he developed the "factual" manner. "September 11th—Lat.81° 40' N.; long. 2° E. Still lying-to amid enormous ice-fields . . ." begins "The Captain of the *Polestar*." While, in "A Physiologist's Wife" and "The Great Keinplatz Experiment," he took as his central characters a type that had always fascinated him: the abstracted intellectual. "Professor von Baumgarten was tall and thin, with a hatchet face and steel-gray eyes, which were singularly bright and penetrating."

It was in 1886, two years after he had become a regular contributor to the *Cornhill*, that Doyle came upon the detective stories of Emile Gaboriau, a French writer of sensational mysteries. In France, the police are regarded with suspicion and dislike; therefore Gaboriau could not make his detective hero a policeman; instead he introduced a retired pawnbroker as the investigator; Tabaret's knowledge of human beings, gained from years behind the counter, serves him well in *L'Affaire Lerouge*. Tabaret is accompanied by an ex-offender, now a policeman, named Lecoq. (Obviously Lecoq's heart is in the right place, because he has been a crook.) As an ex-crook, Lecoq is a master of disguise. He also uses powers of deduction in the manner of Poe's Dupin.

And so, fragment by fragment, the personality of Holmes was assembled. As everyone knows, his first appearance, in *A Study in Scarlet*, was a failure; Doyle had to sell it outright for £25. *The Sign of Four*, commissioned three years later by the American *Lippincott's Magazine*, was hardly more successful. Fame arrived belatedly with the publication of the first two Sherlock Holmes short stories in the *Strand* in the summer of 1891; Doyle received £35 each for the first half dozen. By the time he had allowed himself to be persuaded to start writing *The Memoirs*, he was charging something closer to £100 a story. (For *The Return*, written a decade later, he received five thousand dollars a story from the American publisher.)

Now it is easy enough to understand why the short stories achieved a success that had been denied to the novels. Victorian magazines reached immense circulations. (Aldous Huxley once told me that the *Cornhill*, later edited by his father, had paid George Eliot some incredible sum—I think it was £30,000—for *Romola*.) And a good short story is undeniably easier to read than a novel. (As a boy of twelve, I read and reread the Sherlock Holmes stories, but never derived the same pleasure from the novels.) Doyle could not have had a better showcase for his great detective. Yet no one has ever quite explained why Holmes immediately became one of the most famous characters in the whole realm of fiction. The late Edgar W. Smith once attempted it in *The Baker Street Journal* (and W. S. Baring-Gould quotes it in his *Annotated Holmes*). He begins by pointing out that we love the Victorian atmosphere of the Holmes series, which is obviously true; but then the Victorians themselves must have taken all this for granted. He goes on to say that Holmes personifies "our urge to trample evil and to set aright the wrongs with which the world is plagued," and compares him to Galahad and Socrates. And to me, he seems to be getting further and further away from the essence of the Sherlockian fascination.

I found myself brooding on the question a few years ago, when I succeeded in picking up a small collection of Sherlockiana from a secondhand bookseller—including Vincent Starrett's *Private Life of Sherlock Holmes*; Michael Harrison's *In the Footsteps of Sherlock Holmes*; and Baring-Gould's biography. T. S. Eliot once remarked that he read through the Holmes stories once every two years. I do the same. No one has ever written biographical books about Raffles or Father Brown or Maigret. What is it about Holmes that fills his admirers with such an appetite to go on reading about him?

A partial answer, the beginning of an answer, emerges from the account of Doyle's literary struggles. I cannot think of any other writer of the nineteenth century, with the possible exception of Balzac, with such a passion for the factual detail. It seems possible that Doyle stumbled on the trick through the writing of "J. Habakuk Jephson's Statement." In fact, this story is as romantically preposterous as anything he ever wrote, but it was taken for reality. Gaboriau was influenced by Balzac, and his books have a beguilingly factual ring, at least for the first few pages. In a story, a certain amount of fact is like grit in chicken food—it makes it more digestible and nutritious.

(Rider Haggard made the same discovery when he began writing *King Solomon's Mines*.) Doyle instantly perceived the value of the method, and proceeded to employ it (with the confidence of a duck taking to water) in *A Study in Scarlet*. When Watson meets Holmes in the laboratory at Bart's (about 1881), Holmes has just discoverd an infallible test for bloodstains. Such a test was not actually discovered until 1900 by Paul Uhlenhuth, and first used to convict a murderer in Germany in 1904. Like other men of genius, Doyle had the power to tune in to the spirit of the age; and at the time when he conceived Holmes, crime detection was finally achieving the status of an exact science. In the mid-1880s, Scotland Yard was brooding on whether to adopt the Bertillon system of fingerprinting as a basic method of criminal identification. As a doctor, Doyle had the necessary background for pursuing the science of medical jurisprudence. He might have applied his talents as a police surgeon or pathologist; instead, he wrote stories. But as one reads those first two chapters of *A Study in Scarlet,* one senses that Doyle had struck a rich vein, and could easily spend the next hundred pages discussing crime, medicine, detection, the science of deduction.

The reader catches his enthusiasm. A critic once said of Balzac that no other novelist produces such an illusion of reality, of talking about the real world. This is one of the secrets of the fascination of the Holmes stories. On this level of criminal investigation and medical jurisprudence, they have the ring of authenticity. This is why readers want to go on playing the game, and reading books about Holmes and his cases, like Starrett's *Private Life of Sherlock Holmes*. I believe it may also explain why the various Holmes pastiches by Adrian Conan Doyle, John Dickson Carr, August Derleth, et al, have never caught on. They imitate the style and the mannerisms, but fail to throw in the handful of grit, the illusion of fact; you know they are inventions.

All this may help to explain the popularity of the Holmes biographies, in which the writer tries to sort out Watson's muddled dates; but it hardly begins to explain the fascination of the character of the Great Detective. This is an altogether more complex matter. But you can see the essence of the trick in the passage about the ex-commissionnaire. Watson, vaguely irritated by Holmes's air of intellectual superiority, points to a man on the other side of the street and wonders what he is looking for: "You mean the retired sergeant of Marines?" says Holmes. A few minutes later, the man delivers a letter to them.

"Here was an opportunity of taking the conceit out of him. He little thought of this when he made that random shot.

"'May I ask, my lad,' I said, in the blandest voice, 'what your trade might be?'

'Commissionaire, sir,' he said gruffly. 'Uniform away for repairs.'

'And you were?' I asked, with a slightly malicious glance at my companion.

'A sergeant, sir, Royal Marine Light Infantry, sir . . .'"

And there you have it; Holmes the cool and infallible; Holmes the superman who is never wrong.

Doyle knew that this was what his readers wanted: the satisfaction of an "infallible fantasy." With the storyteller's instinct, he uses the same situation again and again, knowing that his readers will never tire of it, as children never tire of seeing the clown walk into the custard pie. To increase the effect, Watson plays the stooge to an extent that is slightly unbelievable. When a man is really telling a story against himself, he does it with a self-deprecating grin, and tries to soften the effect: "Naturally, I assumed this was mere brag and bounce." Watson tells such stories as if he were his own worst enemy. In the opening chapter of *The Sign of Four*, the whole scene is repeated with embellishments. He begins by "raising his eyebrows" when Holmes describes himself as the only unofficial consulting detective (although Holmes has told him as much in *A Study of Scarlet*), gets irritable when Holmes criticizes the earlier case history, and then becomes angry when Holmes tells him the story of his alcoholic brother from the marks in his watch case. The reaction is overdone. A real man would say: "But that is remarkable, Holmes. Are you *sure* you knew nothing about my brother beforehand?" Watson limps "impatiently about the room with considerable bitterness in his heart," and snorts: "This is unworthy of you, Holmes," accusing him of chicanery. And so, when Holmes explains how he made the deduction, the impact is doubled.

For most readers, these opening sections—in which Holmes demonstrates the science of deduction—are the best part of the story. Of course, we enjoy it as Holmes and Watson rattle off in a cab to catch the 2:15 from Waterloo; but we have to admit that there is an air of sameness about the cases—the attractive girls in distress, the bullying villains who bend pokers (which Holmes immediately straightens again), the sinister figure from the past who comes back to take revenge. (I have never worked out how many of the stories depend on this device, but it must be at least a quarter.) But in the opening pages of the stories, Doyle is at his most inventive, and his most realistic. These are the pages that make us want to to go on reading about Holmes's life and background. Why? Because we like to be assured that Holmes is a real person; that is an important part of the pleasure. That basic *effect*—the hero once more proving infallible—is the effect of the fairy tale. Children love to identify themselves with heroes who possess all kinds of interesting devices for overcoming danger—magic hats that make you invisible when you turn them around, tinder boxes that grant your wishes. They love to identify with brave, but perfectly ordinary, little tailors who pose as conquerors and somehow manage to get away with it. As we get older, the fairy tales fail to satisfy, because we now know that the world is more difficult and demanding than that. Realistic novelists like Flaubert, Balzac, and Stendahl make a virtue of this, and tell us stories of weak heroes who are finally defeated. But we don't really like their tales of defeat, for there is something in us that hungers for triumph and conquest. So if a writer is kind enough to tell us an apparently realistic story in which the hero triumphs like the brave little tailor, our gratitude is immense. Like children, we read and reread the fantasy, blissfully identifying, and reveling in the details that assure us that all this is real. But in order to grasp the full significance of Holmes, I believe we have to see him in an altogether broader perspective. At the risk of seeming too abstract and metaphysical, let me try to explain what I mean.

The novel as we know it came into existence in the year 1740, with Samuel Richardson's *Pamela*. There had been novels before this, but they tended to be either fairy tales or picaresque "true narrations." What Richardson did was to create a highly elaborate daydream about a servant girl who resists all her master's attempts to seduce her, and ends by marrying him. I doubt whether many readers ever identified with Don Quixote or Gil Blas; but every male could identify with the lustful Mr. B., every female with the virtuous Pamela. *Pamela* was a magic carpet to another world—a world of the imagination: at the same time, the sheer mass of its physical and psychological detail convinced the reader of its reality.

Within a decade of the publication of *Pamela*, England had become "a nation of readers" (in Dr. Johnson's phrase). Nowadays we take entertainment for granted; it is difficult to realize what a revolution took place as a result of Richardson's invention. It was as widespread as the tobacco revolution of the Elizabethan age; but to get an idea of its significance, you would have to imagine that Sir Walter Raleigh brought back marijuana from the New World, and that all Europe became pot smokers. This taste for escaping into worlds of fantasy swept across Europe, and literature gained an importance that it had never possessed in any previous age. Rousseau's *New Heloise* was so popular that libraries lent it out by the hour. Scott's novels made sums of money that would be the envy of a modern property tycoon. So did those of Dumas and Hugo, Dickens and Trollope. Reading was a mass-addiction. Middle-class Victorians flocked to Thomas Cook to take them on tours of foreign lands; *every* class of Victorian flocked to the novelists to take them on tours of the imagination. *Pamela* could well have been one of the most decisive steps in the evolution of man since the invention of the wheel.

The trouble is that, after that splendid start, the novel began to find itself in difficulties. Serious novelists like Balzac and Flaubert continued to pursue the line of realism developed by Richardson. But they no longer had the old universal appeal of Richardson and Scott, because they were no longer satisfying the wish-fulfillment fantasy. Everybody agreed that Balzac was a greater novelist than Dumas; but for every one who admired *Père Goriot* or *Lost Illusions*, a hundred read *The Three Musketeers* and *The Count of Monte Cristo* (surely one of the great wish-fulfillment fantasies of all time). Even Dickens made the same discovery; *Hard Times* and *Bleak House* are greater novels than *Pickwick Papers* and *Nicholas Nickleby*, but they were never half so popular; they are too "real," and they lack the element of the wish-fulfillment fantasy.

And so, in the second half of the nineteenth century, literature split into two camps: realists and fantasists. On the one hand you had the Dickens of *Bleak House*, Ibsen and his disciples, Gissing, Zola, Dostoevsky; on the other, Dumas, Stevenson, Haggard, Marie Corelli, and dozens of now-forgotten writers of romances and historical dramas.

From the beginning, Conan Doyle recognized himself as a member of the second group. One critic thought that "J. Habkuk Jephson's Statement" was by Stevenson. Doyle regarded his Holmes stories as entertainments, not to be taken too seriously: he felt that his finest work was to be found in *Micah Clark*, *The White Company*, and other historical novels. But even if, like Winston Churchill, you happen to be an admirer of the historical novels, you cannot help noticing that they are basically escapist fantasies, in which the modern Londoner turns back nostalgically to the days of chivalry, when Robin Hood lurked in the greenwood and crusaders rode around on white chargers. (I remember, a few years ago, seeing a newspaper photograph of Adrian Conan Doyle dressed in armor, carrying a bow and arrow; the accompanying story explained that he hoped to start some kind of movement for the revival of the medieval virtues and martial arts. For the same reason, some modern American businessmen spend their vacations dressed in cowboy gear and reconstruct the gunfight at O.K. Corral.)

Holmes, on the other hand, had his feet planted firmly on the hard pavements of nineteenth-century London. He is a connoisseur of "every horror perpetrated in the century." He is a scientist, and often speaks the dry, abstract language of science. And while this great tide of Victorian London swirls around him, with its crime and violence and misery, he holds aloof in his room in Baker Street, surveying it with the eye of a philosopher. Most emphatically, he possesses what T. S. Eliot called "a sense of his own age."

It is rather interesting to watch the way that his character develops. The famous list at the beginning of *A Study in Scarlet* emphasizes his ignorance of many subjects, including literature, philosophy, astronomy, and politics. He tells Watson that he doesn't know whether the earth goes around the sun or vice versa, and now that Watson has told him, will forget it as quickly as possible. Yet in *The Sign of Four* he recommends Watson to read "one of the most remarkable [books] ever penned," Winwood Reade's *Martyrdom of Man*, a work of historical philosophy. And, later in this novel he discourses on miracle plays, medieval pottery, Stradivarius violins, the Buddhism of Ceylon, and the warships of the future, "handling each as though he had made a special study of it." In other stories we learn that he is the author of a monograph on the motets of Lassus, loves the opera, knows something of painting ("my grandmother, who was the sister of Verney, the French artist . . .") and is a connoisseur of food and wine. ("I have oysters and a brace of grouse, with something a little choice in white wines"—the latter possibly a Montrachet, which makes its appearance in *The Veiled Lodger*.) Doyle's original idea was to make Holmes a rather limited character, like Fleming's James Bond; but he found himself unable to stick to this resolution, and Holmes emerges finally as a kind of "universal man," with an encyclopedic knowledge on every subject, as well as remarkable physical powers. (The prize fighter in

The Sign of Four assures him that he could have aimed high if he had chosen to become a professional boxer.)

Holmes's character develops in another significant way. In the early work he is definitely an esthete; he says things "querulously" and "languidly," his cheeks burn with unhealthy red spots, he injects himself with morphine and cocaine and lies around for days on the settee "with a dreamy, vacant expression in his eyes." His power of imaginative projection is highly developed; in *The Beryl Coronet* he tells Watson that, while his mind has been in Devonshire, his body has, "I regret to observe, consumed in my absence two large pots of coffee and an incredible amount of tobacco." Huysman's novel, *A Rébours*, appeared in 1884, two years before Doyle conceived Sherlock Holmes; its hero, Des Esseintes, also lives a kind of monastic existence in his luxurious rooms, attempting to live a life of the mind and the senses, and behaving as if the outside world could be ignored. In 1889, Doyle had dinner with the editor of *Lippincott's Magazine*, who asked him to write another Holmes novel (*The Sign of Four*). Oscar Wilde was also present and agreed to write *The Picture of Dorian Gray*. It seems possible that they discussed Huysmans's novel; at any event, it plays an important part in Dorian Gray's evolution. Certainly, the Holmes of the early stories has much in common with the esthetic, world-rejecting heroes of the 1880s and 1890s.

Now this is far more significant than it seems. The esthetic hero was a highly interesting phenomenon. He was created by Samuel Richardson, in the person of Lovelace, the demonic seducer of Clarissa Harlowe. Lovelace declared that he cared for nothing but "his own imperial will." He is the proud aristocrat who declines to admit the force of necessity. The Romantics developed this new kind of hero; Schiller's most famous character, Karl Moor in *The Robbers*, declares that man was made for freedom, and that laws were made to be broken by great men. Byron developed the idea; his heroes are gloomy, romantic, proud, sinful, contemptuous of public opinion. Nineteenth-century Russian literature is full of such men. But Des Esseintes, like Dorian Gray and Gilbert's Bunthorne, represents the decadence of the Byronic hero. He ends as a nervous wreck. The world he despises has the last word. Dorian Gray's single-minded pursuit of pleasure ends by destroying him. The novel was violently attacked. Wilde's defenders pointed out that Dorian's self-destruction made it a highly moral tale. But Wilde was not concerned with morality and Mrs. Grundy.

Dorian had to die because that was the artistically logical conclusion of his premises. Villiers de L'Isle-Adam, in his famous play *Axel*, makes his hero express total world-rejection in the magnificent line: "Live? Our servants can do that for us." And the hero and heroine then commit suicide. There was no other logical course for them to take. More than thirty years later, the writers of the "lost generation"—Eliot, Pount, Joyce, Hemingway—were trapped in the same web. *The Great Gatsby* is a daydream about a man who is rich enough to make the world conform to his desires. Like Wilde and Dorian Gray, Fitzgerald was a self-destroyer.

In Sherlock Holmes, Doyle created his own esthetic hero. With his dressing gown, violin, and hypodermic syringe, Holmes is a second cousin of Des Esseintes. When Watson protests, in the name of common sense, against the use of cocaine, Holmes replies, "I cannot live without brainwork. What else is there to live for? Stand at the window here. Was ever such a dreary, dismal, unprofitable world? See how the yellow fog swirls down the street and drifts across the dun-colored houses. What could be more hopelessly prosaic and material?" You almost expect him to add, "Live? Our servants can do that for us." But, unlike Des Esseintes, Holmes has good reasons for going out into the fog. Crime fascinates him, as it did Baudelaire and Dostoevsky. ("Everything in the world exudes crime," said Baudelaire.) But he derives his greatest delight from pitting his wits against criminals. He has not turned his back on the world outside; on the contrary, he regards himself as a last court of appeal.

Quite unconsciously, certainly unaware of what he was doing, Conan Doyle had solved the problem that had tormented and frustrated the novelist since Richardson. He had created a romantic hero, a man whose life is entirely the life of the mind ("I cannot live without brainwork"), yet succeeded in steering him out of the cul-de-sac of despair and defeat that destroyed so many of the best minds of the *fin de siècle* period. Moreover, it was quite logical, without any element of contrivance. When Watson meets him, Holmes is so poor that he can afford only half the rent of the rooms at 221B Baker Street (for all that, as Watson remarks, the terms were exceedingly moderate), although he is certainly not the kind of character who would enjoy sharing rooms with another man. That was around 1881. Seven years later, in 1888, Holmes was a highly successful detective with many distinguished clients (such as the King of Bohemia). It is true that, as late as "The Adventure of Wisteria Lodge" (in 1890), he is complaining that his mind is like a racing engine, "tearing itself to pieces because it is not connected up with the work for which it was built." But one can have no doubt that these slack periods became more and more rare, and that by the mid-1890s Holmes was one of the busiest men in England. By the time of "The Adventure of the Bruce-Partington Plans" (around 1895), he has achieved an altogether new degree of self-control: "One of the most remarkable characteristics of Sherlock Holmes was his power of throwing his brain out of action and switching all his thoughts on to lighter things whenever he had convinced himself that he could no longer work to advantage." This is no longer the man who only three years earlier had explained that his mind was like a racing engine.

I suspect that Holmes's biographers might connect this increased maturity with the Reichenbach Falls episode and its aftermath; and I think they would probably be right. Holmes's *Wanderjahre* in Tibet and the Middle East must have allowed his personality the freedom to develop. (I say *Jahre*, although Holmes speaks of at least two years, for the death of Moriarty occurred in 1891 and "The Adventure of Wisteria Lodge" is dated 1892.) What is more important is that the "death" of Holmes brought Doyle face to face with the implications of the character he had created. We know that he decided to kill Holmes because he was tired of inventing new mysteries for him to solve. But an author does not become tired of his characters while they still have some possibilities of interesting development. Balzac becomes tired of Lucien de Rubempré, who is a weakling, but not of Rastignac or the criminal genius of Vautrin. When a character reaches a certain limit, it is natural for the author to abandon him or kill him off. Shakespeare killed off Falstaff because he had got the best of him; the "return" (in *The Merry Wives*) is a disaster. When Doyle conceived Holmes, it was simply as a fascinating eccentric who might have strolled out of the tales of Hoffmann. The atmosphere of the early stories is phantasmagoric. "'My dear fellow,' said Sherlock Holmes, as we sat on either side of the fire in his lodgings at Baker Street, 'life is infinitely stranger than anything that the mind of man could invent. We would not dare to conceive the things which are really mere commonplaces of existence. If we could fly out of that window hand in hand, hover over this great city . . .'" etc. There is more than a touch of the *Arabian Nights* here. The reader is fascinated because, in fact, it had never struck him that there is anything very strange about London. In the early stories, Holmes is always emphasizing the fascination of the commonplace. "To the man who loves art for its own sake, it is frequently in its least important and lowliest manifestations that the keenest pleasure is to be derived," says Holmes in "The Copper Beeches." Like Poe's Dupin, he is an intellectual esthete, a man whose fastidiousness leads him to prefer the night to the day.

But without fully recognizing what he was doing, Doyle had created a character who embodies a fragment of the superman. The only modern parallel that comes to mind is Tolkein's Gandalf, who is introduced in *The Hobbit* as a comic fairy-tale wizard, and who gradually acquires stature until he becomes the symbolic Magician of *The Lord of the Rings*. Holmes is also a kind of magician. And so, when he returned from Tibet and Persia, he had to be built up into something altogether more universal than the eccentric drug addict of the early tales. In the *Memoirs* Doyle had once tried the experiment of making Holmes fallible ("The Yellow Face"); he never tried it again. (In the earlier "Five Orange Pips" we learn there were three occasions when he was beaten by men; but Watson does not elaborate.) He also provided Holmes with a "superior" brother—but Mycroft is seldom heard of after the adventure of "The Greek Interpreter." Holmes had to be developed into something at once unique and universal. In the early days, Watson records, he had no appreciation for nature and went to the country only to pursue evildoers; in the late adventure of "The Lion's Mane," Holmes mentions how often he yearned for the "soothing life of nature" when living in London. The eccentric esthete gradually disappears, and Holmes slowly takes on the stature of a true magician.

There were many attempts to imitate Holmes or, at least, to follow in his footsteps: Futrelle's Van Dusen, Chesterton's Father Brown, M. P. Shiel's Prince Zaleski, Bramah's Max Carrados, Freeman's Dr. Thorndyke, Agatha Christie's Poirot, Rex Stout's Nero Wolfe (based on Mycroft), Wallace's J. G. Reeder, Morrison's Martin Hewitt. My own favorite is J. G. Reeder, although I realize that many people would plump for Father Brown. When I try to define why these two characters should be so oddly satisfactory, it seems that the answer is connected with their otherworldliness. Both are harmless, innocent men whose superiority springs from their basic natural *detachment* from the affairs of the world. I personally find that more "normal" detectives, like

Poirot or Martin Hewitt, are curiously unsatisfactory. It seems that Doyle's successors have mostly tried to fathom the secret of Holmes's success, and have come to the wrong conclusion. They assumed that the detective has to be "different"; so Van Dusen has Holmes's intellectuality, Poirot has his egoism, Nero Wolfe his esthetic sensitivity, and so on; then there are women detectives, blind detectives, even, I believe, a homosexual detective. (Fleming's James Bond is the nearest anyone has come so far to a sadistic detective.) Shiel's Prince Zaleski is even more of a superman than Holmes; yet he is less interesting, because the stories themselves are somehow unbelievable, slightly absurd. On the other hand, Simenon's perfectly "ordinary" Maigret is one of the most satisfying detectives since Holmes, because one is convinced by the stories. It brings us back to the point already made: that a large part of the fascination of Holmes is that sense of reality. Yet the tales of J. G. Reeder and Father Brown are not noted for their realism. They share another Holmesian characteristic, pinpointed by Watson when he says: "He loved to lie in the very center of five millions of people, with his filaments stretching out and running through them, responsive to every little rumor or suspicion of unsolved crime"; they are "outside" life. If I may intrude a personal note, they are examples of what I would call "outsiders."

And now, it seems to me, we are beginning to approach the psychological root of this question we have set ourselves. Why *should* the audiences of 1891 have been so ready to accept Holmes, when the book-buying public of 1887 had been indifferent? It is not simply that he appeared in a mass-circulation magazine, and that short stories are easier to read than novels. Let us put the question in another way. Why was Poe's Dupin received with relative indifference in 1842? Why was there no frantic demand for whole volumes of Dupin stories? To our eyes, Dupin seems quite as fascinating as Holmes—one of the few fictional detectives who can stand beside him without paling. One of the first to truly appreciate Dupin was the French poet Baudelaire; and *he* sympathized with Dupin's asceticism, his fastidiousness, his dislike of the common daylight. Dickens created the first "detective officer" in Inspector Bucket of *Bleak House* (1852); Wilkie Collins followed with Sergeant Cuff more than a decade later. It never seems to have occurred to either of them that a detective should be some kind of intellectual superman. Their detectives are as ordinary as Maigret.

I suspect the answer lies in that slow evolution of public taste that occurred in the nineteenth century. I say slow, but in historical terms it was like a whirlwind. Richardson taught the European mind to daydream. Intelligent men and women began to live in the imagination in a way that had been impossible for the contemporaries of Rabelais, or even of Pepys. You feel of Rabelais, Montaigne, Shakespeare, Cervantes, Defoe, that they are *realists*; in spite of their genius, they were as down to earth as Julius Caesar or Queen Elizabeth. But when you read Byron or Shelley or Poe, you feel that they weren't entirely able to distinguish between their imagination and the real world. They had become so accustomed to the life of the imagination that real life had become slightly blurred. (And nowadays, when we spend so much time living vicariously through the films and television, this is even more so.) A novel is not only unreal; it is reversible; after the death of the hero, you can go back fifty pages and he is alive again. Or the author can kill him—like Holmes—and bring him back to life again, explaining it was all a mistake. It is easy for someone who has read too many novels, like Flaubert's Madame Bovary, to fall into the habit of feeling that real life is a kind of fiction—even a joke, a story, a lie. In the nineteenth century, many men of genius committed suicide because they lived in a kind of double exposure in which reality and dream kept blending together and blurring each other's outlines. This was what drove De Quincey and Coleridge to laudanum and Poe to alcohol, Beddoes to suicide. Schopenhauer caught the essence of the dilemma in his title *The World as Will and Illusion*; the world was no longer one thing, but two. Friedrich Nietzsche revolted against this pessimism, asserting that "great health" can overcome anything; his "gospel of the superman" appeared, in its first complete version, in 1894. By that time, Nietzsche himself was insane; he died six years later without recovering his reason.

Whether he liked it or not, European man of the nineteenth century was dragged into a new world—a world of double exposures. In the early years of the century, it affected mainly the middle and upper classes, for they were the only ones who could afford to read. By the middle of the century, the serialized novel was reaching millions more readers, and the "outsider" malaise was becoming something of an epidemic—no longer restricted, as in Byron's day, to the rich and the intelligent, but affecting, to a greater or lesser degree, everyone of unusual intelligence.

The older type of hero had demonstrated his skill in dealing with the real world—for example, Robinson Crusoe's desert island. The new intellectual climate of the nineteenth century brought the need for new heroes, men whose skill consists in their ability to conquer the world of the mind. From this point of view, Holmes was an incredible creation, an expression of the spirit of the age rather than of one man's romanticism. He is an outsider; he suffers from the romantic malaise of the century; he smokes too much and injects himself with cocaine. Yet in this world of increasing chaos and violence, he remains a beacon of sanity. In 1888, the Jack the Ripper murders produced a traumatic shock in English society. There had been nothing like them before; earlier murders had been comprehensible, motivated by fear, jealousy, greed. The Victorian imagination was captivated by the crimes of Burke and Hare, Thurtell and Hunt, William Corder (the "Red Barn" murderer), Constance Kent. These savage mutilations of women were beyond comprehension; they did not even recognize them as sex crimes. The Ripper, with his jeering letters to the police, his ability to evade capture, seemed to be a new kind of super criminal, a "fiend from hell." I doubt whether Conan Doyle would have been capable of creating Professor Moriarty before 1888. And although I can offer no proof, I have no doubt that the Ripper was at the back of his mind when he created Moriarty. Holmes was more than a fictional character: he was a response to a deep-rooted psychological need of the late Victorians, a need for reassurance, for belief in the efficacy of reason and for man's power to overcome the chaos produced by this new disease of alienation.

The need is as strong today as it was in 1890, which no doubt explains why Holmes is still so very much alive. And that thought tempts me to explore the whole fascinating question of Holmes as an archetypal "outsider" figure, and the precise operation of the superman wish-fulfillment fantasy—a temptation that must be resisted, for fear of doubling the length of the present essay. But perhaps I may be allowed one comment on the essential nature of wish-fulfillment fantasies. It struck me the other day when I was rereading James Thurber's delightful *Secret Life of Walter Mitty*. Mitty is a henpecked little man living in a small and dull American town. He compensates for the dullness—and his wife's bullying—with fantasies in which he is always cool, heroic, dominant. . . Super-Mitty is always the man who keeps his head when all about are losing theirs. He is the commander of a warship, ordering her to be turned into the storm ("Not so fast! You're driving too fast!" said Mrs. Mitty. "What are you driving so fast for?"). He is a great surgeon who knows precisely what to do when an operation goes seriously wrong. ("Quiet, man!" said Mitty in a low, cool voice.) He is the famous marksman, unjustly accused of murder by the swaggering District Attorney. ("With any known make of gun," he said evenly, "I could have killed Gregory Fitzhurst at three hundred feet *with my left hand*.") He is the RAF's ace bomber pilot, prepared to fly a dangerous mission alone. ("The pounding of the cannon increased; there was a rat-tat-tatting of machine guns, and from somewhere came the menacing pocketa-pocketa-pocketa of the new flame throwers.") And at the end, he is the great spy, defying death to the last. "'To hell with the handkerchief,' said Walter Mitty scornfully. He took one last drag on his cigarette and snapped it away. Then, with that faint, fleeting smile playing about his lips, he faced the firing squad; erect and motionless, proud and disdainful, Walter Mitty the Undefeated, inscrutable to the last."

Our ancestors spent most of their lives dealing with physical problems; they fought, they loved, and they worked, and reality endowed them with a certain strength. Modern man finds himself in an immensely confusing world that offers no oppportunity for the heroic virtues. If he wants to achieve eminence, he needs highly complex disciplines of the mind and emotions, and a great deal of luck. The trouble is that, just as the sound of the trumpet causes the sinews to stiffen, so lack of challenge induces boredom, ineptitude, and a general draining of self-confidence. We can fight this with the imagination. Now, more than at any time in history, man needs "the strength to dream." All these daydreams of Walter Mitty are tension-inducers, and they are an important part of his resistance to the general softening effect of civilization.

Now turn to the Holmes stories. They are almost pure Walter Mitty, and I say this without any undertone of patronage. "He is the Napolean of Crime, Watson. He is the organizer of half that is evil and of nearly all that is undetected in this great city."

Or this:

"I moved my head to look at the cabinet behind me. When I turned again Sherlock Holmes was standing smiling at me across my study table. I rose to my feet, stared at him for some seconds in utter amazement, and then it appears that I must have fainted for the first and last time in my life. Certainly a gray mist swirled before my eyes, and when it cleared I found my collar-ends undone and the tingling aftertaste of brandy upon my lips. Holmes was bending over my chair, his flask in his hand.

'My dear Watson,' said the well-remembered voice, 'I owe you a thousand apologies. I had no idea you would be so affected.'

'Holmes,' I cried. 'Is it really you?'"

We smile at the paragraph when read in isolation, but I still find myself smiling with a lump in my throat as I read it in context. The Holmes stories belong among those works that we know to be full of romantic absurdities, like *The Prisoner of Zenda*, yet which still move us because they are so beautifully done.

Holmes is magnificent because he seems to be, in a sense, larger than his creator. From all we know about him, Doyle seems to have been more like Watson than Holmes. I recall a typical story told at some time by his son, with whom he was traveling on a train, and his son remarked that a certain woman was ugly. Doyle immediately slapped his face, saying: "*No* woman is ugly." The gallantry is marvelously Victorian.

Still, it must be admitted that, in the final sense, there is a dimension lacking in Holmes. And this is because there was something lacking in Doyle himself. He knew it himself. And his artistic instinct was sound when he decided to kill Holmes at Reichenbach Falls. For Holmes is doomed to remain static; his superb qualities of character and intellect can never develop. Crime is, after all, a relatively trivial subject in itself. As Shaw's Undershaft remarks: "What you call crime is nothing: a murder here and a theft there, a blow now and a curse then: what do they matter? They are only the accidents and illnesses of life: there are not fifty genuine professional criminals in London." Undershaft goes on: "But there are millions of poor people, dirty people, ill fed, ill clothed people. They poison us morally and physically . . ." And that is the point: Undershaft *goes on*. Holmes stops at the fact of crime and "evildoers."

It is true that Holmes was never quite the same man after he fell over the Reichenbach Falls (although some of the stories are fine indeed); to engage Doyle's real creative interest, he should have developed. For example, Doyle was always deeply concerned with the problem of life after death; he even dared to convert Professor Challenger into a believer in *The Land of Mist*. Yet, because he had created

Holmes as a skeptic, a "thinking machine," he was unable to introduce this concern into the stories and novels. This might seem to be good sense, for we cannot imagine Holmes attending a séance—at least, not as a believer. But E. and H. Heron recognized the unexplored possibilities in their *Real Ghost Stories* (which began to appear in 1898). They created a psychic investigator called Flaxman Low, obviously based on Holmes, who probes into hauntings and suchlike. Low is as cool and intellectual as Holmes, but he takes for granted that ghosts exist, and investigates psychic phenomena on that assumption. In my own opinion, these are by far the most successful of Holmes's literary progeny (with the possible exception of a couple of stories by Jacques Futrelle).

I suggest this as only one of the possible directions in which Holmes could have been developed. But the truth is that if Holmes had been a real human being, he would have developed in other ways. After the Reichenbach episode, Doyle set out to develop him into a universal man, but his imagination failed him. He was too absorbed in his make-believe world of history—which was not remotely like the reality of the Middle Ages—to attempt to make Holmes a real man in a real modern world. A man with so much interest in crime would have developed an interest in the sociological causes of crime, in the psychology of crime, in the causes of modern man's alienation. Doyle himself investigated a strange case of an animal-disemboweler—the Great Wyrely mystery—but only because an innocent man was accused; he obviously dismissed this sadistic Ripper as an unpleasant madman, without asking himself what could have motivated such a man. The real Holmes would have *wanted* to know. He would also have wanted to know what turns a mathematical genius into a Napoleon of crime. His literary works would not have ended with a monograph on beekeeping or the Chaldean roots of the Cornish language; he would have devoted his retirement to an enormous work on the part played by the sociology of crime in the decline of the West.

In short, Doyle failed to think his creation through to its logical conclusion, thereby demonstrating that he was not the intellectual equal of Sherlock Holmes. But then, perhaps that is just as well. We might draw a lesson from the case of Bernard Shaw. Like Doyle, Shaw made his impact by touching a nerve in the evolutionary consciousness of his age. Although three years Doyle's senior, he achieved fame a great deal later, in the 1905 season of plays at Court Theatre. Shaw's leading characters have an air of ruthless logic that reminds us of Holmes. When someone tells King Magnus that he would like to be able to say "Off with their heads," Magnus replies, "Many men would hardly miss their heads, there is so little in them." That sounds as if it might have been said by Holmes as he scraped away on his violin or filled his hypodermic with a seven percent solution.

Shaw's concern with the superman was more conscious than Doyle's; in fact, he wrote a play called *Man and Superman* in which he formulated the notion that the aim of life is increased consciousness. He developed the idea for two decades, and in *Back to Methuselah* it is embodied in his "Ancients," human beings of some remote future epoch, whose final hope is to become independent of the body and to achieve eternal life. Their ultimate purpose is to develop into a "whirlpool of pure intellect." Shaw's contemporaries rejected the idea with a shudder; they might admire intellect, but they didn't really like it. In a dispute about the sinking of the *Titanic,* Doyle accused Shaw of heartlessness, and most people (including Shaw's biographer Hesketh Pearson) were inclined to agree with him.

Doyle, on the other hand, never made the mistake of trying to think things through to their conclusion. In *The Sign of Four*, Holmes quotes the German Romantic, Richter, and comments: "He makes one curious but profound remark. It is that the chief proof of man's real greatness lies in the perception of his own smallness. It argues, you see, a power of comparison and appreciation which is in itself a proof of nobility." This is a view you might expect of Holmes in his early esthetic period. Yet in spite of his belief in the powers of the intellect, Holmes only becomes more pessimistic with the passage of years. His last appearance is in "The Retired Colourman," in which we find him telling Watson: "Is not all life pathetic and futile? Is not his story a microcosm of the whole? We reach. We grasp. And what is left in our hands at the end? A shadow. Or worse than a shadow—misery." This kind of sentiment reassures the reader, like Shakespeare's speeches on the futility of human existence. It convinces him that, even if Holmes *is* an intellectual superman, the superiority is only skin-deep; basically, he is as helpless and defeated as the rest of us. Unlike Shaw, Doyle was a master of protective coloring. The result is that, while Shaw's reputation has suffered a steep decline since his death, Doyle—and Holmes—is as popular as ever. Human beings love to admire a superman; but they greatly prefer a flawed superman.

6

SCIENCE—AND NIHILISM

In retrospect, I can see that this endless reading was simply a sign of my natural instinct to plunge into the immense inner space of the human mind. But at the time, it seemed—to myself and other people—that I preferred to live in a world of fiction rather than of reality. More than a century after Hoffmann and Poe, I was turning myself into a typical nineteenth-century Romantic, with all that implied in the way of hatred of the "real world," and a preference for the world of imagination.

Fortunately, when I was about ten years old, I discovered an equally fascinating realm—the world of science.

It came about because an aunt presented me with a few issues of a magazine called *Armchair Science*. It contained articles on such subjects as the canals on Mars, and a machine called a cyclotron, used for splitting atoms. On a visit to an aunt and uncle who lived in a nearby town, I talked so much about science that they bought me a volume called *The Marvels and Mysteries of Science*. (It cost five shillings.) It began with a section called *The Wonders of the Heavens* (I have it beside me as I write), with an account of the sun, moon, planets and stars, and continued with a chapter on how the earth began. After reading it, I developed an enthusiasm for astronomy. Like Dickens and Dumas, this appealed to my romanticism. One photograph showed the spiral nebula of Andromeda, with the path of a meteor cutting across the sky like a bolt of lightning. Another showed a huge rock at the edge of the meteor crater in Arizona, forced upright by the impact. As I read about Halley's comet, and the satellites of Mars, and the mysterious red spot on Jupiter (which we now know to be a giant storm), I was no longer a schoolboy living in a dull industrial city, but a scientist who was fascinated by the mysteries of the universe.

I was equally excited by a book called *The Miracle of Life*, presented to me by my grandfather. Although I was less interested in polar bears and duck-billed platypuses than in stars and planets, I was horribly fascinated by a picture of an octopus lying on a rock; like all children, I enjoyed mild thrills of terror. I experienced the same morbid fascination looking at pictures of sharks with open jaws. In a boys' magazine, I had once seen a picture of a man being bitten in half by a shark, with his blood staining the water, and had been shocked and revolted. It always seemed to me a paradox that the world could be so full of beauty—like lilac trees and waterfalls and moonlit nights—and yet so full of danger.

I must digress here to explain that at about the same time, at the beginning of the Second World War, I read an article in a newspaper by Air Marshall Dowding of the Royal Air Force, which claimed to be a communication from a dead pilot, describing how his plane had been shot down, and how he had been amazed to learn that he was still alive, although his body was now dead. After more than half a century, I can no longer recall the details, but I remember that he found himself in a kind of grey twilight, that slowly turned to daylight, and that he then went on to describe how he gradually became acquainted with the world of the afterlife. I remember his description of swimming in water that left his skin completely dry.

I felt no skepticism about this account; it seemed to me as straightforward and reliable as the articles in *The Marvels and Mysteries of Science*. At the age of nine or ten, everything in print is accepted as true.

This, it appeared, was the answer to another question that puzzled me—what happens after we die? It filled in another corner in my gradually-expanding knowledge of the universe. Three years earlier, when I was about seven years old, we had had our first history lesson at school, and I had learned about the existence of dinosaurs. It amazed me that my parents had never bothered to tell me about anything so important, and from then on, I borrowed books from the library and learned about the difference between a diplodocus and a stegosaurus and a tyrannosaurus. The world seemed to be full of important facts that no one had ever bothered to mention. Now I had learned about life after death; I discovered that my grandmother was a "spiritualist," and that there were many books in the adult section of the library about ghosts and poltergeists and haunted houses. As usual, I set out to read them all.

But my interest in the supernatural and my interest in science were at loggerheads. Reading about the depths of the universe, and the world inside the atom, I gradually began to feel contempt for the supernatural. Compared to the question of whether the universe was exploding, the question of whether our souls survived the death of the body seemed rather trivial. Besides, most people struck me as such idiots that it hardly seemed to matter whether they survived death or not. I could not understand why none of the adults around me seemed to share my curiosity about the universe. By the time I was twelve or thirteen, I felt that the question of "survival" was unimportant. It was not until about thirty years later that my interest in the subject began to revive.

When I was eleven, my mother gave me a chemistry set for Christmas. From then on, chemistry seemed the most important subject in the world. I spent all my pocket money on chemicals, and all my weekends in performing experiments in our spare room—which filled the house with the stench of sulphur dioxide or hydrogen sulphide. One experiment always fascinated me: mixing sulphur and iron filings, and then heating them very slightly. As soon as the smallest spot of the sulphur turned into a brown liquid, I could remove the flame, and the reaction would continue until the whole melting-tray was a seething mass of iron sulphide. It reminded me of the way that, during my childhood, some tiny spot of happiness would suddenly form in the mind, and then gradually spread, until my whole being was glowing with a sensation of joy and confidence.

It was also at about this time that my grandfather gave me an old science fiction magazine. Here I was able to unite my two interests—science and the world of the imagination—and I began to collect science fiction magazines with the same obsessive enthusiasm that I had brought to chemistry.

It may well have been in science fiction magazines that I first encountered the name of Einstein. It was obvious that he was regarded as the greatest of modern scientists, and that his theory of relativity was one of the greatest intellectual achievements of the twentieth century. I also read a comment that not more than half a dozen people in the world really understood relativity. Naturally, I was filled with curiosity, and a desire to be the seventh. I looked in the catalogue of the library, and was delighted to find Einstein's book *Relativity: The Special and General Theory.*

I have to admit that my first attempt to read this book was a disappointment. The opening chapter is entitled, *The Physical Meaning of Geometrical Propositions*, and begins:

"In your schooldays, most of you who read this book made acquaintance with the noble building of Euclid's geometry . . . "

Now as far as I was concerned, this was untrue. I was only just then—at the age of eleven—being introduced to geometry, and how to turn a circle into a hexagram with a pair of compasses, and how to work out the area of a right angle triangle. But no one ever mentioned the name of Euclid, and no one bothered to waste time on talking about the "axioms," which would certainly have bored us because they seemed obvious. So Einstein's comment that "For the present we shall assume the 'truth' of the geometrical propositions, then at a later stage (in the general theory of relativity) we shall see that this truth is limited" struck me as totally meaningless. Besides, it seemed to me that what he appeared to be implying was untrue. When he later explained that all the angles of a triangle drawn on the surface of a sphere amount to more than 180 degrees, I felt that this was not being entirely honest; surely, this was a special case that made no difference to the truth of plane geometry, in which the angles always make precisely 180 degrees.

The second chapter of the book had me even more baffled. It was called *The System of Coordinates*, and began by explaining that when we wish to establish the distance between two points on a rigid body, we take a rod whose length we know (a ruler), and mark off the distance between them by using the ruler. That seemed so obvious that I could not see why he bothered to explain it. He goes on to state that "Every description of events in space involves the use of a rigid body to which such events have to be referred. The resulting relationship takes for granted that the laws of Euclidean geometry hold for distances." To which I felt like shouting, "For heaven's sake get on with it!"

But I plodded on. And finally, when I came to Chapter Nine, I began to see daylight. It is called *The Relativity of Simultaneity*, and uses one of Einstein's favorite examples, a train traveling along a railway embankment. Supposing, says Einstein, lightning makes a habit of striking at the same two points along the railway line, and you are given the task of deciding whether the two flashes occur at the same moment. How would you go about it?

One simple method would be to position yourself exactly midway between the two points, and to hold two mirrors positioned at right angles to one another. Now you can actually see the two flashes reflected off the two mirrors, and if they occur at the same moment, then the two lightning strikes occurred simultaneously.

But suppose you are sitting on the roof of a train traveling from point A to point B? Now the light from point A will have to catch up with the train, while the flash from point B will hurry towards it. They will not appear to be simultaneous.

But surely, I thought, this is self-evident? The flashes are simultaneous, but the fact that you are on a moving train disguises this fact.

But Einstein disagrees. The train is what he calls a "coordinate system" (a kind of measuring device, like a graph, with length, breadth and height marked on it). The railway embankment is another coordinate system. Why should you prefer one to the other? Suppose that, instead of a train, you have a long spaceship out in empty space, millions of miles from the nearest star, and you are not sure whether the spaceship is moving or not. Now how do you decide whether the flashes are simultaneous? Of course you cannot. Now let us change the spaceship into a space train on a space embankment—again, millions of miles from the nearest star. You might think that you can now tell whether the train is moving. But no—suppose it is the embankment that is moving, in the opposite direction?

Now, at last, I began to see what Einstein was driving at. We may say that the train is moving relative to the embankment, or that the embankment is moving relative to the train. Both statements are equally true.

At this point I was struck by a terrible thought. Einstein is saying that motion is "relative." On our earth, it is easy to say that the train is moving and the embankment is obviously standing still. But if you look at it from the "universal" viewpoint, like some god whose body stretches between the stars, our earthly viewpoint will seem very parochial.

But for the past two years, I had been studying science because it gave me a comforting sense of incontrovertible fact, of some universal truth, bigger than our trivial human emotions and petty objectives.

When I felt angry at the stupidity of some neighbor, or humiliated by the criticisms of a schoolteacher, I merely had to think about astronomy or chemistry to experience a sense of calm and relaxation. These human problems were trivial and boring; science alone seemed solid and reliable. But now Einstein was telling me that I could find no certainty in science. I was like a devout Christian who has suddenly been convinced that there is no God. I felt as if I had been standing on apparently solid ground, and it had suddenly opened beneath my feet.

But surely, I thought, simultaneousness means something, quite apart from whether your train is moving. If I clap my hands, they strike one another simultaneously. And if someone else claps in unison with me, then that is simultaneous too. The notion "simultaneous" has an intuitive meaning. And can't we explain the fact that, on a moving train, the lightning flash from the front reaches you sooner than the lightning flash from the back by taking the motion of the train into account?

But at this point Einstein produces another paradox.

If I am on a train traveling at fifty miles an hour, and I run along the corridor towards the engine at ten miles an hour, then my total speed is sixty miles an hour. And if the train is traveling at half the speed of light, and I shine a torch towards the engine, then the speed of the light from the torch ought to be one and a half times the normal speed of light. Yet according to Einstein, this is not so. At half the speed of light, time goes slower, and measured by this "slowed-down" time, light would be found to travel at its normal speed.

Again, this notion that time can "flow" at different speeds contradicted common sense, and increased my feeling that Einstein had undermined all my old certainties. I felt intuitively that he must be wrong to declare that the speed of light is a "law of nature." After all, light actually travels slower in water; why should it not also travel faster?

But the problem was complicated by the fact that I wanted to believe Einstein. I enjoyed explaining the theory of relativity to school friends, and answering their objections. So I swallowed his notions about the relativity of space and time, even though they gave me indigestion, and made me feel strangely insecure.

The sense of insecurity suddenly overwhelmed me one day at school, in a clay-modeling class. With a boy called Cyril Flynn, I had been discussing the problem of the expanding universe. But what is the universe expanding into? Presumably into the empty space beyond the stars. But where did that space end? It could not be infinite, yet it was also impossible to imagine that it had an ending. Suddenly, I experienced a sense of sudden danger, a feeling that the world around me was not as solid and secure as it seemed. Children come into a world that has already been prepared for them; they assume that grown-ups know everything. And even when they realize that grown-ups are more ignorant than they had supposed, they continue to believe that all questions have an answer, and that the "eternal verities" remain eternal. Now I had discovered a question that seemed to have no answer, and it made me feel dizzy and afraid.

Everyone knows that it is difficult to concentrate on a book if you feel you are about to be interrupted at any moment. And in the same way, it becomes difficult to live confidently and normally if you feel insecure. All effort might turn out to be pointless. Now it seemed to me that the problems raised by Einstein had destroyed my old sense of intellectual security. Sherlock Holmes and Dupin had symbolized the feeling that the intellect can solve any problem, and that therefore the development of the mind and the acquisition of knowledge is the most important goal to which a human being can devote himself. And now, suddenly, this seemed an illusion. Instead of providing me with a secure vantage point, from which I could look down on the chaos of human existence, science had plunged me into the chaos.

The need for security is basic in human beings. A child may feel bored with his way of life and rebellious towards his parents, but at least they are a part of the normality that surrounds him. For me, this normality now seemed an illusion, like the security that a lamb feels as it nestles against its mother, unaware that they are both destined for the supermarket freezer.

A few years later, in William James' *Varieties of Religious Experience*, I came upon the passage in which the French philosopher Simon-Theodore Jouffroy describes his own loss of faith, and it brought back all my old feelings of anguish and terror.

"I shall never forget that night of December in which the veil that concealed from me my own incredulity was torn. I hear again my steps in that narrow, naked chamber where, long after the hour of sleep had come, I had the habit of walking up and down. I see again that moon, half-veiled by clouds, which now and again illuminated the frigid window panes. The hours of the night flowed on, and I did not note their passage. Anxiously I followed my thoughts as, from layer to layer, they descended towards the foundations of my consciousness, and, scattering one by one all the illusions which until then had screened its windings from my view, made them every moment more clearly visible.

"Vainly I clung to these last beliefs as a shipwrecked sailor clings to the fragments of his vessel; vainly, frightened at the unknown void into which I was about to float, I turned with them towards my childhood, my family, my country, all that was dear and sacred to me: the inflexible current of my thought was too strong—parents, family, memory, beliefs, it forced me to let go of everything. The investigation went on more obstinate and more severe as it drew near its term, and did not stop until the end was reached. I knew then that in the depth of my mind, nothing was left that stood erect.

"This moment was a frightful one; and when towards morning, I threw myself exhausted on my bed, I seemed to feel my earlier life, so smiling and so full, go out like a fire, and before me another life opened, somber and unpeopled, where in future I must live alone, alone with my fatal thought which had exiled me thither—and which I was now tempted to curse. The days which followed this discovery were the saddest of my life."

Now I felt the same: that I was living in a world of people who were blinded by delusions, and that I was the only one who was awake. And my knowledge gave me no advantage—only drained away my vitality and optimism. Nietzsche had experienced the same feeling of emptiness when he read Schopenhauer's *World as Will and Illusion*, and Thomas Mann describes a similar "revelation" in *Buddenbrooks*. There is a sense of coldness, of a loss of inner warmth and vitality.

Now, suddenly, all my old certainties seemed to participate in the doubt. When, as a child, someone had accused me of selfishness, I had occasionally reflected that, seen from a certain point of view, everyone is selfish. Society approves of the philanthropist and disapproves of the criminal; but who is to say that the philanthropist is really less selfish than the criminal? His generosity gives him pleasure and makes him think well of himself; so does the approval of other people. The criminal is prepared to dispense with self-approval for the sake of making a living.

Now the obvious answer to this argument is that the criminal's lack of self-discipline in choosing the path of least resistance is likely to stunt his personal evolution, and since I had no doubt that intelligent and disciplined people are preferable to stupid and lazy people, I could see the fallacy involved. But it seemed to me altogether more difficult to answer the argument that living things are basically machines that have adapted themselves to their environment, and that therefore our sense of values is basically an illusion. When we are hungry, we feel that food is a "value;" when we feel sick, it seems revolting.

In *Man the Machine*, La Mettrie had argued that our lives are merely a series of mechanical responses. This argument always induced in me a kind of despair, since it was obvious that La Mettrie would dismiss any objection as a mechanical response designed to protect our self-esteem. And if we reply, "But in that case, your reply is equally mechanical, and proves that you are also nothing more than a machine," he replies, "Precisely—that is what I have just said."

What made it worse was the feeling that I was the only person in the world who had ever felt such a total sense of the futility of everything. As far as I could see, most people seemed to be fairly contented, and certainly, no one I ever met showed any sign of suspecting that life was merely a shallow surface of meaning over an endless depth of emptiness.

These problems were to haunt me throughout my teens, and to create a deep underlying sense of insecurity—what Camus calls "the absurd." Writers as totally unlike as Nietzsche and G. K. Chesterton experienced it.

But fortunately, I did not spend all my time brooding on the mysteries of human existence. When I spent a long day cycling in the countryside, eating sandwiches beside the river at Warwick Castle or on top of the great cliff at Matlock, I was aware that being a teenager has its compensations.

7

JEFFERY FARNOL
AND HIGH ADVENTURE

When I was thirteen, I worked as a newspaper boy for pocket money. The newspaper shop also had a lending library, from which books could be borrowed for a few pence a week. Often, while waiting for the newsagent to finish sorting the pile of newspapers, I would browse through the books. There was a whole set of a writer of whom I knew little—Jeffery Farnol. Apparently these copies belonged to the newsagent himself, and he warmly recommended them. He suggested that I should begin with *Black Bartlemy's Treasure*, but I thought this sounded too like a boy's adventure story—I was, after all, reading Einstein, Jeans and Eddington—and instead I borrowed *The Chronicles of the Imp*.

From the first few sentences, I was gripped; I read it from beginning to end in virtually one sitting.

It begins with a young man fishing by the side of a stream. He is in love with a girl called Elizabeth (known as Lisbeth), but she has been sent away to stay in a country house—her formidable Aunt Agatha feels that she and the hero have become too friendly. But the young man—his name is Dick Brent—has discovered that the aunt has the design of marrying Elizabeth to the brother of a peer. After learning where Elizabeth is staying from a gossipy socialite, he goes to lodge at the local inn—naturally called the Three Jolly Anglers—and hangs around hoping to catch a glimpse of her.

51

"It is a fair thing," comments the narrator, "upon a hot summer's afternoon, within a shady bower, to lie upon one's back and stare up through a network of branches into the limitless blue beyond, while the air is full of the stir of leaves, and the murmur of water among the reeds."

Now there is not a word here that is not a cliché. Yet it undeniably does conjure up a warm summer day, and the buzz of insects, and a sense of total relaxation.

This, I was to discover, was typical Farnol. He loves to write about fields and rivers and the sky, and no author evokes more nostalgically the delights of the countryside.

His hero is fortunate, for as he lies by the stream, a muddy child appears. His name is Reginald Augustus and he is known as "the Imp." He has just been playing at being a Roman standard bearer, which necessitated jumping into the stream to fight the ancient Britons. And after a few minutes conversation, during which the child confesses that he is very fond of worms and proves it by producing a large and fat specimen from his trouser pocket, the hero discovers that his beloved Elizabeth is at present looking after the Imp and his younger sister Dorothy while their mother is away. The Imp also confides that he has removed Lisbeth's stockings while she was paddling, and has hidden them in a hollow tree. For half a crown, the Imp divulges their exact whereabouts.

At that moment, Lisbeth herself arrives, and is naturally scornful of her suitor for following her. Then there is "a patter of footsteps, and a little girl tripped into view, with a small fluffy kitten cuddled in her arms." (It is clear that Farnol expends a great deal of thought on finding the precise word, and never chooses it without consulting his dictionary of platitudes.) And the two children are taken off to tea.

The hero hurries towards the hollow tree in quest of Lisbeth's stockings, and sees her coming from the opposite direction. He reaches the tree a moment before she does, and retrieves the "soft silken bundle." And although she stamps her foot (as all Farnol's heroines are prone to do), he declines to give them back. In the conversation that follows, he detects the presence of a dimple in the corner of her mouth. "Now if ever there was an arrant traitor in this world it is that dimple; for let her expression be ever so guileless, let her wistful eyes be raised with a look of tears in their blue depths, despite herself that dimple will spring into life and undo it all in a moment." From the presence of the dimple, Dick deduces that she is less angry with him than she pretends, and takes the opportunity to tell her once more that he owns an old Tudor house in Kent with an old-fashioned rose garden which requires the attention of a mistress. He offers her the stockings in return for a kiss, and she appears to be about to yield. In fact, she steals the stockings from his pocket. As she turns to go he begs her to let him keep just one of the stockings; she points out that one stocking would hardly be of any use. But as he turns to go, "there came a ripple of laughter behind me, something struck me softly upon the cheek, and, stooping, I picked up that which lay half unrolled at my feet."

From the first chapter it is perfectly obvious that Lisbeth is more than half in love with him. And since he adores her, it might seem that the story is virtually finished. But that, of course, would not suit Farnol in the least. He is a romantic daydreamer, and loves nothing so much as bringing together a man and a woman, and describing how, with infinite slowness, the woman yields and admits that she loves him. It is a sexual fantasy, but entirely without any crude sexual element. When D. H. Lawrence shows Paul Morel, in *Sons and Lovers*, pulling on his ladylove's stockings, it is perfectly obvious that he finds them sexually exciting. In Farnol, they are simply a soft bundle of silky gauze, and they belong to fairyland rather than to the real world.

There would be no point in going into further detail about the plot of *Chronicles of the Imp*, for it has very little. Selwyn, the peer's brother, whom Aunt Agatha intends Lisbeth to marry, wears highly-polished riding boots and has "a small sleek moustache which was parted with elaborate care and twisted into two fine points"—in short, the archetypal Edwardian villain. Naturally, he tries to commit physical violence on the Imp at an early stage in the book, and is thwarted by the hero. He continues to be thwarted in his designs at regular intervals.

In the key episode of the book, Lisbeth is asleep in the bottom of a boat, watched by the adoring Dick, who lies in concealment. Suddenly, the Imp is inspired to play one of his practical jokes, and cuts the painter. Unfortunately, Dick cannot swim—and if we wonder why Farnol has failed to supply him with this essential masculine attribute, the answer is that he would then rescue Lisbeth by simply jumping into the water. Instead, he rushes downstream, climbs an oak tree, wriggles out along a branch, and succeeds in landing in the boat as it passes underneath. Elizabeth wakes up, jumps to the conclusion that

Dick has cut the painter, and is not amused. To protect the Imp, Dick does not disillusion her. Then they realize that they are coming close to the weir, and that both are likely to be drowned. She allows him to take her in his arms, murmuring "Dick, you will hold me tight, you will not let me go when . . . "

Fortunately, a boat appears and tows them ashore. For the first time in the book, the hero is angry with the Imp; he makes him hold out his hands, and gives him two cuts with a cane. At that moment, Lisbeth appears and asks why the Imp is crying; he tells her that Uncle Dick has "whipped his hands." And as Lisbeth explodes with indignation, the Imp confesses that it was he who cut the painter. Lizbeth asks how Dick got into the boat, and he admits that he risked his life climbing out along the branch of a tree. Full of remorse, she asks, "Oh, Dick, can you ever forgive me?" and he tells her that he will be glad to forgive her on condition that she . . . But before he can propose, little Dorothy appears. Farnol is having far too much fun with his daydream to end it so quickly.

So the book goes on for several more chapters. As in a musical comedy, Dick and Lisbeth have to quarrel, as he becomes convinced that she has decided to marry Selwyn. The misunderstanding gets resolved, and Dick and Lisbeth lose no time in getting married. The last chapter, called *The Land of Heart's Delight*, begins, "Surely there never was and never could be such another morning as this?" and the sentence is repeated half a dozen times in the next few pages. Aunt Agatha, complete with lorgnette, arrives in haste, to be faced with the fait accompli. Fortunately, they are close to the Three Jolly Anglers, from which "wafted to us on the warm still air, there came a wondrous fragrance, far sweeter and more alluring to the hungry than the breath of roses or honeysuckle—the delightful aroma of frying bacon." Farnol seems to have had a passion for bacon—the smell of frying bacon figures in just about all of his books (which number more than fifty). So they all go off for breakfast, and Aunt Agatha unexpectedly confesses that if she had married the man she loved forty years ago, she would have been a far happier woman. And so the book closes as Dick and Lisbeth sail away for their honeymoon, with the Imp, Dorothy and Aunt Agatha waving from the shore.

Now there can be no doubt that *The Chronicles of the Imp* is one of the most sugary pieces of sentimental nonsense ever written. Yet I can still recall, more than half a century later, devouring every page, and closing it with a smile of contentment. At that point I had already written my first short book, *Essays on the Life Aim*, in which I analyzed humanity's proneness to self-delusion, and had—as described in an earlier chapter—experienced despair at the thought of the endlessness of space. But the fact remained that I was thirteen, sexually inexperienced, and full of longing for a member of the opposite sex. Farnol's long-drawn-out romantic daydreams were exactly what I needed. So was his love of the countryside, and his talk about wayside inns and meandering streams and the smell of frying bacon. I was becoming trapped inside my own head, convinced, like Faust, that "we can know nothing." Farnol brought hours of pleasure and relief.

After *Chronicles of the Imp*, the news agent recommended a book called *The Money Moon*. I soon saw why. It is simply a slightly longer version of *Chronicles of the Imp*. Farnol evidently decided that there was far more juice to be squeezed out of the daydream, and shamelessly set about repeating it. The comedian Shelley Berman, commenting on Erskine Caldwell's penchant for semi-pornography, said, "I don't know why that man is seeking success. He could have so much fun just sitting thinking." Where Jeffery Farnol is concerned, this is literally true. He writes as an adolescent fantasizes about romance and greatness: out of the sheer delight of telling himself stories.

The Money Moon is even more preposterous than *The Chronicles of the Imp*. The hero, George Bellew, is a young American millionaire, athletic, square-jawed and strangely friendless. It never strikes Farnol that such a young man—with a yacht and three racing cars—would have more friends than he could possibly handle, and a dozen girls all determined to become Mrs. Bellew. But such perceptiveness would conflict with the demands of the fantasy.

Jilted by the girl he loves, Bellew takes to the open road, like most of Farnol's heroes. And as he sits on a bank eating bread and cheese, a boy crashes through the hedge, "A very diminutive boy with a round head covered with coppery curls." The Imp is back. This time he is called Georgy-Porgy, but since Bellew's name is also George, they decide that he shall be Small Porges while Bellew is Big Porges. Like the hero of *Chronicles of the Imp*, the hero promptly adopts him as a nephew.

The boy explains that he is on his way to Africa to seek his fortune. His Aunt Anthea, who owns a nearby farm, needs money urgently. Mr. Cassilis, the local squire, is trying to persuade her to marry him, but she is unwilling.

Small Porges' new uncle persuades him to return home. On the way they meet Mr. Cassilis who, exactly like Selwyn of the previous book, proclaims himself a villain by his riding boots and small moustache. Farnol adds that his eyes are too close together. He and Bellew take an instant dislike to one another. ("He only smiles like that when he's awful angry," says Small Porges.)

Anthea is, of course, the typical Farnol heroine: "as tall and gracious, as proud and beautiful, as Enid or Guinevere . . . for all her simple gown of blue, and the sunbonnet that shaded the beauty of her face." Bellew naturally falls in love with her at first sight. But, being a Farnol hero, he would not dream of taking advantage of his acquaintance with Small Porges to force his acquaintance on her; he is fading away into the sunset (literally) when she calls him back. She takes him for a tramp, and tells him that if he goes to the house, cook will give him a good meal. Then she sees his face, realizes he is a gentleman, and blushes. "Now that their eyes met, it seemed to Bellew as if he had lived all his life in expectation of this moment." He tells her that he is a friendless American in search of lodgings, and after wrinkling her nose ("for a lodger was something entirely new in her experience") she offers him a room.

In real life this would raise questions of propriety—a handsome young man moving into a farmhouse with a beautiful girl in her early twenties with only her young nephew as chaperone. (Farnol never explains how Anthea came to be in charge of Porges.) But all Farnol cares about is getting them in close proximity, so the daydream can get started. So Bellew moves in to Dapplemere "in the glory of the afterglow of an August afternoon, breathing the magic air of Arcadia."

The farm, of course, dates from the days of Henry the Eighth, and possesses latticed windows, a great old hall, spacious chambers and broad stairways. He soon meets Aunt Priscilla, Anthea's delightful housekeeper; a one-armed soldier who adores her but does not dare to speak; as well as a farm laborer called Old Adam, a benevolent witch, and various other quaint country characters.

The central event of the book is a sale of Anthea's furniture. The unpleasant man who owns the mortgage on the house—who bears the Dickensian name of Grimes—is hoping to buy most of it, for he is hoping to repossess the house. Bellew, of course, frustrates this by giving Old Adam enough money to bid for most of the items; he himself joins in to outbid Grimes by paying a vast sum for an antique sideboard.

Now Anthea has already drooped her long lashes often enough to convince us that she is attracted by Bellew, and now that he has bought back her furniture for her, one might suppose that the path of true love would run smooth. But that would break the romantic spell long before Farnol is ready. So Old Adam manages to give Anthea the impression that Bellew is engaged to a childhood sweetheart, and intends the furniture for his own use. Her affronted pride leads her to decide to marry the wicked squire.

Things eventually sort themselves out. But Farnol has decided on a far more dramatic climax than in *The Chronicles of the Imp*. The benevolent old witch has told Anthea that she will marry a man who bears "the tiger's mark," and that "by force she will be wooed and by force she will be wed." Bellew has on his arm three long scratches inflicted by a tiger. When the villainous landlord tries to foreclose, Small Porges saves the day with a sack full of gold coins (which Bellew has planted in the orchard). When even this fails to soften Anthea's heart, Bellew seizes her as she stands on a bridge in the moonlight, carries her to his car, and takes her to a church where they are married by special license. Naturally, she yields gracefully, with appropriate blushes, dimples, and drooping of her long eyelashes, and she tells him, in her "low, thrilling voice, 'I have loved you—from the—very beginning.' And with a soft murmurous sigh she gave herself into his embrace."

One might have expected that even the reviewers of this time—about 1912—would have had some harsh things to say about such a gushing and unashamed wish-fulfillment fantasy. But on the contrary, they seemed to have reveled in the sentimentality. "One of the most delightful youngsters we have met in fiction," said the *Lady* of Small Porges, "will be appreciated by all lovers of little folk and their ways." "The story has all the charm of the country spring time," said the *Librarian*. Even the *Lancet* declared that "To those who can enter with sympathy into the mind of childhood, the book will prove delightful."

Although written after *The Imp*, *The Money Moon* came out earlier. *Chronicles of the Imp* was, in fact, Farnol's first novel, and had been universally rejected. But the story of the success that followed its rejection is every bit as romantic as one of Farnol's own daydreams.

John Jeffery Farnol was born on February 10, 1878, at Aston, near Birmingham. His mother encouraged him to write, but his parents nevertheless decided to turn him into an engineer, and apprenticed him to a brass foundry. Then they relented, and allowed him to attend art school. Farnol fell in love with an American girl, married her, and moved to New York. There he became a scene painter in the Astor Theatre, but was scarcely able to support his wife, who moved back with her parents at Englewood, New Jersey. Nostalgia for the English countryside is visible in *Chronicles of the Imp*. (A far greater novelist, John Cowper Powys, was to write his finest evocation of the English countryside, *A Glastonbury Romance*, while pining for England in New York State.)

Undeterred by publishers' rejections, Farnol went on to write another novel of the countryside, this time set in the days of the Regency. It begins, "As I sat of an early summer morning in the shade of a tree, eating fried bacon with a tinker, the thought came to me that I might some day write a book of my own, a book that should treat of the roads and by-roads, of trees, and wind in lonely places, of rapid brooks and lazy streams, of the glory of dawn, the glow of evening, and the purple solitude of night; a book of wayside inns and sequestered taverns; a book of country things and ways and people. And the thought pleased me much."

The narrator of *The Broad Highway* is the scholarly but powerfully-built Peter Vibart. And the book opens with a lawyer reading his uncle's will. "And to my nephew, Maurice Vibart, I bequeath the sum of twenty thousand pounds in the fervent hope that it may help him to the devil within the year, or as soon after as may be."

To his other nephew Peter, Sir George has left only ten guineas, with which to buy a copy of Zeno or any other stoic philosopher. (Farnol offers no reason for this disinheritance, but his own reason was certainly that otherwise he would have had no plot.) But he adds that the remaining five hundred thousand pounds of his estate shall go to whichever of his nephews succeeds in marrying Lady Sophia Sefton, the well-known beauty, within a year.

Unoffended, Peter takes the ten guineas and sets out on the open road (which, if not quite Farnol's only plot, was at least his mainstay, utilized again and again). Within a short time he has been divested of his ten guineas and his watch by a footpad under a gibbet. He goes into an inn to spend his remaining two pence, and hears a pugilist named Tom Cragg denying angrily that he has been beaten by Maurice Vibart—known as "Buck." To prove it, Cragg offers a bet of ten shillings that he can beat any man present. Peter promptly takes him up on the offer, hoping to obtain the money for a night's lodging; but to his surprise, Cragg goes pale when he sees him, and winks heavily. In fact, Cragg is the first of many people who mistake Peter for his cousin Maurice.

Peter sells his embroidered waistcoat to a farmer for ten shillings, and goes on his way. By now, the reader acquainted with *The Pickwick Papers* will recognize it was one of Farnol's main inspirations. Like Dickens, he loves creating "characters"—literary tinkers, philosophical yokels, and suchlike—and recording their manner of speaking. Farnol writes with just as much inventiveness as Dickens, but lacks his sheer dramatic genius. And whenever his imagination flags, he introduces a damsel in distress.

In a tavern where he is spending the night, Peter hears a woman sobbing. A beautiful girl has been locked in her room by a would-be seducer. As the footsteps of the villain sound on the stair, Peter clambers through her window. The door opens; he strikes a man in the dark, then Peter and the abducted maiden flee. It seems that she has been lured away from home by Sir Harry Mortimer, an unpleasant character we have encountered earlier in the story.

In a dark wood, for the only time in his books (as far as I know), Farnol makes his hero fall prey to temptation; as the lovely girl offers him her hands in gratitude, he seizes her and tries to kiss her. His hat falls off, and when she sees his face, she also mistakes him for his wicked cousin Maurice. His conscience pricked, he strikes a tree with his fist, skinning his knuckles. From now on, he behaves like all Farnol's heroes, with impeccable chivalry.

They are now close to the estates of Lady Sophia Sefton, and the alert reader senses that it cannot be long before she enters the story. Peter approaches a temperamental blacksmith called Black George (or Jarge) for a job. (Farnol had himself been a blacksmith during his apprenticeship.) The blacksmith agrees to hire him if Peter can beat him in a hammer-throwing contest. Each shall have three throws. Peter wins the first, then the smith exerts himself and throws the hammer far beyond Peter's range. Peter deliberately makes an appearance of all-out effort, and throws far short of the smith's distance. The smith is deceived, and makes less effort next time. This time Peter beats his throw. And so Peter becomes the apprentice of Black George, and goes to live in a "haunted" cottage in the woods. (The ghost proves to be a Scots piper.)

One stormy night, a beautiful girl knocks at his door. She is pursued by a villain, a gentleman who is determined to possess her. He and Peter fight, and Peter wins by luck, when his opponent falls and strikes his head on a stone. When Peter sees his face by lamplight, he recognizes his cousin Maurice Vibart.

After the unconscious Maurice has been transported away by a postilion, Peter collapses. The beautiful lady, who introduces herself as Charmian, nurses him. (The reader, of course, guesses that she is Lady Sophia Sefton.)

Now Farnol has engineered his favorite situation—the hero and heroine living in close proximity, so they can take their time falling in love. (It was a device that Farnol probably learned from Jane Austen.) To add piquancy, he is pretending to be plain Peter Smith, a blacksmith, although she can see from the fact that he reads Virgil in Latin and Homer in Greek that he is a gentleman and a scholar. And although she sees through his subterfuge (his real name is written in front of the Virgil), she also insists that she is plain Charmian Brown, poor and friendless. He takes her word for it, in spite of the fact that under her coarse brown cloak she is wearing expensive silk stockings.

The book ought now to be nearing its end—surely they cannot take all that long to fall in love? In fact, it is only halfway finished, for Farnol gets such keen pleasure from his absurd situations that he wants to make them last forever. Given his own way, he would take three volumes to make his hero and heroine fall in love, even if he managed to contrive a way of making them share the same bed.

Black George conceives the mistaken idea that Peter is hoping to steal his own ladylove, Prue, who runs the inn kitchen, and he has another of his "spells" and vanishes. When he finally encounters Peter, he insists that they fight, and although Peter puts up a good show, he is no match for George's enormous strength, and is beaten unconscious. This is fortunate, for he and Charmian have just quarreled, and now he is bruised and battered, all her womanly tenderness wells to the surface, and she once again becomes his nurse.

It never strikes Farnol that having his hero and heroine living together in a cottage is improper; he has devised the whole plot to make it seem normal and natural. And so their fingers occasionally touch, she blushes and drops her eyes, and he tells her that, from all he has read of women in books, he never intends to marry one.

Finally, the moment cannot be delayed any longer. After a dozen or so misunderstandings, she confesses she loves him, and they go off and get married. End of book? No, not at all. For Peter's wicked cousin Maurice, who has sworn to come between then, is found murdered, a bullet through his head. Charmian confesses that she flung open the door and fired a pistol to frighten away an intruder. Realizing that his beloved is likely to end on the gallows, Peter hastens to take the blame on himself.

"'Some day,' said I, 'Some day if there is a just God in heaven, we shall meet again . . . '

"With a broken cry, she drew my head down upon her breast, and clasped it there . . . "

Peter flees to London. He is caught by Bow Street Runners, but escapes. Finally, exhausted and bruised, he collapses on the doorstep of his friend Sir Richard (who had been present at the reading of the will). There Charmian is waiting for him, and he finally learns that he has married Lady Sophia Charmian Sefton. When he wakes up—three days later—Sir Richard tells him the news that the real murderer, a man whom Maurice Vibart had wronged, has confessed. All that remains for Peter is to rush back to the cottage in the dell and take his wife in his arms.

For a first novel (or rather, a second) *The Broad Highway* is quite a remarkable achievement. Farnol writes naturally and well. He is particularly good at dialogue, and often drags out to a page and a half an exchange that ought to take a few lines. But he is always readable, with a natural gift for fast action. In retrospect, *The Broad Highway* is full of absurdities; on the romantic level, it is only one step above the kind of cheap fiction written for teenagers. Yet it is carried off with a panache that sweeps the reader on from page to page, even while he is wincing at its atrocious banalities. It is incomprehensible that it was not accepted by the first publisher who saw it.

In fact, it was rejected by three American publishers—two without comment, one on the grounds that it would only appeal to English readers. An actor offered to show it to Little, Brown in Boston, but forgot, and when he returned to New York, it was still in the bottom of his trunk. Farnol sent the manuscript to his wife in Englewood, suggesting that she read it then burn it. But she sent it to a literary friend in England, Shirley Byron Jevons, and he instantly recognized its merit, and took it to the publisher Sampson Low. A director showed it to the critic

Clement Shorter, who was a devotee of the books of George Borrow, by whom Farnol was also undoubtedly influenced, with their heroes who enjoy life on the open road. Shorter also recognized its merit. *The Broad Highway* came out in 1910, in the midst of the golden Edwardian era, and became an instant bestseller. Offered to Little, Brown in Boston, it instantly disproved the New York publisher's comment that it was too English. The book sold 600,000 copies in a year, and made Farnol rich. He returned to England a celebrity.

But what was he to do as an encore? Would he prove to be a one-book author? Never at a loss, Farnol pulled *Chronicles of the Imp* from a drawer, and rewrote it as *The Money Moon*, making the hero an American to appeal to his American audience. It is, as we have seen, a wish-fulfillment fantasy, whose attraction lies in the idea of an anonymous millionaire who becomes the lodger of a beautiful girl with heavy debts (Farnol never ceased to love the notion of people masquerading, their identities concealed). The critics loved it. So he offered his publisher *Chronicles of the Imp*. And in spite of its close resemblance to *The Money Moon*, it was just as successful. The public could not get enough of Farnol's brand of wish-fulfillment fantasy.

The Amateur Gentleman, which followed in 1913, is in its way quite as good as *The Broad Highway*. This time its hero, Barnabas Barty, is unexpectedly left seven hundred thousand pounds by a deceased uncle who has made a fortune in Jamaica, and decides to go to London to become a "gentleman." He is only an innkeeper's son. But, like all Farnol's heroes, he speaks with such a literary touch that no one seems to guess that he was not a born gentleman, and as "Mr. Beverley" he makes a considerable impression among the Regency bucks.

Naturally, Barnabas would not dream of doing anything so commonplace as taking public transport to London, which in those days would have been a coach, or even riding a horse; he has to set out on foot.

"It was upon a certain glorious morning some three weeks later that Barnabas fared forth into the world; a morning full of the thousand scents of herb and flower and ripening fruits; a morning glad with the song of birds. And because it was still very early, the dew yet lay heavy, it twinkled on the grass, it sparkled in the hedges, and gemmed every leaf and twig with a flaming pendant."

Within a mile or so, he has decided to take a shortcut across a field, and finds a beautiful girl lying unconscious, " . . . her tumbled hair made a glory in the grass, a golden mane." There is, of course, "a small polished riding boot with its delicately spurred heel," and Barnabas devours with his eyes "the gracious line that swelled voluptuously from knee to rounded hip, that sank in sweetly to a slender waist, yet rose again to the rounded beauty of her bosom." But approaching her from the other side is a Regency buck, whose curling lip proclaims him a villain, and who addresses Barnabas as "my man" and orders him to take himself off. His dishonorable intentions are revealed by the "slow smile" that spreads over his face as he contemplates the "defenseless beauty."

Barnabas, of course, refuses to go, even when the villain threatens to thrash him, and the two of them fight. Barnabas knocks him unconscious with a blow to the chin (he has been trained as a pugilist, which serves him well later in the book), and carries off the defenseless beauty to a nearby stream, where she "raises her curling lashes" and asks "Where am I?" When, in due course, Barnabas tells her he is going to London, the reader entertains a suspicion that they will meet again.

And so it goes on, preposterous beyond words, full of unlikely twists of plot, yet quite obsessively readable. Barnabas, of course, has no difficulty being mistaken for a gentleman in London, and ends by marrying the voluptuous beauty, whose name is Lady Cleone Meredith.

What kind of life Farnol led as a best-selling author is unrecorded—the few biographical facts are contained in Clement Shorter's introduction to *Chronicles of the Imp*. I have not even seen a photograph of him. All that is certain is that he continued writing busily until his death in 1952, at the age of seventy-four, and that he continued to play an infinite number of variations on his two or three themes. A novel from any period of his life reads like a novel from any other period. In *The Quest of Youth*, a middle-aged baronet named Sir Marmaduke decides that he needs exercise, and takes to the open road. Weary, he climbs a hayrick and falls asleep. He soon learns that he is sharing it with a pretty Quaker girl, Eve-Ann, who is running away from home to join her lover. The lover proves to be another treacherous Regency buck, who is soon sent packing by Sir Marmaduke. After that, there is an encounter with a wicked squire, who also has designs on the pretty Quaker. Just before Sir Marmaduke and the squire are due to fight a duel, the squire is found dead, killed by a blunderbuss, which is now in the hands of the Quaker girl.

It would greatly simplify the story if Eve-Ann explained that she did not kill the squire, but Farnol prefers a plot with as many complications as possible. So the noble baronet (who is known to the girl as simple John Hobbs) breaks his own gold-headed cane and leaves it by the body, to give the impression that he is the murderer. Then he and Eve-Ann take to the road, and make for London.

Naturally, true love does not run smooth, and in the last chapter, Sir Marmaduke is gloomily back at home, believing that Eve-Ann is about to marry his nephew. But when his nephew appears and admits that Eve-Ann has rejected him, Sir Marmaduke hurries to her cottage, where she flings herself into his arms.

As I reread Farnol, it becomes obvious that he never advanced beyond the year 1910. He remains a figure of the placid Edwardian era, like Mr. Toad of *The Wind in the Willows*. His work breathes an air of innocence—the kind of innocence and romanticism that can also be found in Anthony Hope, G. K. Chesterton, Stanley J. Weyman, P. C. Wren, Rafael Sabatini and J. Phillips Oppenheim. Reading their works, full of chivalrous gentlemen, and ladies whose long eyelashes are always drooping demurely on cheeks that have the consistency of a peach, it is hard to believe that the twentieth century held in store horrors like Auschwitz, the atom bomb and the serial killer.

All the same, I find it hard to feel any great nostalgia about the Edwardians. Their basic values were sound—they believed in honor and decency—but I find that their world is curiously stifling. They are trapped in a kind of perpetual adolescence. When I read Raskolnikov's comment in *Crime and Punishment*—that he would rather stand on a narrow ledge forever and ever than die at once—I suddenly catch a glimpse of the real potentialities of human existence, and the possibility of a continual consciousness of freedom, and Farnol's sunlit world suddenly looks as artificial as a stage set.

Still, I have to admit that I owe Farnol an odd debt of gratitude. His sweet, demure ladies became fixed in my mind as a kind of archetype. When I met my wife Joy nine years later, I was instantly captivated by her graceful walk and pleasant voice and sweet-natured smile, and felt impelled to pursue her until she agreed to break her engagement and come to London with me. It was only later that I realized that the archetype to which she corresponded had been shaped by Edwardian heroines, particularly those of Jeffery Farnol. So clearly, his works were by no means as unsound a guide to living in the real world as they seemed at the time.

8

ON KEEPING A DIARY

It was in one of Shaw's prefaces that I first came upon a reference to a young Russian artist, Marie Bashkirtseff, whose posthumous diaries had caused a scandal when they were published in 1890 because she talked confidently about her genius and her determination to be a famous artist. She had died at the age of twenty-four.

I borrowed the book from the Leicester Public Library, which possessed a first edition. (There was probably no second edition.) I gazed for a long time at her picture opposite the title page—a beautiful girl of sixteen, leaning sideways, with both elbows resting on a cabinet and gazing at the camera; I assume this is a daguerreotype. Naturally, she became the subject of my daydreams.

Marie had been born in Poltava, in the Ukraine, on November 11, 1860, the daughter of a wealthy Russian landowner. Regrettably, her father was a philanderer who continued to sow his wild oats after marriage, so that his wife left him after only two years. So Marie was deprived of the father figure that is so essential to all young girls at an early age.

When Marie was ten, her mother's family set out on a grand tour of Europe—Vienna, Baden-Baden, Nice. During a later stay in Rome, she was fascinated by the great artists: Leonardo, Michelangelo, Raphael. Ever since the age of four she had believed she was destined for greatness; now she decided that she would be a great artist. At seventeen, she became an art student in Paris. She wrote: "I am enchanted: the streets were full of students coming out from the schools. The narrow streets! These musical instrument makers, and all kinds of things! Ah, heavens! how well I understood the magic, if I may call it so, of the Latin Quarter!"

In spite of the fact that her life so far had been fairly devoid of discipline, she now began to work hard at her art. Unlike so many of the other art students, she lived in an elegant home and wanted for nothing. Then she moved into her own atelier, which comprised a whole floor, and had shelves full of expensive books. And finally, at the age of twenty-three, celebrity arrived when her painting, "Le Meeting," was exhibited in the Salon of '84 and attracted wide attention. It was reproduced in illustrated magazines all over the continent, and journalists wrote about her in the society columns. Unfortunately, the tuberculosis that was to kill her in less than a year was already advanced.

The painter she admired more than any other, Jules Bastien-Lepage, had become a close friend, and he was also dying of tuberculosis. Marie was probably in love with him, and his death almost certainly hastened her own.

I must admit that I read the journal with puzzlement. What seemed so strange was that this lovely girl, who was already pursued by admirers in her mid-teens, should have wanted to keep a diary in which she confided her desire for fame. Where someone like myself was concerned, it was easy enough to understand—at sixteen, I was convinced of my own genius, and afraid that I would spend my life in oblivion. I craved experience, and envied Marie her travels from the age of ten. Moving from Vienna to Baden-Baden to Nice, it was hard to see why she needed to keep a journal.

What I was failing to grasp was that all intelligent young persons need to see their own face in a mirror, to create a sense of distance from their own lives. Keats, for example, does it in his letters, which are addressed to himself as much as to his correspondents. And Marie also addressed herself on paper as she might have talked to her image in a mirror.

I had been keeping a journal since the age of sixteen; in fact, I had kept a diary since I was thirteen or so. But that was a tiny notebook, with only enough space to enter the main event of the day, such as "Went to cinema to see Wizard of Oz." What I wanted was to be able to set down my thoughts and feelings. So one Saturday morning, after

I had worked in the school lab all morning, I went to the newsagent near my bus stop and bought a lined notebook with cardboard covers. And to that I confided my hopes and dreams and frustrations.

Yet there is something oddly unsatisfying about keeping a diary—as absurd as sitting in a room and addressing yourself to an empty armchair.

Now the Colin Wilson I became aware of through keeping a diary was a bored, sexually-frustrated teenager. Yet a part of me told myself that this was not me—that when, for example, I achieved those curious moods of delight and relaxation, this "I" vanished, and I felt oddly free of myself. In fact, it struck me that what I was trying to do, by keeping a journal, by reading poetry and listening to music, was to get away from "me"—to escape from my "personality." And this insight struck me as so important that I carefully wrote on the cover on my journal, in block letters: ESCAPE FROM PERSONALITY.

Of course what worried me most was what worried John Keats and Marie Bashkirtseff—that I might die "before my pen has reaped my teeming brain." It seemed perfectly possible that, in spite of my certainty of my own genius, I might die of some illness, or perhaps even in a street accident, before I had even glimpsed the meaning of life. My moods of happiness and self-confidence convinced me that I had a "destiny" to become a famous writer, and to be remembered as one of the most important thinkers of the century. But at other times it seemed that this was mere self-deception—not because I was not a "genius," but because there is no such thing as destiny. You may as well say that every raindrop that falls from the sky has a "destiny." At these times it seemed apparent that the universe is meaningless, and that these "melting moods" (as William James calls them) are an illusion, a piece of self-deception.

At about the same time that I discovered the journal of Marie Bashkirtseff, I discovered another diarist who fascinated me—and whose name, like Marie's, is now virtually forgotten. I see from my own copy that *The Journal of a Disappointed Man* by W. N. P. Barbellion, was first published in Penguin paperbacks in 1948, so I must have been seventeen when I came upon it. The Journal was first published in 1919, and was a considerable success. Its last words are, "Barbellion died on December 31"—1917. In fact, the author added these words, in much the same spirit that Tom Sawyer attended his own funeral, to see what effect they produced. The effect was flattering—the *Journal* was well received and widely read. So Barbellion did receive a certain recognition before his death—of disseminated sclerosis—in 1919; he even received a letter of appreciation from H. G. Wells.

Barbellion was not the real name of the author of *The Journal of a Disappointed Man*; he was actually Bruce Frederick Cummings, and he was the son of a successful local journalist who lived and worked in Barnstaple, Devon. He was the youngest of six brothers, and was always in delicate health.

Cummings was born on September 9, 1889, and was therefore almost twenty years younger than Marie Bashkirtseff. He was a born naturalist, who spent his days roaming around the Devon countryside studying birds, insects and newts.

It seems strange that such a child, totally fascinated by the world around him, should have decided to keep a diary. The answer is that, like Marie Bashkirtseff, he had a great deal of vitality, and had an obscure conviction that he would one day achieve something important. When the journal begins, in his thirteenth year, Cummings records such simple matters as finding a lame seabird and getting his trousers wet wading across an inlet of the tide. But by the time he is fifteen he is writing, "I am thinking that on the whole I am a most discontented mortal. I get bursts of what I call 'What's the good of anything?' mania. I keep asking myself incessantly till the question wears me out. 'What's the good of going into the country naturalizing?' 'What's the good of studying so hard?' 'Where is it all going to end?' 'Will it lead anywhere?'" And when he is seventeen he writes, "As long as he has good health, a man need never despair. Without good health, I might keep a long while in the race, yet as the goal of my ambition grew more and more unattainable, I should surely remember the words of Keats and give up, 'There is no fiercer Hell than the failure of a great ambition.'"

In fact, I was also reading a great deal of Keats at the time—the letters, edited by Lord Houghton, and again recognized myself in this ambitious spirit who knew himself to be a great poet, but wondered if he would ever be recognized.

The main difference, as I saw it, between myself and diarists like Marie Bashkirtseff, Barbellion and Keats was that they still managed to lead far more interesting lives than my own. Keats, the son of a stablekeeper, nevertheless traveled to Scotland and Devon and the Isle of Wight, whereas I had never spent more than a day at the seaside.

When I was fifteen, my grandfather gave me a bicycle, and I began taking long rides on Sundays, some of them as much as eighty miles in a day (although my average was closer to fifty). So it seemed to me that my life was altogether more dreary—more like one of those bored and frustrated Chekhov heroes, in a story like *My Life*. I seemed to be continually conscious of a sense of unused energy, as frustrating as constipation. And reading Marie Bashkirtseff and Barbellion and Keats only increased the frustration.

Barbellion, in fact, succeeded in becoming a member of staff at the Natural History Museum in South Kensington, part of the Royal College of Science where Wells had been a pupil thirty years earlier. But he was already ill—the doctor who diagnosed the sclerosis advised his brother not to tell him, because the knowledge that he would die in a year or so would have depressed him too much.

He also fell in love with a girl in the same lodging, and he married at the age of twenty-six, four years before his death. So at least Barbellion experienced some degree of fulfillment.

Barbellion recognized himself in a description of Lermontov by Maurice Baring—"Proud, overbearing, exasperating and exasperated . . . He could not bear not to make himself felt and if he felt he was unsuccessful in this by fair means he resorted to unpleasant ones. Yet he was warm-hearted, thirsting for love and kindness and capable of giving himself up to love if he chose . . . At the bottom of this lay, no doubt, a deep-seated disgust with himself and with the world in general, and a complete indifference to life resulting from large aspirations which could not find an outlet and recoiled upon himself." And I, in turn, recognized myself in Barbellion—particularly the profound depressions, the tendency to wonder whether life was meaningless, like some grey, dull day that went on unendingly.

Yet I also recognized that there are marvelously sunny days, when everything seems good, and believed that, sooner or later, my life would change.

I envied Barbellion his marriage, and Marie Bashkirtseff her many admirers—although, in the manner of a well-brought-up young lady of the nineteenth century, she undoubtedly died a virgin. (In our own time she would have lost her virginity almost as soon as she started art school.) And of course, I wondered what would have happened if I had met Marie when we were both in our teens. Would she have recognized genius in me? Would she have found me attractive?

The answer, I realize in retrospect, is no. Marie was a flirt, and she was—as her editor Matilde Blind admits—inclined to jealousy and envy of her fellow artists. A girl who is inclined to jealousy and envy is also inclined to emphasize her superior social position, a trait I have always found irritating. Besides, Marie was one of those women of high vitality who in middle age become incorrigible talkers—usually about themselves—and exhaust everyone around them. And no doubt she would also, in the manner of Russian ladies, have put on weight.

So I can see, in retrospect, that I would probably not have found Marie attractive in the long run, although I would certainly have found myself enthralled by her vitality. Two people with a high opinion of themselves might become friends, under the right circumstances, but I doubt whether they can fall in love.

Yet as a symbol, as a daydream, Marie Bashkirtseff played an important part in my mid-teens. Her early death made her more like a figure of tragedy, a kind of female John Keats.

I remember how, when I was in the RAF, and stationed near Birmingham, I called on an aunt and uncle who lived there. I had a cousin Rhoda, a few years my senior, whom I had admired as a child, and who was now engaged to a young man who was obviously going to do well in business.

They had a Christmas party in 1949, and I was there. But I felt out of place among all this Dickensian mirth and pulling of crackers. Quite suddenly, I thought of Marie Bashkirtseff, and as I murmured the word "Marie," had difficulty preventing tears from coming to my eyes. She had become for me an important symbol of the "outsider," the person who feels a stranger in society.

Of course, at the age of eighteen, you have no idea of the kind of girl you would like to marry. It would have been impossible for me at the time because although I had begun to learn self-discipline through the *Bhagavad Gita* and the Buddhist scriptures, my personality was still basically unformed. Dreaming of beautiful and talented Russian girls, I could not then imagine that my first sexual experience would be—as I shall recount later—with a working-class girl for whom even I seemed a figure of glamour and sophistication. Yet that experience would be vital for me, in revealing me to myself. It enabled me to recognize, for example, that I am a highly protective person, and that this protectiveness would be bound to form the basis of any long-term relation. In short, it enabled me to understand what type of girl would be my ideal.

It was another four years before I finally came to meet her, and I believe that I recognized her immediately as the one I had been waiting for. I had returned to my hometown after a period of trying to live in Paris, and had taken a job in a big store that needed extra staff for the "Christmas rush." We were sent up to a kind of classroom on the top floor to learn how to use a cash register. The girl who shepherded us into the lift was very slim and attractive, although not conventionally pretty, her nose being perhaps a little too prominent. I had no doubt that she would have the awful accent that characterizes midlanders, full of ugly gutturals—an accent that I had gone to some trouble to get rid of. But when she stood in front of the class—only about four of us—and began to speak, her accent bore no traces of any local origin; it was pleasant and precise without being affectedly upper class.

But what attracted me most was her smile, which was infinitely sweet and good-tempered. As I looked at her, I felt my heart sink. Two or three years before, I would have become hopelessly infatuated. Now, as I noticed a ring on her finger, my buddhistic training made me aware that this would be pointless. But I still allowed myself to appreciate her smile and the graceful way she moved as she turned to the blackboard.

Her name was Joy Stewart, and she had been to Trinity College in Dublin, studying French language and English literature. And—as I learned when I spoke to her in the canteen—she was engaged to be married, to a fellow student, a geologist who was about to sail for Canada and set up a home.

I had become friendly with another new employee, an ex-army officer of about my own age, called Martin Halliday, who preferred to be called Flax. And Flax was intent on seducing a pretty girl called Pat, who happened to be Joy's closest friend, and who worked on the cosmetics counter. Pat had broken off a previous engagement because she had discovered that her future husband had been unfaithful, and now she gently but firmly declined to be lured into Flax's bed. He tried a more roundabout method, inviting Pat and Joy and myself to go over to his flat on a Saturday evening, and spend the night there. It was the opportunity I had been looking for, and as Joy and I lay on a rug in front of the fire, listening to music, I told her that I thought she was the most wonderful girl I had ever known. She was obviously not displeased, but she told me later that she did not believe a word of it, convinced that my intentions towards her were as straightforward as Flax's towards Pat.

Soon after that weekend, Pat allowed herself to be seduced. But Joy very firmly kept my advances at bay. However, since Pat was now spending most of her spare time with Flax, Joy allowed me to see a great deal of her, and we spent many of our evenings at a teetotal club drinking tea and eating sticky buns.

Her personality was something of a contradiction. She had an air of efficiency, and seemed so cool and controlled that I assumed she was several years older than she was, and was startled to discover that she was a year my junior. But she was also gentle, good-natured, and—as I came to realize—basically rather shy.

I understood the contradiction when I eventually came to meet her parents. Her gentle, kindly nature was inherited from her father, an accountant. Her mother was the dominant one of the family, the kind of woman who might easily have been the headmistress of a "girls" school. Her mother was—inevitably—Joy's chief role model, hence the air of efficiency and self-possession, which was at odds with her underlying gentleness and shyness.

In due course, I persuaded Joy to break off her engagement and to find herself a job in a department store in London, where I had already moved. Her parents were shocked and upset when they learned that she was no longer engaged, and it was many years before they came to accept me. Her father once told me that I would "end in the gutter."

Yet I believe that, from an early stage, we each had the feeling that we were perfectly suited to one another. Years later, when Joy drove up to Oxford to see my daughter Sally—who was visiting her brother—Sally asked her whether she had not felt worried and insecure about breaking off her engagement, and committing herself to an unknown who had no profession and who supported himself by taking casual laboring jobs, and Joy answered, "No, I somehow knew it would be all right."

On another occasion, when I asked her, "Weren't you ever worried that I might not make a success as a writer?" she said, "No, I was always certain you would."

So I suspect that Joy and I were somehow "intended" for one another, and that we recognized this almost as soon as we met. I do not, of course, think we are unique—I have met many other couples who seemed to me specifically designed for one another. I have also met a great many couples who very obviously made the wrong choice. But I have never ceased to regard Joy as the most fortunate thing that ever happened to me.

Sometimes, I wonder if the same is true for Joy. As a writer, I am not unduly difficult to live with, being, on the whole, good-tempered, affectionate and cheerful. But I have to admit that I am inclined to bursts of impatience, a consequence of my obsessive and workaholic temperament. And every time I get into a state of impatience and behave like a bear with a sore head, I realize how lucky I am to have found anyone so serene and patient and good-tempered. I am sorry that I had to make someone else unhappy by stealing Joy, but have never had the slightest doubt that she was the ideal person for me.

This lengthy digression is not entirely self-indulgence. It seems to me that one of the basic problems of human beings is summarized in Nietzsche's phrase "How one becomes what one is." Until that happens, we are in no position to make important choices, because our essential being is still in a state of flux. The diaries of Marie Bashkirtseff and Barbellion were written by people in a state of flux, and who were vaguely aware that they had still not "discovered who they were."

This is not a matter of age—another famous diarist, Frederic Amiel, had still not discovered "who he was," even when he died at the age of sixty-one (in 1882). And the reason, I think, can be found in this comment on the penultimate page of his *Journal Intime*, "21 March 1881. This invalid life is too Epicurian. For five or six weeks now I have done nothing but wait, nurse myself, and amuse myself, and how weary one gets of it."

And this, I think, goes to the heart of the matter. H. G. Wells was also an invalid in his late teens, spending his days in bed writing an early version of *The Time Machine*. But Wells had a powerful sense of purpose. In one of his early novels, *Love and Mr. Lewisham*, the protagonist is obviously the young Wells, working as a schoolmaster in a private school; over his washstand dangles a timetable, that begins at five o'clock in the morning with three hours of French, then, after eating breakfast in twenty minutes, memorizing passages of Shakespeare. On other days it will be other languages, including Latin, until he has acquired at least five. I remember being inspired by this when I first read the novel in my mid-teens. (I still get up at 6 a.m. and read for two hours while the rest of the house is asleep.)

Wells was driven by a desperate sense of purpose—to escape the failure that had engulfed his father and forced his mother to become a housekeeper; this explains why he achieved a clear sense of "who he was" while still relatively young. The difference between his single-minded drive and Amiel's insecure sense of his own identity lies in the fact that Amiel came of a well-to-do family, and that although orphaned at the age of twelve, he was able to spend his student years in Berlin and Heidelberg, traveling during the vacations all over Europe. By the age of twenty-eight he was a professor in Geneva, and spent all his life in the academic profession. Yet he was also a lonely "outsider," too intelligent and fastidious to make much impact on his contemporaries. He lacked Wells' belief that "if you don't like your life you can change it."

This is even more apparent in one of the strangest journals of the twentieth century, *The Inman Diaries*, subtitled *A Public and Private Confession*, published by Harvard in 1985, and running to around 1600 pages. Arthur Inman, born in 1895 in Atlanta, Georgia, was the son of wealthy parents. In his early twenties, he had an inexplicable breakdown in health—"My nervous system went on strike," as he put it. Then, like Proust, he more-or-less took to his bed, in a large and comfortable flat in Boston. There he advertised for young women to come and talk to him. His intention was not to seduce them—although this happened more than occasionally; what he wanted was to live their lives vicariously. He had also decided—as the editor of the *Diary* puts it—"that the only way for him to win fame, perhaps even immortality, would be to write a diary unlike any ever written, an absolutely honest record of himself and his age." So he spent virtually forty years in bed, listening to his "talkers" (as he called them), frequently persuading them to remove their clothes and climb into bed with him—although in later years he preferred mutual masturbation to the act of sex—and writing his endless diary, which finally ran to millions of words (and had to be greatly abridged for publication). Inman finally grew tired of this stifling life at the age of sixty-eight—he was suffering from migraines and hallucinations, and shot himself on the same day that President Kennedy was killed.

It was, oddly enough, also the day that Aldous Huxley died, for Inman is almost a Huxley character, living—and suffocating—inside his own head. His first seduction—of a girl named Alma—is typical: "She reached down with one hand and felt me. 'There's no doubt you're a man, old dear. None.' 'Physically, yes. But it's the mental quirk that stalls me . . . ' . . . She moves very quickly, pulling her skirts up and her drawers off. 'All right. Don't think bad of me afterwards.' When I had rolled on top of her and she had inserted me into her, the thing began. I swear I felt no passion, no sexual elation . . . I thought the darn thing would never end. . . . It got monotonous . . . Gee, but wasn't I sore. I didn't see any fun in the darn thing. I guess I have got a mental quirk."

Yet even with such frank and amusing passages, reading the *Diary* is a strangely claustrophobic experience, and it is easy to see why Inman finally killed himself. To live for year after year without motivation means that you become a slave of the mechanical part of you, the "robot." And when we are in a "robotic" state, life loses its savor, and all its values suddenly disappear.

It is easy enough to make them reappear: any act of serious concentration will do it. As soon as we focus on anything with a sense of purpose, the robot is switched off, and the "real you" appears. And suddenly, everything you look at is interesting. This is what happened to Dostoevsky as he stood in front of a firing squad, and the insight it brought remained sharp and clear for the rest of his life.

But it is not necessary to face some desperate emergency to achieve this state; we only have to focus intently enough. I have merely to recall clearly some past crisis to "wake myself up." Our minds are too passive, and we fail to see the danger of this passivity, and how it robs us of our lives.

We need to understand this situation. If you were floating in the sea, wearing a glass helmet with an air supply, and your head occasionally sank beneath the surface, you would understand what was happening. You would not ask which was true, which gave you the most accurate view of reality—being below or above the surface; you would know. Well, the "robotic" state is like being below the surface. Yet we continue to wonder which is true: the cheerful condition we experience on spring mornings, or the sense of "life failure" we feel when we are tired and depressed. The answer should be obvious: that the condition of life failure is another name for robotic consciousness, and that, compared to "fully awake" consciousness, it is subnormal. Yet men commit suicide—like Arthur Inman—because they fail to grasp this simple and obvious truth.

When I was about eighteen, I destroyed all the diaries I had kept since I was sixteen. I felt they were neurotic and claustrophobic, and that the "self" they reflected was a false self. I have never regretted the decision. If I want to recall something of the Colin Wilson who wrote them, I have only to read Marie Bashkirtseff or Barbellion, and my sixteen-year-old self is suddenly real again. It might be said that I killed him when I burnt the first half dozen volumes of my journals.

9

FAUST AND
"ABSURD GOOD NEWS"

It was about the time that I was thirteen or fourteen that I began
to catch glimpses of an answer to the problem of nihilism that
had reduced me to such a state of despair and exhaustion.

In a secondhand bookshop, I found the Everyman edition of
Goethe's *Faust*. Even the awful translation could not disguise the
tremendous vitality of the poetry:

> *And swift, unutterably swift,*
> *Earth rolls around her pageant splendid;*
> *Day, such as erst was Eden's gift,*
> *By deep, dread night in turn attended.*
> *And all the towering cliffs among,*
> *In spreading streams upfoams the ocean,*
> *And cliffs and sea are whirled along,*
> *With circling orbs in ceaseless motion.*

But when I came to Faust's opening speech, in his "high vaulted,
narrow Gothic chamber," I realized with a shock that the young Goethe
had experienced my own glimpse of meaninglessness.

> *I have studied, alas, philosophy,*
> *And jurisprudence, and medicine too,*

And worst of all, theology,
With ardent labor through and through.
As here I stick, as wise, poor fool
As when my steps first turned to school.
Master they style me, nay doctor, forsooth,
And nigh ten years, o'er rough and smooth,
And up and down, and acrook and across,
I lead my pupils by the nose,
And know that in truth we can know—aught!

"Das wir nichts wissen konnen"—that we can know nothing: the words made my heart sink. Yet there was also immense comfort in knowing that someone else had recognized the futility of human knowledge.

There followed a passage that I soon learned by heart:

Would thou, full orbed moon, didst shine
Thy last upon this pain of mine.
Thou whom from this my desk so oft
I watched at midnight climb aloft.
O'er books and papers thou didst send
Thy radiance, melancholy friend.
Ah, could I, on some mountain height,
Float onward, steeped in thy dear light,
Round mountain caves with spirits hover,
Or float the moonlit meadows over,
From fumes of learning purse my soul,
Bathe in thy dew, and so be whole.

Like Faust, I also felt that I had dehydrated my soul with logic and reason. But whenever I read this passage, I experienced a cooling sensation, like plunging a blistered finger into cold water, and a sense of relaxation and serenity. In fact, Goethe does not use the word "float," but "gehn," which might easily be translated "walk." But this image of floating peacefully over moonlit meadows always brought a tremor of sheer joy.

I was discovering something that I had half forgotten since childhood: that I could use the imagination to release physical and emotional tensions. This still strikes me as the most interesting and unique characteristic of modern man.

Opening his textbook of magic, Faust's eye falls upon the symbol of the macrocosm, and he experiences a surge of joy. He then speaks the lines that struck me as the most important in the poem:

> *The spirit world is never closed,*
> *Our sense is shut, your heart is dead.*
> *Rise, scholar, and bathe unafraid*
> *Your earthly breast in morning red.*

These lines seemed to me so significant that I found a copy of Faust in German and learned them by heart. They expressed an insight that I had glimpsed again and again, and which a favorite author of my childhood, G. K. Chesterton, had called "absurd good news." There is a sense in which our despair is always superficial. Just as we are feeling that the whole world is dark, some trickle of joy flows into the soul and makes us want to laugh aloud.

Faust then uses his textbook of magic to conjure up the Earth Spirit. His first glimpse terrifies him. But just as he is recovering his courage, and expressing his sense of closeness to the spirit, it answers, "You're like the spirit you grasp with your mind, not like me," and vanishes.

Faust cries in despair, "Not like you? Who, then?"

His student Wagner hears him talking, and comes in to ask him if he is reciting some Greek tragedy. Ten minutes conversation with his dull but well-meaning disciple are enough to plunge Faust into gloom. When Wagner leaves, he decides that it is time to commit suicide. But as he is raising the cup of poison to his lips, the sound of the Easter bells bursts into his room. Suddenly he is reminded of childhood happiness and "absurd good news." The impulse to kill himself vanishes like an evil spirit, and he exclaims, "The earth takes me again!"

It was a process with which I was familiar: fatigue, misery, despair—and then, as the sun shines out from behind a cloud, or the rain suddenly patters against the windows, the flash of delight, and the realization that reality is infinitely rich. But to see it expressed so clearly deepened and clarified the insight. It enabled me to grasp exactly what had happened to me, and to understand how that sense of futility and emptiness was in itself an illusion, a kind of mistake, like accidentally substituting a minus for a plus in a calculation.

Let me try to express this insight as I would explain it now, fifty years later.

The problems of life demand from us continual effort. In order to make an effort, we have to concentrate our energies, like a runner waiting for the crack of the starter's pistol. The psychological process involved is rather like the release of petrol vapor into the cylinder of an engine. A spark plug causes the vapor to explode, and it drives the piston.

When we feel bored or insecure, it is as if the cylinder is leaking, so that most of the energy escapes. But it is we who summon energy, driven by a sense of purpose. And if most of the energy escapes, we lose the sense of purpose, and it becomes an enormous effort to summon more energy. Further effort seems futile when the energy is being wasted.

As we slip into this sense of futility, life begins to seem unreal. It is hard to see that any effort is worth making. We feel disconnected from reality. Problems and difficulties only increase our sense of unwillingness to make an effort. And this in turn makes us feel more helpless, and increases the sense of futility. It is a kind of vicious circle.

On the other hand, consider what happens when we are full of energy and vitality. We want something, and imagination pictures what it would be like to achieve our desire. We brace ourselves, and hurl ourselves towards our objective, driven by energy like a bullet from a gun.

In states of "futility," the imagination becomes enfeebled by a sense of unreality, and no longer pictures its objectives. So the energy we summon is inadequate, and most of it escapes. This in turn deepens the sense of futility.

But here it is, the intellect that is betraying us. Our reason seems to assure us that all effort is futile. But that only applies to positive objectives—for example, writing a letter. But suppose, as you were trying to summon the energy, that you suddenly remembered that you had left a saucepan of potatoes on the stove, and that they might have boiled dry. You leap to your feet and rush to the kitchen. For although your reason assures you that life is futile and that all our efforts are directed towards illusions, you still know that a burnt saucepan and a kitchen full of black smoke and a burning smell are definitely not illusions.

Any sense of sudden crisis makes you realize that the sense of futility is a lie. Although you may not feel any strong desire to do anything positive, there are still a thousand possible crises that you would make an effort to avert.

Colin Wilson

And when a threatened crisis has forced you to "brace" yourself, and then the crisis goes away, you observe that the sense of futility has vanished. You sigh with relief, and suddenly, life is self-evidently wonderful. All that has happened is that you have closed the "leaks" through which your energy was escaping. Your sense of values comes flooding back. And you suddenly realize that this sense of normality is not an illusion. Living organisms are intended to respond to life, and as they respond, they experience a clear perception of values. In such moments, these "values" are seen as perfectly clear and real—for example, the importance of not having a kitchen full of black smoke. Moreover, once you have been galvanized into recognizing the desirability of not having a kitchen full of smoke, you can also see the desirability of having a clean and tidy kitchen rather than a dirty and untidy kitchen. These values are not illusions; our despair is due to fatigue—or boredom—which causes us to "leak," and which creates a kind of color-blindness towards values.

The real problem is our lack of imagination. If sudden crisis can reawaken me to a sense of values, then it should be possible to awaken these values by thinking about crisis. This "galvanizes" us, and, like an electric current passed through the leg of a dead frog, causes the muscle to contract, producing a sudden flow of energy.

This ability increases with practice. Just as a healthy body can galvanize itself into physical activity, leaping out of an armchair and hurling itself across the room, so a healthy mind can "contract" at the thought of a sudden emergency, and achieve a state that psychologists call "readiness potential."

I imagine Nietzsche's superman as a being who has achieved such a high degree of readiness potential that he is completely free of the laziness and sloth that turns most human beings into robots.

10

SEX AND
THE ETERNAL FEMININE

But I have not yet finished discussing the significance of *Faust*. For Goethe goes on to raise the question that most human beings find more fascinating than any other: sex. When he makes his bargain with Mephistopheles—who introduces himself as "the spirit that negates"—Faust is promised "more pleasure in an hour than in a year's monotony." And he agrees that:

> *If to the moment I should say*
> *Tarry awhile, thou art so fair,*
> *Then you can throw me into chains.*

Faust is willing to sell his soul for a pleasure so intense that it will raise him to a god-like level of consciousness.

Then he encounters Gretchen as she comes out of church—a pretty country maid with pink cheeks and a demure manner. As soon as he sees her, he decides that she is what he wants, more than anything in the world. Is it love at first sight? Not precisely—merely desire at first sight—an instant and powerful attraction. As far as Faust in concerned, she is not a real girl, but a symbol of the eternal feminine.

She rebuffs his attempt to engage her in conversation, but the cunning Mephistopheles soon finds a way to bring them together in a neighbor's garden. She falls in love and gives herself to him.

But is Faust not intelligent enough to see the disadvantages of becoming her lover? What if she becomes pregnant? Does he really want to marry her, and introduce her to his colleagues as his wife? The sexual illusion makes him blind to these problems.

"Beim Himmel, dieses Kind ist Schon!"

("By heavens, this child is lovely!")

And he turns to Mephistopheles and says,

"Hor, du must mir die Dirne schaffen!"

("Listen, you must get me that girl.")

He wants her so badly that he tells Mephistopheles, "If this sweet young thing doesn't lie in my arms tonight, our pact is off."

Mephistopheles, of course, is delighted to see how easily Faust is being taken in by the sexual illusion. He even takes the risk of warning him, "What have you got when it's enjoyed?" But all Faust cares about is possessing her. And having achieved this, he takes no further interest until, a long time later, he learns that Gretchen has been condemned to death for killing her baby. Then, at last, he feels miserable and conscience-stricken. Galvanized into realism, he can see that pursuing the sexual illusion is a recipe for disaster.

Yet it is clear that he has not learned his lesson. For when Mephistopheles shows him Helen of Troy, his desire is so powerful that he faints. Mephistopheles obligingly summons Helen from the underworld; she and Faust fall in love, and she bears him a child. But I suspect that when she finally dissolves away in his arms, leaving behind only her garments, this is Goethe's way of saying that once again, sex has failed to provide Faust with a joy so intense that he will cry, "Linger awhile, thou art so fair!"

But did Goethe grasp the true power—and the danger—of the sexual illusion? Probably not. He lived in the age of Romanticism—in fact, was one of its founders. For him, the sexual illusion presented only its most alluring face: beautiful women who could be idealized.

It is necessary to make an effort of imagination to place ourselves in the mid-1770s, when Goethe conceived Faust. We have to try and transport ourselves to a time when there were no magazines showing naked girls in alluring positions, no television advertisements trying to capture male attention by showing glimpses of girls taking off their clothes. Goethe's age was not prudish about sex—as we can see from the *Walpurgisnacht* of Faust. But its attitude was more realistic and down to earth.

I first read Faust at a time when my own adolescent sensuality was awakening, and I could understand why Faust thought it was worth selling his soul to the devil to possess a girl as desirable as Gretchen.

It is necessary to explain that, sexually speaking, I had been a late developer. I was about six or seven when some school friend had told me "how babies are made," but I was shocked, and disinclined to believe anything so indecent. And I can remember, a year or so later, when an older boy that I liked and trusted referred to sex, I asked incredulously, "You don't believe all that filthy stuff, do you?" I suppose I was rather a puritanical little boy. This was not because adults had told me that sex was sinful or wicked. It was simply that, when I listened to school friends talking about sex, and boasting about what they had done—or hoped to do—to little girls, I felt that they were defiling themselves. My puritanism was natural and instinctive.

But by the time I was thirteen, I had found myself a girlfriend—she went to the girls' school that was attached to the College of Art and Technology next door to our secondary school—and soon became aware of the stirrings of sexual desire. At thirteen, her breasts were fully developed. And her previous boyfriend had told me how, when he made some joking comment about the color of her knickers, she had said, "You mean these?" and raised her dress to her waist. The very thought made the blood pound in my head.

But I was far too gauche to do more than kiss her goodnight, and she finally threw me over and went back to her previous boyfriend. (In due course they married, and he became a policeman.)

Left at a loose end, I settled down during the long August holiday of 1945 to write my first book. It started as an attempt to summarize my knowledge of physics and chemistry. But I had acquired at a church bazaar a six-volume work called *Practical Knowledge for All*, which contained courses on biology, geology, psychology, philosophy, and even aeronautics, and so I decided to extend my range. I learned as I wrote, and had soon forgotten the emotional upset of being jilted. The *Manual of General Science* finally extended to six small notebooks, but when I began one on mathematics, I ran out of motivation.

By this time—at the age of fourteen—the sexual hormones were doing their work, and I was experiencing a permanent fever of interest in the opposite sex. Our French mistress often sat on her desk, with her feet on a desk on the front row; the boy who sat there claimed to be able to see up her skirt, and the very thought made me flush with desire.

One night, pressing my thighs into the bed, and imagining that the French mistress was underneath me, I experienced a flood of pleasure, and discovered that I had made a small damp stain on the sheet.

Nothing in my childhood daydreams prepared me for the sheer imaginative intensity that could be induced by sexual fantasy. A newspaper photograph of a girl in a bathing suit, a shop window full of women's underwear, could create a flood of desire that startled me. At least I was sensible enough not to feel guilty about it. I recognized that these were the normal changes that took place in adolescence, and that they were nothing to be ashamed of. At first I was inclined to try and escape these powerful impulses by being determinedly "clean-minded." But since every glimpse of a schoolgirl's legs as she climbed ahead of me to the top deck of a bus brought an explosion of desire, it seemed pointless to try.

Besides, this amplification of the imagination by sexual fantasy was as exciting as a voyage to a strange country. It was so much more powerful than ordinary imagination that it seemed virtually a new faculty. It seemed amazing to be able to look at a picture of a woman in her underwear in one of my mother's magazines, and soar into a state of sexual excitement that invariably ended in orgasm. But then, I was experiencing a general intensification of the imagination. After seeing the film *Dangerous Moonlight*, the Warsaw Concerto could induce a state of dreamy ecstasy; so, after a film called *Concerto*, could the Rachmaninov Second Piano Concerto. The opening of Tchaikovsky's First Piano Concerto always brought an image of a young man with a knapsack on his back, tramping away from his hometown to face the world, and refusing to look over his shoulder. Through *Palgrave's Golden Treasury*, I discovered poetry, and found that certain poems—like Cowper's *Poplar Field* and Gray's *Elegy in a Country Churchyard*, could create a sense of floating, as if I had turned into a balloon. Coleridge's *Ancient Mariner* was such a revelation that I insisted on reading parts of it to my younger brother Barry.

When I was about thirteen, my grandfather allowed me to borrow his bicycle every Sunday, and I used to set out when the air was still cool and fresh, and explore places like Warwick and Stratford on Avon and Matlock. Cycling along the empty roads at eight o'clock in the morning, I found that I experienced a marvelous sense of the sheer complexity and endless fascination of the world that lay around me, and my imagination conjured up wonderful adventures, and love affairs with girls like Faust's Gretchen or Dumas' Mercedes. I borrowed Stendhal's *Scarlet and Black* from the library, and was fascinated by this tale of an inexperienced youth who seduces a married woman.

The problem was that with real girls, I was gauche and tongue-tied. As a child, I had often thought how embarrassing it must be for a man to have to ask a girl, "Will you marry me?" And now it seemed equally inconceivable that I could ever bring myself to do the things that I daydreamed of all the time.

So the years between the ages of fourteen and eighteen were a period of sexual fantasy that never achieved the slightest degree of reality. Nowadays of course, many young people lose their virginity before they even reach adolescence. Yet I doubt whether our modern degree of permissiveness would have made any difference to me. My personality was only half formed; in a sense I was like a chicken that has only just hatched out of the egg. And endless new intellectual adventures—like discovering music, poetry, philosophy, psychology, and the world of Elizabethan playwrights—went a long way towards compensating for the sexual frustration. But—like all adolescents—I hated the feeling of being awkward and embarrassed, and tripping over my own feet, and saying the wrong thing. I longed for the day when I would feel relaxed and self-assured. But even by the time I was eighteen, and went into the RAF to do my eighteen months National Service, this was still as far away as ever.

Since this is supposed to be an account of the books in my life, and not an autobiography, I shall not speak here about how I left school at the age of sixteen, and became a factory worker, then a laboratory assistant, then a civil servant. For the moment I need only say that, after a brief period in the RAF, which came to an end when I succeeded in deceiving the authorities into believing that I was homosexual, I found myself back in civilian life in the spring of 1950, when I was eighteen and a half. The labor exchange sent me to a fairground that was advertising for labor, and I was given a job selling tickets on a kind of gambling machine called a spinner; when enough tickets were sold, a great beam swept around in a circle over my head, and lights flashed behind a glass panel, illuminating its numbers. When the beam came to a halt, the light rested on the winning number.

On my second or third evening there, a young girl—who looked about twelve—asked, "Do you want to sell yourself?" She had a pretty, oval face, and a cold sore on her lip. When the fairground closed, I walked her home and kissed her goodnight. She was, in fact, fifteen years old, and her name was Sylvia. Her family lived in a slum district not far from the fairground. I met her the next day, and took her on a bus trip to some woods seven miles away. We kissed several times, and she introduced me to the technique of kissing with the tongue, which I found strange but pleasant. Although sexually excited, I—of course—would not have dreamed of trying to go further. But as we walked back to the bus stop, she took my hand, which was resting on her waist, and placed it on her small, flat breast. And as we kissed goodnight at the corner of her street, she pressed herself tight against me and moved her pubis against my erection.

Things moved quickly. I lost my job at the fairground for taking the evening off, but it seemed worth it. That evening I took her to a remote park, and as we kissed and became increasingly aroused, she unzipped my fly and grasped my erect penis. But I was still too shy to make any attempt to explore beneath her skirt.

Two days later, on a Sunday, we took a bus out into the country, and soon found a spot in a remote field, at the side of a stream. I was wearing khaki shorts, and within a few minutes they were open from the waist. I reached clumsily up her skirt, and my hand found its way inside her knickers. My inexperience was so total that I thought the female sexual organs were situated above the pubic bone—having occasionally seen female babies undressed, and mistaking the visible fold of flesh for the vagina. Sylvia appeared not to notice my ignorance, and firmly pushed my hand further back. A few minutes later, as I clumsily tried to mount her, she made me lie on my back, removed her knickers, then sat astride me, reaching behind her to grasp my penis; then sat down on it slowly, gasping with pain. With her other hand she pulled down the front of her vest, because her stomach was covered with a strawberry rash.

I had expected excitement culminating in ecstasy; instead, I noted that I was feeling perfectly calm, and that the sensation of her body enclosing my penis was not very different from the feeling of my own hand. I learned what I had always suspected—that the most important part of sex is mental. A moment later, as she slowly moved up and down, her two hands now on my chest, I had to tell her to move off quickly.

We made love about half a dozen times that day—after the first time, in the normal position. Each time, I withdrew hastily. But still, as we walked back towards the bus, I was anxious in case some of my sperm had stayed inside her and made her pregnant. It was as if the fates were determined to teach me that sexual relationships are fraught with problems and anxieties.

Now that, at last, I had experienced the reality of sex, I could see that, quite apart from anatomical inaccuracies, it bore almost no relation to my daydreams. The romantic fantasies of embracing a Gretchen were now replaced with the reality of a pretty but perfectly ordinary girl with whom I had nothing in common, and who talked about how soon we could get married. That idea struck me as absurd. Even as a child, I had decided that I had no intention of spending my life supporting a wife and family. So now I simply explained that, since I was not yet nineteen, and she was hardly fifteen, we should put off thoughts of marriage until far in the future.

But it was at this point that I realized that the real allure of sex is not physical but psychological. The German jurist Rosenstock-Huessy says, "Even a man who believes in nothing needs a girl to believe in him." And it did not take me long to realize that what made Sylvia so addictive was not that she was willing to surrender her body (which, I must confess, struck me as a kind of miracle), but that she accepted me at my own valuation as a genius. I sometimes caught her looking at me with an expression of abject surrender in her eyes, as "bobbysoxers" at that time gazed at Frank Sinatra.

And since, as Sartre points out, we see ourselves through the gaze of others, the stimulus to my ego was enormous. I felt as if life had suddenly decided to pay the interest on all the efforts I had made to remain optimistic in the past four years, and that after a kind of emotional poverty, I was suddenly rich. During my teens, I had often suspected that my obsession with books and ideas had doomed me to a life of frustration and loneliness. And now, as Apuleius says in *The Golden Ass*, it was as if the apple bough of love had bent down over me and invited me to help myself.

The only problem was not only that Sylvia was determined to marry me, but that she was extraordinarily jealous. She swore that she would kill any other woman who tried to take me from her. She often took offense at some innocent remark, and burst into tears. (I met her again, forty years later, and she had still not changed very much—still the same tendency to live on a kind of emotional switchback.) After some pointless quarrel that I failed to understand, I often found myself longing for my own "high-vaulted, narrow Gothic chamber," and the life of books and ideas.

Sylvia's determination to get married—and a few pregnancy scares—finally rang alarm bells, and I fled from her, and hitchhiked across France. When I came back, Sylvia had found someone else—a quiet, shy boy who adored her and wanted nothing more than to marry. And marry they did, and Sylvia passed out of my life, leaving me feeling oddly regretful, yet quite certain that marriage to her would have been a disaster.

The whole experience left me once again confronting the problem of illusion and reality. What had my daydreams of Gretchen to do with the reality of sex?

To begin with, Gretchen is the male's dream of "the eternal womanly"—pretty, shy, demure, virginal, childlike, adoring. Sylvia was certainly pretty, childlike and adoring. But she was not shy or demure—she was a charming chatterbox, and when I met her in later years, had become a relentless nonstop talker. Neither was she virginal in the usual sense. I am not referring to the fact that she had been raped in a park by several boys when she was thirteen, but that she simply enjoyed sex as much as any male. I soon realized that the male sexual organ fascinated her, and that if it had been socially permissible, she would have unzipped the fly of every good-looking male to examine his endowment.

In my teenage daydreams, the girl was always submissive; she raised her arms as I removed her dress, lay down quietly on the bed, and lifted her buttocks to allow me to remove her knickers. She looked like Goethe's Gretchen, and had a gentle smile and innocent eyes. Her submissiveness made her infinitely exciting. (When, many years later, I met Marilyn Monroe, I recognized her as a kind of embodiment of this adolescent daydream, and realized that this was the secret of her appeal.)

There are, in fact, a few women who conform to this picture—to some extent. But it is only to some extent. Beneath the surface they remain complex, human, unpredictable. Joyce's Molly Bloom, in *Ulysses*, with her frank sexuality and preoccupation with everyday trivialities, is closer to the eternal womanly than Goethe's Gretchen.

Yet Gretchen is installed in the male psyche as the image of woman. Men wear the image like Kant's blue spectacles, and cannot see womankind without them.

It seems to me that it is to this image that men make love, rather than to real women.

Which explains the basic problem of human sexuality. The image of the eternal feminine arouses the male to an intense pitch of desire. The result is that the sexual act itself is bound to seem something of a disappointment. When I worked on a farm, I saw a vet impregnate a cow by inserting his arm into its vagina, and squeezing sperm from a plastic tube, and the actual physical reality of sex reminded me of this crude process. Inevitably, then, the sheer intensity of the desire leaks away in the act of consummation.

This is the reason that most of the "great lovers"—the Don Juans and Casanovas—have been so fickle. It is not natural immorality; it is simply that the fulfillment seems an anticlimax compared with the pursuit. They feel that they are the victims of a confidence trick—that sex is rather like some gorgeous-looking, exotic fruit, which when bitten tastes just like an ordinary apple or pear.

To a large extent they are right. And to understand why, we need to look closely at the phenomenology of sexual experience. When a male is in an intense state of sexual excitement, he has only one desire: to discharge this excitement with the aid of a willing partner. His sexual energy is canalized, and flows in its narrow channel like a fast stream, without "leakage."

Now when we are in this state, we feel that the object of desire is genuinely desirable. It is not some kind of illusion. Millions of male cinemagoers have felt this as they looked at Greta Garbo or Marilyn Monroe or Grace Kelly; millions of women have felt it as they looked at Rudolph Valentino or Clarke Gable or Elvis Presley. And the fact that they share it with so many others convinces them that this person is genuinely "desirable"—that is, it seems to be a perception rather than just a "feeling."

This is what philosophers call a "value." Plato thought that there were permanent realities behind the world of experience—for example, the notion of a circle exists independently of any real circle. So does a chair or a table. So does a hammer and a nail.

Now it is not all that easy to distinguish between genuine values and illusions. We may feel we are "dying of hunger" two hours after breakfast; our stomach is telling us lies. We may feel that a certain person is totally decent and reliable when, in fact, he is a plausible crook; our emotions are telling us lies. Yet when we respond to a magnificent sunset, or a marvelous view from a mountaintop, we do not feel that this is illusion; we feel that "beauty" has a reality quite apart from any beautiful object.

Now Goethe ended Faust with the words:

> *Das Ewig-Weibliche*
> *Zieht uns hinan.*
> *(The Eternal Feminine*
> *Draws us upward and on.)*

He obviously felt that what we feel when we fall in love, or respond to the beauty of a member of the opposite sex, is another "real value," like a circle, not just a "feeling." (Perhaps he should have written "the eternal sexual," since women seem to respond to an "eternal masculine" just as males respond to the "eternal feminine.")

Now consider again what happens in sexual excitement. In Aldous Huxley's *Antic Hay* there is a scene in which the hero spends the night with a girl who fascinates him. But he finds the sensation of lying beside her so exquisite that sex would be an anticlimax—"to desire would have been to break the enchantment;" instead, he caresses her slowly from head to foot, until they both fall asleep. Faust must have felt like this the first time he made love to Gretchen. His will, his desire, would have been so powerful, so totally controlled, that he would have felt no kind of doubt that she contained the essence of every woman since time began; there would be no kind of ambiguity, no "leakage."

The same, of course, is true of all desire. By focusing our full attention on the object of desire, we experience it far more intensely. Conversely, when we do something without proper attention, half the experience leaks away—that is why a connoisseur holds wine up to the light, sniffs it, and rolls it around the glass, before he actually tastes it. He has no intention of allowing half the experience to escape.

Now unfortunately, this is one of the major problems of the human race. Our lives are so complicated that we cannot afford to give our full attention to everything we do. Besides, there would be no point. It is far better to allow my fingers to type these words, so my mind can be free to think about their meaning. But the result of this division of labor is that we live a great deal of our lives "mechanically."

The trouble is that we cannot evolve as human beings while we are living mechanically; evolution depends on "real living," living that is done while you are fully alive and awake. Holidays wake us up, make us aware of "values" behind the repetitive face of reality. That is why we need holidays—to make us "pay attention," and remind ourselves that life is far more interesting than we thought. Yet even so, most of us fail to reach our full potential because we spend ninety percent of our time living "mechanically."

Human beings find sex so fascinating because it has the power to free us from our mechanicalness. That is why Don Juan is willing to devote his life to its pursuit: because he feels that it offers the surest route to personal evolution. (I certainly felt that I "evolved" more in two weeks with Sylvia than in the previous four years.) But Don Juan keeps changing the object of his attentions because even lovemaking can become partly robotic, and he finds that the answer is to start all over again.

And now, I think, we can begin to see that the question raised by Faust's experience with Gretchen is one of the most momentous questions that can be asked by a philosopher. By freeing us from our mechanicalness, sex seems to offer us the secret of evolution and immortality. When a male experiences the kind of focused attention that Faust experiences as he holds Gretchen in his arms, he seems to glimpse new vistas of consciousness, stretching into the distance like some pathway lined with stars. He can see that if he wants to experience this promise of the "eternal feminine," he must develop a far more powerful type of consciousness. Conversely, he can also see that if he wants to develop a more powerful type of consciousness, he could use sex as a discipline to attain this end.

11

PLATO AND
THE SEXUAL ILLUSION

When I was thirteen or fourteen, I heard a radio performance of Clifford Bax's play *Socrates*, part of a BBC
series called *Saturday Night Theatre*. I had never read
Plato, but had assumed—from Joad's account in *Practical Knowledge
For All*—that he was an obscure philosopher who talked in abstract
language about an invisible world of forms or ideas. Bax's play made
me aware that, on the contrary, he wrote with a force and clarity that
made him seem as contemporary as Shaw.

The play is in six scenes, and depicts how Socrates offended some
of his fellow citizens so much that they drew up an indictment accusing
him of atheism. After a scene in which Socrates offends his chief
accuser Meletus—by alluding to the fact that he has given a bad silver
coin to a blind beggar—Bax presents the trial and condemnation of
Socrates, and finally his execution. But a long second scene concerns
a party given by the young dramatist Agathon, in which a number of
guests make speeches on the nature of love. It was this scene that
impressed me most, with Socrates' magnificent speech in which he
pretends to be quoting from a woman called Diotima, on the ultimately
divine nature of love; he is followed by Alcibiades—a latecomer,
slightly the worse for drink—who makes a speech in praise of Socrates.

I found it all so fascinating that the next day I went to the library
and spent an hour looking at the works of Plato. I discovered that Bax

had adapted the trial and death of Socrates from two dialogues called the *Apology* and *Phaedo*, and that the party scene was called the *Symposium*. This had, fortunately, been newly translated by Michael Joyce, and was far more colloquial and readable than the classic translation by Jowett.

I took it home and read it straight through—delighted to discover that a Greek philosopher should be so lively and amusing. But I was interested to observe that Bax had censored Plato, removing all references to love between men and boys, which—I now learned with amazement—the Greeks took for granted.

In retrospect, I am inclined to believe that the reasons for the Greek preference for boys and youths should be sought in the Greek social structure. Women played no active part in the Athenian state or Athenian society; girls and matrons were kept in seclusion. But there were plenty of girls available for men whose taste lay in that direction. The lowest order could be found in brothels, and were known as pornai (hence pornography). Males could go and examine them virtually naked and take their pick. If they wanted a "mistress," they could hire her and take her home for days, weeks or months. Next came auletrides, or flute players—Bax represents one of them entertaining the men in his version of the *Symposium*. They were entertainers, not unlike the Japanese geisha, who might be called upon for sexual services. Finally, there are the hetairai, or "companions," who might be compared to the courtesans of nineteenth-century Paris, or to the Alexandria depicted by Anatole France in *Thais*. But although they might be the mistresses of statesmen, they had no civil rights, and were not allowed to enter any temple except that of Aphrodite.

So in Athens, there was no chance of a young man falling in love with the girl next door and having a tender Romeo-and-Juliet love affair. He entered into marriage—probably arranged—and then his wife stayed home and brought up the children in virtually Mohammedan seclusion. (It is important to realize that the Greeks are closer to Arabs than to Europeans.) Her husband went to the baths, drank with his friends, and lived in a virtually male society. If a man thought of taking a lover, it was usually a boy or an older man. Even if not naturally homosexual, he would find it easy enough to acquire the taste, and to be swept up in the hysteria about beautiful young men.

All this helps to understand things about the *Symposium* that I, as a young working-class boy, found baffling.

The first speaker is Phaedrus, who declares that the love between virtuous men and youths is of the highest type of love, and that an army of homosexuals would be formidable, since lovers would be determined to prove their bravery in the eyes of their lovers.

Next, Pausanius argues that there are two kinds of love: "earthly" and "heavenly." Earthly love is of the body, and such lovers (Pausanius remarks disapprovingly) are as much attracted by women as boys. On the other hand, young men should not feel ashamed to give themselves to lovers who are virtuous and who try to educate their minds.

By this time, I was feeling slightly disoriented, and was almost relieved to read the speech of the physician Eryximachus, who argues that it is right to indulge sound and healthy desires, and wrong to indulge bad and morbid desires. I found myself wondering how I should regard the fantasies that kept me in a continual state of sexual arousal, and that brought me regularly to orgasm. Certainly, they seemed highly indecent, and I would have blushed if my father or mother could have guessed what was going on in my head. So how did Eryximachus distinguish between healthy and morbid desires? It was the first time I had given any careful thought to this question.

The discourse of Aristophanes came as a surprise. Bax has him making a comic speech about the grotesqueness of the human body, with a head like an inverted flowerpot on a stake and a patch of discolored turf called hair. But in the *Symposium*, Aristophanes has something altogether more interesting to say. Once upon a time, he says, there were three sexes, male, female and hermaphrodite, and the hermaphrodites were globular, with four arms, four legs, four eyes, and two sets of private parts. These creatures were so dominant and energetic that they tried to scale the heavens and attack the gods. So Zeus decided to slice them all in half, so they became human beings as we know them today. And that meant that these divided beings had such a powerful desire to reunite with their lost halves that they spent their whole lives seeking for a partner, and ceased to be a challenge to the gods. And this, says Aristophanes, explains why lovers press themselves together, as if longing to become part of one another; they recognize their incompleteness.

This seemed an altogether better attempt to explain the desires that led me to press my loins into the mattress. It was quite obviously a sense of incompleteness. But did that mean that what I was really seeking was a "soul mate?" That struck me as untrue. What fascinated me was the world of science and knowledge. I certainly wanted a member of the opposite sex—but not as a soul mate. My desires were quite obviously physical; quite simply, my loins ached with a kind of sexual electricity, and I longed to discharge it into the loins of a member of the opposite sex.

After the speech of Agathon, describing love as a youthful god who is good and beautiful, Socrates finally gets his turn. He begins by questioning Agathon. If love is a desire for goodness and beauty, is this not an admission that love does not possess goodness and beauty? This struck me as a mere piece of wordplay, for it is not love itself who falls in love, but a human being. Besides, what had my desire to possess a naked girl to do with goodness and beauty? The simple truth was that I would like to make use of her body.

But in the speech that follows, Socrates also has an answer to this objection. His teacher Diotima, he claims, argued that love is a craving for loveliness, and that its essential nature is a desire to procreate. This is why poets write poetry, musicians write music, artists paint pictures or sculpt figures out of marble.

It is, of course, inevitable that we should fall in love with beautiful bodies. But this is only the first step. The next is to fall in love with beautiful minds. And at that stage, the lover recognizes that institutions and laws are also beautiful. The sciences are even more beautiful, since they are concerned with the beauty and truth of the universe. But the ultimate aim is the contemplation of beauty itself—not the beauty of any particular thing, but the idea of beauty, which transcends all human limitations. We then recognize that when we love a thing or a person, this is only because we can see the reflection of absolute beauty.

The speech moved me deeply—far more than in Bax's abridgement. Lying in my bed, in a working-class house in an industrial town, I felt as if Plato was someone who might have lived next door; in the world of ideas, time is an illusion. The basic aim of human life, I could see, was to transcend our mere humanity. And when, later, I read Shelley's translation of the *Symposium*, in a volume of his collected works, I recognized him as a kindred spirit—someone who wanted to transcend the world of material reality, and to see beyond it to a world of timeless ideas. Unfortunately, he was too involved in emotion and self-pity.

After Socrates has made his speech, there is a loud knocking on the door, and Alcibiades comes in, admitting that he has drunk too much wine. He is pressed to join in, and instead of a eulogy on love, announces that he will deliver a eulogy on Socrates. And he begins with a shameless account of how, many years before, he set out to seduce Socrates, climbing into his bed one night. But when they woke up in the morning, he had no more "slept" with Socrates than if he had been his father or elder brother.

Next, he tells a story about when he was on campaign with Socrates. One day, Socrates began brooding on some problem at sunrise, and stood there lost in thought. Midday came, and he still stood there. The soldiers were so curious that they brought their bedding into the open to see if he stood there all night. At dawn Socrates roused himself, made a prayer to the sun, and went on his way.

When Alcibiades has finished his speech, a crowd of revelers arrives, and they all proceed to get drunk. By dawn, only Socrates, Agathon and Aristophanes are still awake, drinking wine out of an enormous bowl which they pass from one to the other. Socrates is arguing as lucidly as ever, and finally he is the only one left awake. No one has ever seen Socrates drunk. As the sun comes up, he goes to the public bath, then spends the rest of the day in his normal manner, returning home in the evening.

Plato's aim is obviously to create a portrait of an intellectual superman, and as far as I was concerned, he succeeded. Socrates became my first real hero. When I had finished the *Symposium*, I had an odd sense of being two people—one an awkward adolescent, painfully aware of my immaturity, and one a disembodied mind, inhabiting the same world as the great minds of the past.

Plato's discourse on love has continued to preoccupy me ever since. In due course, I made my own attempt to state the problem—primarily in *The Origins of the Sexual Impulse* and *The Misfits*, and more recently, in a novel called *Metamorphosis of the Vampire*. I had no intention of contradicting Plato—only supplementing what he had to say, in the light of modern biology.

According to the Gnostic philosophers, there are two Gods: one the supreme Lord of Eternity, the other a limited demiurge to whom the Deity assigned the task of creating the universe. It has always seemed to me that it was this demiurge, or one of his less competent assistants, who was responsible for creating the sexual urge.

It probably seemed a good idea at the time. Animals must be persuaded to reproduce themselves, and the simple and obvious solution is to make the act of reproduction so pleasant that they will value it above all other experiences. So the female who is ready for sexual intercourse produces a smell so alluring that males will fight to possess her. Dogs will wait for days, without food, outside the home of a bitch in season.

Yet even animal sexuality is not wholly a mechanical affair of stimulus and response. A bull has been known to copulate with seven cows, one after the other. But if a cow with whom it had already copulated is reintroduced, it ignores her.

The phenomenon is known as "the Coolidge effect," named after an anecdote about President Calvin Coolidge, of whom it is told that, on a visit to a government farm, he was separated from his wife, who was taken off on a separate tour. Viewing a chicken pen, Mrs. Coolidge asked the man in charge how many times a day the cock copulated with the hens. "Dozens," said the man. "Tell that to the president," said Mrs. Coolidge. Later, when the man passed on the message, the president asked, "Is it always the same hen?" "Oh no—a different one each time." "Tell that to Mrs. Coolidge," said the president.

So the male animal has an inbuilt tendency to choose different sexual partners. This obviously has a biological purpose—to make it impregnate as many females as possible. But from the point of view of the bull or the cock, it must look as if the female who has not yet been possessed is desirable because she is "forbidden"—exactly the same feeling that a predatory male experiences when he looks at a woman and wonders what she would be like without her clothes.

Now at some point in her history, the human female ceased to be seasonal, and became sexually available all the year round. The reason is probably that when the males of the tribe returned from long hunting trips, they wanted sex whether their mates were in season or not. The women who objected to nonseasonal sex would produce less offspring, and so gradually disappear through a process of natural selection.

The male would not find his mate any less interesting because she failed to appeal to his sense of smell, for he would have found visual stimuli—like large breasts, shapely hips and buttocks, sensuous lips—just as exciting. But in any case, sex is not simply a matter of responding to an attractive female. The virile male, as I have said above, accumulates a kind of sexual electricity in the loins, which longs to discharge itself through sexual release, just as static electricity discharges itself when it comes into contact with a conductor. So what happens when he enters a female is not unlike what happens when we touch the door handle of a car that has built up a static charge.

There is one obvious difference. Static electricity discharges instantaneously. If a male discharged as quickly as this, both he and the female would find the experience disappointing. So sexual intercourse involves a deliberate attempt to control the excitement for as long as possible. This is why, as the Latin tag has it, "man feels sad after coitus." The orgasm, and the loss of sexual interest that follows, seems a kind of betrayal.

Static will discharge itself through any conductor. If nature had stuck to this design, a bull would copulate with the same cow a dozen times, and would impregnate only one female when it might have fathered a dozen calves. So, as we have seen, the male animal has an inbuilt preference for "strange" females. And nature accomplishes this by making the strange female seem "forbidden"—the "Tom Sawyer painting the fence" effect.

In short, nature makes sex alluring by associating it with a sense of "naughtiness." So when Faust sees Gretchen coming out of church, dressed in her Sunday best and looking demure and virginal, he feels that possessing her is the most important thing in the world. Taken to her bedroom by Mephistopheles, Faust goes into raptures, and declares that he is in love, but the cynical Mephistopheles knows that what it really amounts to is a desire to spend a night in her bed.

Gretchen is baffled by his interest in her, for she feels—quite rightly—that she is just an ordinary country girl. She fails to realize that Faust's desire is not "personal"—the desire for an intellectual or spiritual partner—but simply a response to a sexual magic that women exercise unconsciously. In short, Faust is a victim of the sexual illusion, which produces upon the human male imagination the same effect that the smell of oestrum produces on bulls.

And here is the central point I wish to make. There seem to be two kinds of sex. The first and most straightforward is "animal sex," of the kind that takes place when a bull couples with a cow. For "animal sex" to take place, a virile male merely needs to find himself in bed with a woman. When it is over, he falls asleep.

The other kind is romantic sex, which depends upon the sexual illusion. This could also be called "magical sex," for it focuses on the *idea* of the opposite sex. And this "magical sex" can be blown to a far fiercer glow than "animal sex." Faust probably spent the whole night lying awake beside Gretchen, far too excited to fall asleep, just as if he had swallowed a magic potion.

In the modern age, this "magic potion," on which the demiurge has relied so heavily to ensure the propagation of the species, has led to disaster. Throughout history, males have been inclined to promiscuity, but it is only in the twentieth century that the illusion has produced its own type of crime—sex murder. We often describe sex killers as "animals," but this is unjust to animals, whose sex lives are governed by rigid natural laws. The problem with the sex killer is that he is not an animal; he is a human being whose imagination has been inflamed by the sexual illusion. Women seem to him infinitely desirable; like Solomon, he would like to have a thousand concubines. In short, he is like a drug addict or an alcoholic, hopelessly in thrall to a desire that torments him and gives him no peace.

This was clearly not an effect foreseen by the demiurge. He was only concerned with making sure that men and women should find one another mutually enthralling, and fall into bed. When women dispensed with the alluring smell of oestrum, the demiurge quickly replaced it with romantic sexuality. The love potion drunk by Tristan and Isolde is actually a symbol of this romantic illusion that works through the imagination; the lover finds her glove or handkerchief almost as exciting as the presence of the beloved.

Now we can see that it is only a single step from this kind of romantic associationism to what the psychologist Alfred Binet labeled fetishism, in which the male finds some object associated with a woman—most frequently her underwear—as exciting as her naked body. The fetishist, stealing women's panties from a clothesline, has been enslaved by the same magic potion that intoxicated Tristan and Isolde.

The problem, of course, lies in the fact that sexual anticipation can be used as a powerful stimulant. Whenever we want something badly, we perform a mental act which is like pulling back a spring; the more we want it, the further we pull the spring. The same thing happens with our appetite for food. There is obviously a world of difference between a workman opening his box of sandwiches and a gourmet sitting down to dinner in a good restaurant, and this difference lies in the fact that the gourmet has pulled his spring back further.

But then, this aspect of his meal—increasing the pleasure by anticipation—can only be carried to a certain length. Every mouthful of food he eats, every mouthful of wine he swallows, diminishes his appetite.

This is the fundamental and important difference between the sexual appetite and the appetite for food. When the sexual gourmet prepares to enjoy himself, the "foreplay" does not diminish the appetite—on the contrary, it can increase it.

Finally, there is the fact that the sexual appetite only vanishes with the orgasm. It is rather as if the gourmet remained ravenously hungry until the last mouthful of the meal, then achieved a kind of orgasm of sensual satisfaction as he swallowed it.

Now this fact—that the sexual appetite can be fully sustained until the climax—means that the "anticipation" becomes, so to speak, the major part of the meal. For animals, sex always remains simple, like a workman eating his sandwiches. But a highly-sexed human being can spin out the anticipation and foreplay almost indefinitely.

Sexual energy, that tingling sexual "electricity" in the loins, could be compared to money; unlike animals, human beings have a choice about how they spend it. Sexual excitement fires the imagination, and imagination plays an important part in all human sexual activity. Lovemaking involves only one physical partner at a time, but it can involve any number of mental partners.

Now compared to the rest of us, sexual obsessives—like Ted Bundy or Albert Desalvo (the Boston Strangler)—are sexually "wealthy." (Desalvo was capable of having a dozen orgasms a day.) The normal man or woman might be compared to a child who goes to a fairground with a certain sum of pocket money, and has to carefully decide how much to spend on the various attractions. By comparison, Desalvo was like a child who has been given a hundred dollars by a wealthy uncle. No matter how hard he tried, he would still find it difficult to get rid of that much money. He can go on the roundabouts, the swings and the dodgems, and eat cotton candy and ice cream until he is sick, and still he has a pocketful of money.

The sexual obsessive soon becomes bored with the usual range of sexual entertainments, and craves more exciting ways of disposing of his (or her) sexual pocket money. But sex is, after all, an oddly limited activity. The only way it can be extended is through "forbiddenness." For example, all sex contains an element of sadomasochism; the male is "imposing his will" on the female, and she is "yielding" by permitting it. But in normal sexuality, the sadomasochistic element is so slight as to be almost unnoticeable. The sexual obsessive sets out to increase satisfaction by amplifying the sadomasochistic element. The sight of a woman who is tied and gagged increases the stimulus. The next step might be beating her. And sooner or later, sexual murder becomes a logical development.

Since the sexual responses themselves are transformed and intensified by fantasy—the vast majority of sex killers have become sex killers through indulging in fantasy—imagination can, in effect, turn human beings into sexual alcoholics.

The serial killer has taken one further step into "sexual alcoholism." To him, it seems to offer the key to higher states of consciousness, a new level of personal evolution. Frustration means that our development is blocked; stagnant energies accumulate inside us, like dirty water in a blocked sink. When the blockage is removed, we experience a sense of relief and happiness as the water flows away. And in such moments, it becomes clear that human beings need the "flow experience" to change and evolve.

Now sex seems to offer the possibility of an altogether higher level of evolution. To begin with, it can fill us with a sense of purpose that transcends all our normal drives. A man can be bored and half asleep, but a mere glimpse through a window of a woman who is removing her blouse or unzipping her skirt is enough to shock him into wide-awakeness.

And here we come to the central problem. As we have seen, the greater the "forbiddenness," the "naughtiness," the greater the drive. Nabokov's Humbert, lusting after ten-year-old Lolita, experiences a far greater intensity of desire than he can feel for more "achievable" adult women. The novels of Jerzy Kosinski—whose life was spent in seduction—make it clear that the idea of rape and incest excites him far more than more "normal" forms of sex.

Moreover, everyone who has experienced intense sexual excitement will admit that it would seem a waste to dissipate it in the usual sexual climax; it seems to demand the same kind of tasting and prolonged appreciation as a great wine. The mere act of copulation does not seem "forbidden" enough to do justice to the excitement. We feel a natural desire to control it, to draw it out, to "amplify" it, as teenagers like to amplify the sound of rock music.

E. T. A. Hoffmann went to the heart of the matter when he remarked in *Murr the Tomcat*, "Every man really has an innate inclination to fly, and I have known serious, respectable people who in the late evening fill themselves with champagne, as a gas to ascend to the heights, as balloon and passenger at the same time." This innate inclination to fly explains the ecstasies and miseries of the nineteenth-century Romantics. In our modern age, we could find a more precise analogy in the hovercraft, which floats on a cushion of air, prevented from "leaking" by a kind of curtain.

In the same way, any kind of deep concentration can generate an inner power that can raise us off the ground. When we are deeply absorbed in something, our minds cease to "leak," and we leave behind the normal "worm's-eye view," and soar up into a bird's-eye view of existence. The same thing happens on spring mornings, or as we set out on holiday; it is as if our minds cease to plod along on the level of material reality, and seem to soar up into the air.

The result is an odd sense of becoming what we really are. Yeats expressed it in *Under Ben Bulben*:

> *Know that when all words are said,*
> *And a man is fighting mad,*
> *Something drops from eyes long blind,*
> *He completes his partial mind,*
> *For an instant stands at ease,*
> *Laughs aloud, his heart at peace . . .*

In these moments when man turns into a hovercraft, he "completes his partial mind," and seems to understand who he really is. Our unconcentrated usual state of mind could be compared to the moon in its last quarter; in moments of "completion," the moon suddenly becomes full.

There are many ways of achieving this state. Wordsworth achieved it contemplating nature. Van Gogh obviously achieved it as he painted *The Starry Night*. A racing driver probably achieves it driving at a hundred miles an hour. And, as Yeats remarks, it can happen when we are "fighting mad."

Now it is because it provides a ready access to this state of "completion" that sex is so popular. Moreover, the state can be achieved with a minimum of effort and inconvenience—even without the presence of a member of the opposite sex. The human power of imagination enables us to "bottle up" the energy of sexual desire, to compress it, as the chamber of a rifle compresses the gases released when the firing pin strikes the bullet, and to direct this energy into sexual release.

In 1972, an American pharmacologist named Andrew Weil caused a sensation with a book called *The Natural Mind*, in which he argued that human beings have an innate psychological drive to higher forms of consciousness, and that this is as natural as hunger and the sexual urge. This, he argued, is why children like to spin until they are dizzy, and why people get drunk and take drugs. He went on to suggest that these "highs" can be achieved naturally by meditation, which creates a channel between the conscious and the unconscious mind.

What I am trying to point out is that one of the easiest ways of achieving "highs" is through the misuse of sex. As any frustrated teenager with a pile of sex magazines realizes, he can create a kind of virtual reality, in which he performs "thought experiments" that may progress from undressing the girl next door to committing incest with every woman in his family and violent rape on every girl in his class at school. The more he learns the trick of intensifying his sexual fantasy, the more his imagination seeks new limits of "forbiddenness." In his fantasy world, he can be a combination of Haroun Al Raschid and Ivan the Terrible. The more he fantasizes, the more he can cause his sexual desires to respond to extremes. As William Blake remarks:

When thought is closed in caves
Then love will show its root in deepest Hell.

And all this is due to the fact that "imaginative sex"—the specifically human form of sex—can offer a far more ready access to states of intensity than music, poetry, philosophy or even religion.

This happens through the same process that occurs in every type of "high." In *A Suggestion about Mysticism*, William James argues that so-called "mystical states" are merely an extension of the ordinary field of consciousness. What happens in such states is that "the present coalesces . . . with ranges of the remote quite out of its reach under ordinary circumstances." And he describes how he himself has experienced states of consciousness in which "I seemed all at once to be reminded of a past experience; and this reminiscence, ere I could conceive or name it distinctly, developed into something further that belonged with it, this in turn into something further still, and so on, until the process faded out, leaving me amazed at the sudden vision of increasing ranges of distant fact of which I could give no articulate account." In short, it was a kind of "bird's-eye" vision.

We can see the same process in poetry; for example, Shelley's poems produce a breathless sense of excitement because he moves so fast from image to image, so that the reader actually seems to become the west wind or a raincloud or a skylark.

Great music produces the same effect, bringing a rush of associations that seem to raise us higher and higher, until we feel as if we are looking down on the world, like Faust floating over moonlit meadows.

And sexual excitement works in precisely the same way, bringing a rush of erotic associations. The composer Percy Grainger wrote, "I love to wade and swim in a sea of overwrought ceaseless sexual thought." And in this "overwrought" state, everything becomes permissible.

In quantum physics there is a concept known as the "ultraviolet catastrophe." When you strike a piano key, each string causes the others to vibrate. Now we know that all energies blend into one another—radio waves into heat, heat into light, light into x-rays, and so on. So when you switch on your electric fire, why does it now send out x-rays and gamma rays and cosmic rays? Max Planck discovered the answer: that light comes in "packets," which are, to all intents and purposes, particles.

But in states of intense sexual excitement, a kind of "ultraviolet catastrophe" does take place, and this is why "normal sex" can so easily degenerate into perversions like sadism, masochism, and sexual murder.

The point can be illustrated by the recent case of the Gloucester builder Fred West, in whose back garden and cellar police found nine bodies of young girls. Like so many sex criminals, West had been turned into a "sex maniac" by head injuries from two serious accidents in his teens. He treated his daughters as a harem—having regular sexual intercourse with one of them from the time she was nine—and murdered another daughter to prevent her from reporting his rapes. It was the rape of yet another daughter that led to his arrest and final downfall. His wife Rose was a lesbian and a nymphomaniac who declared that no man or woman could ever satisfy her. Both loved to take part in sexual orgies—often with girls who had been kidnapped, and who ended buried in the garden. Like Percy Grainger, Fred and

Rose West also liked to wade in a sea of overwrought sexuality. And we are left with the paradox that there seems to be no clear dividing line between sexual perversion and creativity.

I conclude that all this is some kind of mistake on the part of an incompetent demiurge, who decided to use "imaginative sex" as a bait to persuade us to propagate the species—a mistake which might be compared to encouraging children to use petrol to light fires.

It can be seen why, although I regard the *Symposium* as one of the great philosophical studies on the nature of love, I am inclined to feel that there was a great deal Plato did not even begin to understand about sex.

12

SHAW

At this point I must speak of another work that made on me a greater impact than anything I had read so far. At the end of the war—I think it must have been in the autumn of 1945—the BBC launched a new radio wavelength—the "Third Programme," devoted to classical music and drama.

I think it was sometime during its first week that I tuned in, and heard the familiar voice of the actor Esmé Percy declaiming:

"Friends and fellow brigands. I have a proposal to make to this meeting. We have now spent three evenings in discussing the question, 'Have anarchists or social democrats the most personal courage?' We have gone into the principles of anarchism and social-democracy at great length . . . "

It was the beginning of the third act of Shaw's *Man and Superman*.

Two years earlier I had been to see the film of *Caesar and Cleopatra*, and been impressed by it; but since it was a historical drama, and I was not deeply interested in history, I had felt no inclination to read more of Shaw's plays. But *Man and Superman* was "modern," and it was also funny.

The brigand making the speech is Mendoza, who calls himself "President of the League of the Sierra." His band of intellectual cutthroats lie in wait for travelers in the Sierra Nevada, in Spain, and pass the time by debating like a university political club.

Soon they are interrupted by the arrival of a car. It is John Tanner, M.I.R.C. (Member of the Idle Rich Class) and his chauffeur Henry (or, as he calls it, 'Enry) Straker.

Mendoza introduces himself grandiosely, "I am a brigand: I live by robbing the rich." Tanner replies, "I am a gentleman: I live by robbing the poor. Shake hands."

When Mendoza informs Tanner that he has been kidnapped and will be held to ransom, Tanner replies, "I am rich enough to pay anything in reason." Mendoza is impressed, "You are a remarkable man, sir. Our guests usually describe themselves as miserably poor."

And now Mendoza proceeds to tell Tanner and 'Enry the story of how he became a brigand. He was in love with a beautiful girl, who rejected him. He reads some appalling poetry he has written to her. But when he reveals her name—Louisa Straker—'Enry is indignant; she is his sister, and he feels she has been insulted.

Finally they all calm down and go to sleep. Then there is sheer emptiness: "omnipresent nothing," and the sound of a violin playing a phrase from Mozart. And as a little light steals into the scene, a man is seen sitting in the void. It is John Tanner's ancestor Don Juan (they are both played by the same actor). After more mysterious strains of Mozart, an old woman enters, explaining that she died that morning. "Where am I?" she wants to know. "In hell, Senora." That is impossible, she says; she feels no pain. In that case, says Don Juan, "There is no mistake; you are intentionally damned." The wicked are quite comfortable in hell, since it was made for them.

Don Juan explains why he is in hell; he killed an old man who was defending his daughter's honor. The old lady declares that her father was killed in identical circumstances. But when Don Juan tells her that, since she has no body, she can now become whatever age she likes, she loses no time in becoming a young woman again. And they instantly recognize one another. She is Dona Ana, the lady whose father (in Mozart's opera) was killed by Don Juan in a duel, and whose statue later dragged the famous seducer off to hell.

Soon, they are joined by her father, the Commander, who prefers to keep the form of a statue because it is so handsome; he has come from heaven, but confesses that the place bores him. In fact, he has come there to tell the Devil that he has finally decided to leave heaven and join him.

The Commander sends for the Devil (who turns out to be Mendoza's double) by sending out great rolling chords of Mozart's music.

Ana is baffled. Is it possible to choose whether you prefer heaven or hell?

The Devil assures her that indeed it is.

"Then why does not everybody go to heaven?" she asks.

"Because," says her father, "it is the most angelically dull place in all creation."

The Devil concurs. "There is a notion that I was turned out of it; but as a matter of fact, nothing would have induced me to stay there. I simply left it and organized this place."

Ana nevertheless decides to leave for heaven immediately. She demands that her father should go with her. "You cannot stay here. What will people say?"

"People!" says the statue, "Why, all the best people are here—princes of the church and all."

For it seems that heaven is the home of the intellectually serious; hell is the home of those who prefer amusement. Don Juan wants to go to heaven so that he can enjoy "the contemplation of that which interests me above all things: namely, Life, the force that ever strives to attain greater power of contemplating itself." "In heaven," says Don Juan, "there is the work of helping Life in its struggle upward. Think of how it wastes and scatters itself, how it raises up obstacles to itself, and destroys itself in its ignorance and blindness. It needs a brain, this irresistible force, lest in its ignorance it should resist itself."

I listened, electrified. Shaw was talking about the problem that had been obsessing me since I had read Einstein: why are human beings alive? And what are we supposed to do now that we are here? Shaw was saying that the purpose of life is more consciousness: to understand itself.

The Devil interrupts to remind them that when he was "arranging that affair of Faust's," he had said that all man's reason has done is to make him beastlier than any beast. "One splendid body is worth the brains of a hundred dyspeptic, flatulent philosophers." And he launches into a great tirade to demonstrate that man is the most murderous, destructive creature who has ever walked the surface of the earth.

Don Juan is inclined to agree. And yet, he points out, man has one interesting peculiarity. "You can make any of these cowards brave by simply putting an idea into his head." Man differs from the animals because he is not driven merely by a desire for survival; he has a craving for ideas, for ideals, for meaning.

It was now about eleven o'clock at night, long past my bedtime. Yet I found it all so exciting that I went on listening. I suddenly felt that, for the first time, I had encountered a mind that was like my own. I had admired Einstein; but he was only concerned with physics. Shaw was addressing a far more profound problem: what we are supposed to do with our lives. And the answers he gave sounded self-evidently true: to use the brain, the intellect. Only one man, says Don Juan, has been universally respected, "the philosophic man: he who seeks in contemplation to discover the inner will of the world, in invention to discover the means of fulfilling that will, and in action to do that will by the so-discovered means. Of all other sorts of men I declare myself tired. They are tedious failures."

And now Don Juan goes on to describe how his search for meaning led him to art and music and poetry, and finally the worship of Woman.

"Yes: I came to believe that in her voice was all the music of the song, in her face all the beauty of the painting, and in her soul all the emotion of the poem."

Dona Ana says scornfully, "And you were disappointed, I suppose. Well, was it her fault that you attributed all these perfections to her?"

Yes, says Don Juan, "for with a wonderful instinctive cunning, she kept silent, and allowed me to glorify her: to mistake my own visions, thoughts and feelings for hers."

Yet, "when the barriers were down for the first time, what an astounding illumination! I had been prepared for infatuation, for intoxication, for all the illusions of love's young dream; and lo! Never was my perception clearer, nor my criticism more ruthless. The most jealous rival of my mistress never saw every blemish in her more keenly than I. I was not duped: I took her without chloroform."

"But you did take her," says Dona Ana dryly.

"Yes, that was the revelation. Up to that moment I had never lost the sense of being my own master; never consciously taken a step until my reason had examined and approved it . . . " And now, as he stood face to face with Woman, prepared to make his excuses and withdraw, "Life seized me and threw me into her arms as a sailor throws a scrap of fish into the mouth of a seabird."

This, for Don Juan, was the great revelation: that there is a far more powerful force than our human reason; that behind this facade of everyday social existence, there is a creative will that drives philosophers to think and artists to create. And, of course, Don Juans to seduce.

This was exactly what I wanted—and needed—to hear: that all my brooding on the meaning and purpose of life was not a waste of time. Shaw had suddenly justified my existence, and made me feel that, like Don Juan, I also had a purpose. That purpose made me feel bored, alienated, utterly miserable and frustrated; yet if I could recognize and accept it, it could also provide my life with meaning.

What had happened, in the two hours I had been listening to *Man and Superman*, was that I had begun to learn to accept myself, to cease to feel myself an "outsider." (Ten years later, writing a book about "outsiders," I was instinctively attempting to perform the same service for others who felt as I did.)

When I went to bed that night, well after midnight, I felt an odd mixture of exhilaration and anxiety. I felt overwhelmed by Shaw's flow of language and ideas. Yet I had never been entirely free of a certain fear that—as Yeats put it:

> *Knowledge increases unreality, that*
> *Mirror on mirror mirrored is all the show . . .*

—the suspicion that, if one thinks too deeply, one is bound to end by looking down into a void.

Since childhood I had slept in the same bed as my brother. In the middle of the night, I woke up and found that the blankets had slipped off us. I reached out and touched him; he was as cold as a corpse, and for a moment I believed him dead. Suddenly, it seemed to me that this was a punishment for prying too deeply into the meaning of life. But when I covered him up, he became warm again, and my anxiety vanished, and with it, my suspicion that the hidden forces of the universe wish to prevent us from indulging in too much questioning.

The following evening, *Man and Superman* was repeated. This time I listened to it from beginning to end—five or six hours. I went to bed glowing with an absolute certainty that Shaw was the greatest mind of the twentieth century—possibly of any century. I had read H. G. Wells and G. K. Chesterton, but never anyone who spoke of ideas with the assurance and confidence of Shaw. It seemed to me astonishing that his greatness was not more widely recognized. I spoke of him to the English master at school—a man I greatly admired—but he was dismissive; he seemed to think that Shaw was in some way superficial. The other masters to whom I mentioned Shaw seemed to agree. Finally, I stopped mentioning Shaw, because it infuriated me to hear him dismissed by men who did not possess a quarter of his intellect.

I borrowed *Man and Superman* from the library, and read and reread it until I almost knew it by heart. Its most important sentence seemed to me to be Tanner's statement: "The artist's work is to show us ourselves as we really are. Our minds are nothing but this knowledge of ourselves; and he who adds to such knowledge creates new mind as surely as any woman creates new men." It still strikes me as the most important sentence Shaw ever wrote.

I have to admit that, by comparison with *Man and Superman*, I found Shaw's other plays something of a disappointment. Someone told me that his greatest play was *Back to Methuselah*; I borrowed it from the library, but found it oddly dull. Shaw's lengthy satire on politicians bored me, and I began to see why my schoolmasters thought that Shaw was often shallow and complacent. Like some headmaster, he seemed to have become so accustomed to everyone laughing at his jokes that he assumed that anything he said was witty.

But it was mostly the later work that I found dull. *Saint Joan* simply struck me as overrated; *In Good King Charles's Golden Days* went on too long and seemed to get nowhere. Even *The Apple Cart*—which I now regard as one of his finest plays—seemed to me rather pedestrian.

In the following year—1946—to celebrate Shaw's ninetieth birthday, Penguin books brought out a dozen paperbacks of his plays, and I was finally able to acquire my own copy of *Man and Superman*. By this time I had read all Shaw's plays, from *Widower's Houses* to *Good King Charles*. (*Buoyant Billions*, his last play, had not yet been written.) I loved the early plays—particularly *Arms and the Man*, *Candida*, *The Devil's Disciple*, and *Caesar and Cleopatra*. It seemed to me that after *Man and Superman*, written in 1903, when he was forty-seven, there was a falling off. *John Bull's Other Island*, *Major Barbara* and *The Doctor's Dilemma* disappointed me because Shaw had not returned to the theme of human evolution and "creating new mind." *Getting Married* and *Misalliance* seemed to me to display a drift towards self-indulgence, the certainty that he had his captive audience who would listen to whatever he had to say because he was the latest fashion. (By 1910, Shaw was already one of the most famous writers in Europe, and it had all happened within five years.) He would produce one more first rate comedy—*Pygmalion*—and one more flawed masterpiece—*Heartbreak House*—before garrulity began to take over.

I must admit that I envied Shaw. He had arrived at precisely the right time, when Nietzsche and Ibsen were beginning to question nineteenth-century values. The conventionality of the Victorians made an easy target; their city walls had already been weakened, and it only took a trumpet blast to make them tumble to the ground.

Sometime in 1946, when I was fifteen, I made my first attempt to write a full-length book (as opposed to the compiled summaries of the *Manual of General Science*); it was called *The Quintessence of Shavianism*, the title shamelessly lifted from Shaw's *Quintessence of Ibsenism*. I wrote it on Saturday afternoons, sitting at the table in the house where my mother had grown up; now I had a second younger brother, as well as a sister, I went there to get some peace—my grandfather had died in the previous year, and my grandmother was glad of the company. I still have the book in a filing cabinet somewhere, but I do not think I could bear to reread it—the clumsinesses of my earlier work fills me with a sense of shame, and I only refrain from destroying it because I feel I have no right to disown my past.

Twenty years later, I was commissioned by an American publisher to write a book about Shaw, and into that I finally put my balanced view of the man who had exercised so much influence on my life. By that time I had become aware of the garrulousness that mars so much of the later work, and the vanity that made perceptive critics patronizing, and the failure to develop beyond the age of about sixty—a book like Stephen Winsten's *Days With Bernard Shaw*, written when the sage was in his eighties, portrays a man whose mind is caught in a time warp, and who talks endlessly about his days in the Fabian Society. Yet when I came to reread the plays—to write about them in *Bernard Shaw: A Reassessment*—I still found myself falling under the spell of the magic that had captivated me when I first heard *Man and Superman* on the radio. And when I came to teach a course on Shaw at the University of Washington, in Seattle, I found that it cost me the utmost self-discipline not to read whole plays aloud to my students—*Widowers' Houses, Arms and the Man, Mrs. Warren's Profession, The Devil's Disciple, John Bull's Other Island*. It was obvious to me that, in spite of my dislike of his vanity and complacency, his work still reduced me to a state of uncritical admiration.

Eventually, it seemed to me that, in spite of its faults, *Back to Methuselah* is, as Shaw believed, his "world classic." That is because it recognizes so clearly that the basic human aim is to achieve higher intensity of consciousness, and that this will automatically entail living longer.

Now oddly enough, Shaw's notion of the importance of longevity, and of the eventual conquest of matter by spirit, has either been ignored or derided. Critics obviously find the notion of his "Ancients"—beings who have become independent of most physical needs—curiously repellent. Aldous Huxley even produced a satire on the idea in *After Many a Summer*, where an old aristocrat who has achieved a kind of immortality has degenerated into a human ape. Yet Huxley must have understood as well as anyone that Shaw was not talking primarily about longevity, but about how we might achieve greater intensity of consciousness.

When I was twenty-four years old, and *The Outsider* was due to be published in a few weeks time, I met the novelist Iris Murdoch at a party, and when she asked me about my basic purpose, I replied, "To live to be three hundred." Understandably, she thought I was joking.

The problem is: what could bring it about? Shaw thought it would "just happen." What he failed to grasp was that living longer would have to entail a higher level of purpose, and that such a level does not "just happen;" it has to be achieved by effort. If we could achieve the full support of the unconscious mind, we could do practically anything; but the only way to gain this support is by impressing the unconscious mind with a sense of urgency. Gurdjieff understood how easily human beings relax their sense of purpose and become "mechanical."

Even when I was young, I recognized the paradoxical nature of the problem. Human life is a continual striving for "success," and without success, we tend to become victims of what Shaw called "discouragement." Yet with success (as Arnold Toynbee pointed out in *A Study of History*) human beings tend to "rest on their oars." This is why highly successful civilizations go into decline. I have an article about longevity in my file, that points out that orchestral conductors tend to live far longer than the average man. And, oddly enough, that people whose names are in reference books like *Who's Who* also tend to live longer. In other words, longevity is related to the sense of purpose.

Interestingly enough, mathematicians also tend to live longer than average, which affords another interesting clue. The peculiar disciplines of mathematics mean that a mathematician spends far more time "inside his own head" than the rest of us. And this lack of dependence on physical reality means that he is less prone to boredom.

In other words, the majority of human beings could be compared to those old-fashioned motor cars whose engines needed a swing on a starting handle, inserted in a hole underneath the radiator. Most human beings are like this; before our minds can achieve a state of full alertness, we need to be "started" by some stimulus from the external world.

Old-fashioned cars were soon replaced by vehicles with "self-starters," that merely required the push of a button or the turn of a key to start the engine. But "self-starting" human beings (or what Nietzsche called "self-rolling wheels") do not yet exist. The nearest thing so far is the pure mathematician, and perhaps the religious ascetic, who spends his days attempting to achieve control over his mind.

Yet it seems to me that we may not be as far from the "self-starting" human being as we assume. In my own experience, an act of total concentration can actually cause the engine to "turn over," even if it fails to start. Again, if I use my imagination to summon some possible disaster, the engine begins to stir into life.

The problem, at the moment, is that our equivalent of a battery is not strong enough—or perhaps not sufficiently highly charged—and, above all, that we fail to make the kind of effort required. Such an effort requires imagination—precisely what the critics of *Back to Methuselah* lacked.

It seems to me that, in conceiving *Back to Methuselah*, Shaw was one of the most far-seeing minds of the twentieth century. Regrettably, he thought of it too late. If he had written it ten years earlier, *Back to Methuselah* would probably be the greatest of Shaw's works.

But we should not allow the failure in execution to blind us to the fact that the vision that led Shaw to write *Back to Methuselah* was the most important of his life.

13

ELIOT AND
THE PYTHON'S TAIL

It was a comment by my English master, Mr. Harris, to the effect that T. S. Eliot was the most difficult of modern poets, that led me to borrow the *Collected Poems, 1909-1935* from the public library—the notion of a "difficult" poet was a challenge to someone who had a reputation as the fifth-form "intellectual." A glance at *The Love Song of J. Alfred Prufrock* and *The Waste Land* revealed that Mr. Harris was not exaggerating.

By this time I was already reading poetry, having been introduced to it by the literature chapters of *Practical Knowledge for All*. I read Keats, Wordsworth—even Milton, whose *Paradise Lost* was being broadcast canto by canto on the radio on Sunday evenings—and whose magnificent, sonorous English was well suited to being read aloud. I soon knew Keats' *Bright Star* sonnet, and Wordsworth's *Westminster Bridge*, and Shelley's *Ode to the West Wind*, and Poe's *Raven* and *Ulalume* by heart. For an adolescent in the throes of continual frustration and emotional torment, they were marvelously soothing.

It did not take me long to recognize that, in spite of his obscurity, Eliot was as romantic as any of the poets of the 1890s:

> *They are rattling breakfast plates in basement kitchens,*
> *And along the trampled edges of the street*
> *I am aware of the damp souls of housemaids*

Sprouting despondently at area gates.
The brown waves of fog toss up to me
Twisted faces from the bottom of the street,
And tear from a passer-by with muddy skirts
An aimless smile that hovers in the air
And vanishes along the level of the roofs.

This reminded me of the *Autumnal* of my favorite fin de siècle poet Ernest Dowson:

Pale amber sunlight falls across
The reddening October trees,
That hardly sway before a breeze
As soft as summer: summer's loss
Seems little, dear! on days like these.
Let misty autumn be our part!
The twilight of the year is sweet
Where shadow and the darkness meet
Our love, a twilight of the heart
Eludes a little time's deceit.

Also in the local library I found *The Achievement of T. S. Eliot* by F. O. Matthiessen, and was fascinated—and puzzled—to discover that it treated Eliot as a writer of stern classical discipline. Here I found nothing about the sense of emotional devastation of *The Waste Land* or the despair of *The Hollow Men*—only a comparison of Eliot's "technical devices" with those of Donne, and of Eliot's *Tradition and Individual Talent* with Matthew Arnold's *The Study of Poetry*. It was all very puzzling, and I, who thought of myself as well-read, had never heard of Laforgue or Corbiere or Gerard de Nerval.

I lost no time in borrowing Eliot's *Selected Essays* from the library, and found them dry, precise and slightly mordant in tone—he dismisses Shaw, Chesterton and Bertrand Russell in casual and scathing asides. It was through Eliot—and Matthiessen—that I heard of T. E. Hulme, and borrowed his *Speculations* from the library.

And what was I—who only a year ago had still intended to be a scientist—doing reading Eliot and Hulme? It was basically because I felt the need of some discipline to replace the discipline of science. Romantic poetry was not enough; I felt the need of more solid, intellectual fare.

I left school in July 1947, at the age of sixteen; I might, if I had tried, have obtained a scholarship to a university, but my father was determined that I should contribute to the household budget. (My brother Barry had already been at work for six months, employed by a local butcher as a delivery boy.) In any case, it would not have been a good idea, for I had already lost interest in science.

The local labor exchange suggested that I should apply for a job with the chemical giant ICI. But for that I needed a Matriculation Certificate. And although I had passed my School Certificate examination, I only had four credits—one less than I needed to matriculate. The answer was to take the math exam again, in which I only had to pass. In the meantime, I applied at the Labor Exchange for a temporary job, and was sent to a wool warehouse where they needed someone to unpack the wool—which arrived in hanks—and repack it when it had been wound onto spools.

I detested the job, feeling exactly as Dickens felt in his blacking warehouse or Wells in his drapery emporium. It was a small building of two stories, the ground floor used for the reception of crates of wool, while the upper floor was full of the machines that wound it onto bobbins. The employees were all local women, mostly housewives, and since this was a slum area, most of them had been working since they were thirteen or fourteen. One of them had such a smell of stale urine that I held my breath as I passed her.

Working from eight in the morning until six in the evening, and for five hours on Saturday morning, I was plunged into gloom and depression. I felt trapped. It seemed outrageous that someone who had been regarded as one of the brightest students of his year should be working for forty-eight hours a week in a factory, with apparently no prospect of escape. Even being accepted by ICI would be no solution, since my interest in science had vanished.

As far as I could see, there was only one possible solution—and that seemed so remote and unattainable that it made my heart sink: to become a writer. So I began writing short stories, and sending them off to magazines. They were all promptly returned, and disappointment always left me shattered for days.

It was now, in this state of deep depression, that Eliot's poetry took on a new importance. In my states of blackest depression, I read *The Waste Land* and *The Hollow Men* and found that they brought a kind of grim relief:

A rat crept slowly through the vegetation
Dragging its slimy belly on the bank
While I was fishing in the dull canal
On a winter evening round behind the gashouse . . .

The poem seemed an indictment of modern civilization. In retrospect, I can see that it was nothing of the sort—merely an expression of Eliot's despair, expressed with a power that would have been beyond the verbal skills of the poets of the 1890s.

A woman drew her long black hair out tight
And fiddled whisper music on those strings
And bats with baby faces in the violet light
Whistled, and beat their wings
And crawled head downward down a blackened wall
And upside down in air were towers
Tolling reminiscent bells that kept the hours
And voices singing out of empty cisterns and exhausted wells . . .

It is difficult to say why this imagery evokes a sense of despair, and it is probably meaningless to ask—like asking why the music of Mahler often creates the same sense of despair and spiritual struggle.

In *The Hollow Men*, the despair rises to a climax:

This is the dead land
This is cactus land
Here the stone images
Are raised, here they receive
The supplication of a dead man's hand
Under the twinkle of a fading star.
Is it like this
In death's other kingdom
Waking alone
At hour when we are
Trembling with tenderness
Lips that would kiss
Form prayers to broken stone.

Eliot's poetry springs, of course, from a profound and dangerous emotional exhaustion—dangerous because this kind of depression verges on mental illness. When the vital powers become too depleted, the result is a vicious circle of pessimism and misery, where the pessimism deepens the misery and the misery deepens the pessimism. Coleridge describes such a state in *Dejection: An Ode*:

> *A grief without a pang, void, dark and drear,*
> *A stifled, drowsy, unimpassioned grief,*
> *Which finds no natural outlet, no relief,*
> *In word, or sigh, or tear—*
> *O Lady! in this wan and heartless mood,*
> *To other thoughts by yonder throstle woo'd,*
> *All this long eve so balmy and serene,*
> *Have I been gazing on the western sky,*
> *And its peculiar tint of yellow green:*
> *And still I gaze—and with how blank an eye!*
> *And those thin clouds above, in flakes and bars,*
> *That give away their motion to the stars;*
> *Those stars that glide behind them, or between,*
> *Now sparkling, now bedimmed, but always seen:*
> *Yon crescent moon, as fixed as if it grew*
> *In its own cloudless, starless lake of blue;*
> *I see them all, so excellently fair,*
> *I see, not feel, how beautiful they are.*

In Eliot's early poetry, like the *Rhapsody on a Windy Night* and *Morning at the Window* (quoted earlier) we get a sense of fin de siècle melancholy and world weariness rather than despair; but by the time of *The Hollow Men*, it is obvious that Eliot is on the verge of a nervous breakdown, and that poetry has become a kind of lifeline connecting him to sanity. This becomes even more clear in *Ash Wednesday*:

> *Because I do not hope to know again*
> *The infirm glory of the positive hour*
> *Because I do not think*
> *Because I know I shall not know*
> *The one veritable transitory power*
> *Because I cannot drink*
> *There, where trees flower, and springs flow,*
>   *for there is nothing again . . .*

"Nothing again"—that sudden collapse of feeling and response, like a sudden loss of memory, is an accurate description of the state called schizophrenia—not, of course, split personality, but a sense of alienation from reality, and consequent loss of all motivation:

> *The air which is now thoroughly small and dry*
> *Smaller and dryer than the will*
> *Teach us to care and not to care*
> *Teach us to sit still.*

What has happened is that Eliot has escaped mental breakdown through a kind of move towards religious conversion. Yet he is still unable to believe that religious conversion can provide a solution:

> *...Will the veiled sister pray*
> *For the children at the gate*
> *Who will not go away and cannot pray...*
> *Will the veiled sister between the slender*
> *Yew trees pray for those who offend her*
> *And are terrified and cannot surrender...*

In this state of exhaustion, which Sartre calls "nausea," and Shaw "life failure," the world seems self-evidently meaningless, so that religious conversion, in the usual sense, would seem to be mere self-deception. So the poem ends with a kind of prayer, directed not at God the Father or the Son, but at some unspecified female figure, "blessed sister, holy mother, spirit of the fountain, spirit of the garden." *The Hollow Men* had ended with a counterpoint between the statements "For thine is the Kingdom" and "Life is very long."

> *For thine is the Kingdom*
> *For Thine is*
> *Life is*
> *For Thine is the*
>
> *This is the way the world ends*
> *This is the way the world ends*
> *This is the way the world ends*
> *Not with a bang but a whimper.*

121

In *Ash Wednesday* the poet is finally able to bring himself to finish the sentence:

> *Sister, mother*
> *And spirit of the river, spirit of the sea,*
> *Suffer me not to be separated*
>
> *And let my cry come unto thee.*

At the age of sixteen, I felt myself to be in Eliot's situation; I was suffering from the same emotional frustration and exhaustion, and felt the same craving for relief, for rain on the parched ground. *The Waste Land*, *The Hollow Men*, and most of all, *Ash Wednesday*, brought this sense of relief, and consequently seemed to me among the most profoundly moving poetry ever written.

I should immediately qualify this by saying that I never thought of Eliot as a "great poet," like Milton or Wordsworth or Shelley; it was simply that he spoke to me more directly and powerfully than any other poet.

It followed, of course, that I was also deeply influenced by his intellectual views. In his essay on Baudelaire I found a quotation from T. E. Hulme, the poet and essayist who had been killed in the First World War:

"In the light of these absolute values, man himself is judged to be essentially imperfect and limited. He is endowed with Original Sin. While he can occasionally accomplish acts which partake of perfection, he can never himself be perfect. Certain secondary results in regard to ordinary human action in society follow from this. A man is essentially bad, he can only accomplish anything of value by discipline—ethical and political. Order is thus not merely negative, but creative and liberating. Institutions are necessary."

Now although this seemed totally opposed to Shaw's belief that men can become godlike, I saw no real contradiction. Nothing seemed more clear to me than the certainty that most men are weak and stupid—in Nietzsche's phrase, which haunted me throughout my teens, "human all-too human. " So the shallow optimism of some of Wells' utopian novels—such as *Men Like Gods*—is based on a false view of human nature. Man is capable of some sort of greatness—but only, as Hulme says, through discipline. Shaw also recognized this when he wrote, "And the greatest of these is self-control." The notion of self-discipline became my major obsession.

At this time I thought a great deal of entering a monastery, and if England had still possessed a living monastic tradition—as Japan still does—I have no doubt that I would have become a monk. As it was, I read Thomas Merton's *Seven Storey Mountain*, the autobiography of a young man whose deep sense of dissatisfaction with modern life finally led him to become a Trappist monk, with a kind of envy. I also read books like Douglas Hyde's *I Believed*, the story of an atheistic Communist who finally joined the Catholic Church, with deep sympathy. Like Eliot, I looked back on the Middle Ages with nostalgia, and when, after my stint in the RAF, I hitchhiked to Strasbourg, I spent a great deal of time in the cathedral, feeling as if I had been transported by a time machine back into the Ages of Faith.

But I am losing the thread of my story. I was saved from the wool factory when I went back to my old school one day to borrow some books on mathematics, and was told by the headmaster that there was a job as a laboratory assistant available if I could gain the necessary credit in mathematics. I took the exam again and achieved the required mark. I ought to have been deliriously happy at escaping the wool factory—but now knew that I would never be a scientist. When I accepted the job, I felt like a confidence trickster, for I knew that I had no intention of taking the science degree that the position entailed. Besides, I now found science a bore, and as I attended night classes in analytical chemistry or applied mathematics, I found it incomprehensible that I had ever found either of them interesting.

After almost a year of this, exam results showed that I had lost interest in science, and the headmaster, a kindly and sympathetic man, gave me notice.

After that, the young lady at the Labor Exchange who had been deputed to advise me, suggested that I join the Civil Service. For the next year, between the age of seventeen and eighteen, I became a tax collector, sitting in an office and filing forms which I found totally uninteresting. At the urging of my parents, I took exams to become an established civil servant—and felt a grim despair when I passed.

I was rescued from the Civil Service by National Service. In those days, shortly after the end of the Second World War, every male of eighteen years of age had to spend eighteen months in the armed forces. At first I found the discipline enjoyable. Then I was assigned to an office as a filing clerk, and it became as boring as the Civil Service. It seemed as if some malign fate had determined that I should remain frustrated and unfulfilled.

Yet during this long period of misery and depression, which lasted for more than two years after I left school (and during which I once seriously contemplated suicide), I had made one immensely important discovery.

In my last year at school I had discovered an anthology called *The Bible of the World*, which contained chapters from all the world's major scriptures: Christianity, Judaism, Hinduism, Islam, Buddhism, Taoism, even Zen. For many years now I had been contemptuous of religion, associating it with church, Sunday school and morning assemblies. But *The Bible of the World* was a new challenge; I could see that world religions had far more variety than I had supposed, and I wanted to learn all about them, just as I had learned about astronomy and relativity and philosophy. I was particularly impressed by the *Tao Te Ching*, which seemed to me far more profound than any Christian scripture.

In Eliot's essays I came across a reference to the *Bhagavad Gita*. There was an abridged version of it in *The Bible of the World*, but in a rather uninspiring prose translation. Now, in a local bookshop, I came upon a new translation of it by Christopher Isherwood. This exercised upon me a more profound influence than any book I read in my teens.

The *Bhagavad Gita* is a section from the Hindu epic the *Mahabharata*. At the beginning, Prince Arjuna is forced to lead his soldiers against an army which contains many friends and relatives; he experiences revulsion, and refuses to fight. His spiritual adviser Krishna—who is, in fact, an avatar, or incarnation of God—tells him to put his doubts behind him. "There never was a time when you, nor I, nor any of these warriors, did not exist, nor is there a time when we shall cease to exist. That which exists can never be destroyed; that which does not exist can never come into existence."

He goes on to explain that men find themselves surrounded by illusion, blind to the fact that the individual soul—atman—is the same in essence as God, Brahman. So all is well. Death and misery are illusions. Our job is not to be taken in by the delusions, but to remain detached and controlled.

I felt as if I had been awakened by a thunderclap. Now, suddenly, I could see what was wrong with me. Because I felt so profoundly bored and dissatisfied with my job as a factory worker, then a lab assistant, I had plunged into a state of passivity, allowing my will to become slack. And when the will is slack, we feel trapped in the present. We feel suffocated, as if we have been deprived of air. But we have not really been deprived of air. The real problem is that we are breathing so shallowly that we suffer oxygen starvation. Our energies become stagnant; we long for release, for the "flow experience." This is what Eliot is writing about in *The Waste Land*, with his bored socialites who ask, "What shall we do tomorrow? What shall we ever do?"

It occurred to me that I could escape this suffocation by taking a deep breath, so to speak—by deliberately setting out to use my will. I began to sit cross-legged in my bedroom, meditating for half an hour at a time, as prescribed by the *Gita*. I began to get up at dawn and went for a long run before I went off to work. When I was a lab assistant, I often walked the five miles or so to school. And the sense of suffocation vanished, just as I had known it would.

The problem, I could see, was that human beings suffer from "tunnel vision." We allow ourselves to become "stuck in the present," as if there is no reality beyond it. This was also Faust's problem—a sense of stifling to death.

Dostoevsky's Svidrigailov, in *Crime and Punishment*, expresses this same sense of suffocation when he tells Raskolnikov that he dreamed of eternity, and that it was like a tiny room full of cobwebs. He is expressing one of the most basic fears of intelligent human beings: that life is limited and futile and meaningless. I called this "the Svidrigailov effect."

The Easter bells make Faust aware that this is untrue; that there is another reality "out there," far greater than the limited reality inside our own heads.

It has often seemed to me that the truth of this matter is symbolized in the python's tail. The python has enormous powers of constriction, and can suffocate a large animal. But before it can use its powers of constriction, its tail must be wrapped securely around some stable and solid object like a tree. Unless it is "anchored," the python is unable to use its enormous strength.

When we are bored, we are like a python who cannot find a tree to wrap its tail round. All our strength is wasted. But the moment we experience a clear sense of some other reality—like Faust hearing the Easter bells—our tails wrap around it, and we can exert our strength.

Now clearly, it is extremely important to know that there is "another reality" beyond the present. In the late nineteenth century, the Russians seemed to enjoy writing about characters who feel that the present is the only reality, and that they have been doomed to boredom and impotence. Dostoevsky's Stavrogin, in *The Possessed*, commits suicide because he can find nothing to do with his enormous willpower. Chekhov's plays and stories are full of such characters; so are the stories of Leonid Andreyev and Mikhail Artsybashev (of whom I shall speak later). More recently, Sartre and Samuel Beckett have dealt with the same dilemma.

In *The Outsider*, the problem is epitomized by T. E. Lawrence and Ernest Hemingway. Both tried to escape "the suffocation" by subjecting themselves to danger. Hemingway spent his life looking for trees to wrap his tail round. Yet his alcoholism and suicide reveal that he failed to grasp the general solution—that the sense of claustrophobia, and the panic it brings, is a delusion. There is always a world of reality "out there."

The history of this sense of life failure (what I have called the "Ecclesiastes effect"—"vanity of vanities, all is vanity") can be seen clearly in the past two and a half centuries. The Romantics found that they greatly preferred the world of imagination to "everyday reality"—but when we let go of everyday reality, we also let go of the tree that enables us to exert pressure on reality. So the Romantics suffered from boredom and the "Svidrigailov effect." Byron was the first major figure to actually allow it to undermine him to the point of destruction. Hemingway's instinct led him to the right solution: to find some "other reality" to wrap his tail round—in fact, he stumbled on it accidentally when he became an ambulance orderly in the First World War. But Hemingway lacked the intellectual insight to understand why action brought a sense of freedom, and his failure—as we shall see—eventually cost him his life.

Shaw had always been aware of the "Hemingway solution;" in *Heartbreak House*, Shotover tells Ellie, "You are looking for a rich husband. At your age I looked for hardship, danger, horror and death, that I might feel the life in me more intensely."

Eliot's religious conversion—after *Ash Wednesday* he became a member of the Church of England—reveals the operation of this same instinct to find a tree. He recognized that in the Middle Ages, the Church provided the basic symbol of another reality. But all his early work reveals that he had always been aware of the need for "another reality," and all his most powerful effects depend upon it:

The host with someone indistinct
Converses at the door apart,
The nightingales are singing near
The Convent of the Sacred Heart,

And sang within the bloody wood
When Agamemnon cried aloud,
And let their liquid siftings fall
To stain the stiff dishonored shroud.

Yet Eliot, like Hemingway, lacked the intellectual power to grasp the general solution to the problem, and to recognize that joining the Church of England was no more satisfactory than traveling around the world looking for "hardship, danger, horror and death."

It was on a snowy day in Washington, D.C., in 1966, that I suddenly grasped the general solution. I was thinking of T. E. Lawrence, and how the war in the desert brought him freedom from "the thought-riddled nature," and Hemingway's search for situations that would bring a sense of danger. The reason is obvious. When we are in some situation of danger or inconvenience, we can see quite clearly that what we want most of all is for it to go away. And the relief that follows when the problem disappears brings a sense of freedom, and makes us aware of the rich potentialities of the present moment.

While the danger is still present, we feel that if only it would go away, it would be easy to maintain that sense of relief and gratitude indefinitely. In fact, the sense of relief seldom lasts more than a few hours—or days at the most. Then we slip back into the habit of taking the present for granted.

Yet whenever we experience danger or inconvenience, we feel once again that it ought to be perfectly easy to maintain a sense of gratitude.

Why this inconsistency?

The answer is obvious. We habitually overestimate the power of memory and imagination. Our problem is that relief fails to penetrate deep enough into the unconscious mind. Auden remarked, "Even war cannot frighten us enough."

And this is largely our own fault. I am, for example, writing this on a rather out-of-date word processor. If I believe that I have accidentally erased a file, my first reaction is shock and alarm. For a few moments I contemplate the sheer inconvenience of having to retype the work of hours or days, and my heart sinks. In those few moments I feel that I would be willing to face a great deal of inconvenience to escape this problem.

Then I type the name of the file, press "confirm," and to my relief it appears on the screen. I heave a sigh and thank God. But then I begin working again, and within minutes, the crisis is forgotten.

Yet I can see, in the few moments when I am tense with anxiety, that I can choose my response to learning that I have not erased the file after all. I can promise myself that I will remain grateful for the rest of the day.

It is pointless to complain about the feebleness of the imagination. We ourselves are to blame. We feel instinctively that the imagination could be amplified by a great enough effort.

And as I thought about that, I saw that the imagination is often amplified spontaneously. The most obvious example is the experience of Proust that led him to write *À la recherche du temps perdu*, and which is described at the beginning of *Swann's way*: how, returning home one evening, weary and slightly depressed, Marcel tasted a little cake called a madeleine, dipped in herb tea, and suddenly felt "an exquisite pleasure" invading his senses. "I had ceased to feel mediocre, accidental, mortal." After dipping and tasting the cake again, he realizes what has caused the sensation of delight. When he was a child, his Aunt Leonie used to offer him a piece of her madeleine dipped in herb tea. And the taste has brought his childhood flooding back to him.

The madeleine has made him aware of the reality of his childhood, like a time machine carrying him into his own past. And it is this realization—that the past can be revived and relived—that leads him to begin writing his vast autobiographical novel.

The historian Arnold Toynbee describes how a parallel experience led him to begin the *Study of History*: how he had spent the morning climbing Mount Taygetus, in Greece, and sat in the ruined citadel of Mistra, meditatively chewing a bar of chocolate. Mistra had been a ruin for a century, since the Turks invaded the town in the Greek War of Independence. Quite suddenly, this ceased to be mere history; it was as if he could actually see the Turks pouring through a gap in the wall and sacking the town. The past had become as real as the present.

Clearly, what Proust and Toynbee had experienced was precisely this "greatly intensified form of imagination" that I had been thinking about. Realizing that I would need to find a name for it—or risk forgetting all about it—I labeled it "Faculty X."

Faculty X is the power to suddenly grasp the reality of other times and places. And it is the key to many other modern writers besides Proust. Eliot's work depends on contrasting the boredom of the present moment with the sense of "other realities." Joyce's re-creation of Dublin while he was living in Trieste was an attempt to summon Faculty X. The same is true of Hemingway's evocations of the past in a book like *A Moveable Feast*.

It is as if modern man has become aware of the possibility of another type of consciousness: not simply an escape into the dreamworlds of the Romantics, but an odd ability to live in two realities at once: the present, and "other" times and places.

Our remote descendants may see the dawning of this new faculty as the most important event of the twentieth century, and the beginning of a new phase of human evolution.

14

JOYCE

I had heard of James Joyce through Matthiessen's *Achievement of T.S.Eliot*, which refers to Joyce's attempt to give "a shape and a significance to the immense panorama of futility and anarchy that is modern life" through the "mythical method" of *Ulysses*, which Matthiessen compares to *The Waste Land*. This led me to believe that Joyce was a writer who shared Eliot's outlook on the modern world. So, when I came upon a book on James Joyce, by Louis Golding, in our local library, I took it home and read it eagerly.

My initial reaction was disappointment. As far as I could see, Joyce had nothing whatever in common with Eliot. His work seemed to be basically autobiographical, and I felt that writers who wrote disguised autobiography lacked the self-discipline to write about something more significant.

This impression was confirmed when I came upon Eliot's little anthology, *Introducing James Joyce*. The opening story from Dubliners—"The Sisters"—bored me, and the extracts from *A Portrait of the Artist as a Young Man* failed to change my opinion about Joyce. I read the extract from *Ulysses* with some interest, having learned from Golding that the book had been banned; I was disappointed that it contained no obscenities. And I found the extracts from *Finnegan's Wake* incomprehensible, and on the whole pointless.

But, since Eliot regarded him as a major writer, I decided that the fault lay in myself. When I discovered from the catalog that the library possessed a copy of *Ulysses*, I placed my name on a waiting list. And again I was bored and disappointed. Where was the point in describing a single day in Dublin hour by hour? What I wanted from literature was to be introduced to other people's lives—the kind of lives I wanted to live—not told in boring detail, about a man going to the butcher's to get himself a kidney for breakfast.

I came upon the first piece of "obscenity" during Mr. Bloom's walk back from the butcher's, where a cloud covering the sun causes him to think of the Dead Sea. "Now it could bear no more. Dead: an old woman's: the grey sunken cunt of the world." The image made me wrinkle my nose with disgust.

After I had returned the library copy—which was wanted by another reader—I asked casually in a local bookshop whether it was still in print, and was startled when, a few weeks later, the bookseller handed me a copy. It was printed on a kind of thick, grey paper—wartime economy paper—that made it about six inches thick, and the binding was poor. It cost me a pang to part with twenty-one shillings—virtually my week's wages as a lab assistant—but having a copy of my own at least made me determined to read it from beginning to end.

I was bored and depressed with my job at school—the physics master disliked me and took every opportunity to show it—and *Ulysses* made things worse. But Shaw acted an as antidote. And, gradually, I began to recognize that *Ulysses* was an extraordinary feat of disciplined writing. And Joyce certainly taught me a great deal about writing and about the need to find the exact word.

I found *A Portrait of the Artist as a Young Man* easier to read and far more interesting. Joyce's struggles and problems seemed to have been very like my own—or, for that matter, Bernard Shaw's. I was familiar with boredom and frustration, and with those curious bursts of relief and pure happiness that would leave me suddenly confident and sure of my destiny. For that, obviously, was Joyce's problem—the fear that his life might be wasted. I read again and again the passage at the end of Chapter 4, in which Stephen escapes from his school friends and walks to the seashore. "His soul had arisen from the grave of his boyhood, spurning her graveclothes. Yes! Yes! Yes! He would create proudly out of the freedom and power of his soul . . . ."

He wades into the sea and sees a girl standing before him, her skirt tucked into the waistband of her knickers. "She seemed like one whom

magic had changed into the likeness of a strange and beautiful seabird."
He experiences a tremendous surge of happiness and affirmation. "He
turned away from her suddenly and set off across the strand. His cheeks
were aflame, his body was aglow, his limbs were trembling. On and
on and on and on he strode, far out over the sands, singing wildly to
the sea, crying to greet the advent of the life that had cried to him. Her
image had passed into his soul forever and no word had broken the
holy silence of his ecstasy."

Such a passage made it obvious that Joyce was as much a romantic
as I was myself and that writing *Ulysses*, with its precision of language
and exactitude of description, had been a deliberate act of self-discipline.

There was a passage in *Ulysses* that I always read with satisfaction:
the scene in the teashop, where Buck Mulligan and Haynes, the English
visitor, discuss Stephen. Mulligan comments "They drove his wits
astray by visions of hell"—he is referring to Stephen's fear of being
damned after becoming a habitué of brothels—"He will never capture
the Attic note. The note of Swinburne, of all poets, the white death and
the ruddy birth. That is his tragedy. He can never be a poet."

Haynes enquires: "Does he write anything for your movement?"
(meaning the Irish literary movement, whose stars were W.B. Yeats,
J.M. Synge and AE—George Russell). And Mulligan replies: "Ten
years. He is going to write something in ten years."

Haynes comments: "Seems a long way off. Still I wouldn't wonder
if he did after all."

What Joyce wrote in ten years was, of course, *Ulysses*, the most
significant novel to appear after the First World War. When *Ulysses*
received such tremendous acclaim, Joyce must have reread the passage
with quiet satisfaction. Buck Mulligan, after all, was his one-time
"friend" Oliver Gogarty, the friend of W.B.Yeats and others of the
Celtic Twilight movement, upon which Joyce had failed to make an
impact. Now *Ulysses* had made an impact greater than Yeats, Synge,
Russell and the rest put together.

This is why I became a Joyce enthusiast—because Joyce seemed
to me one of the few modern writers who set out to turn himself into
a major writer by sheer self-discipline. *Ulysses* was a triumph of the
will.

In the Central Library I also found *Finnegan's Wake*, but soon gave
it up. But when, about two years later, in the summer of 1949, I had

become an established civil servant and had been posted to the small town of Rugby (scene of *Tom Brown's Schooldays*), I found Campbell and Robinson's *Skeleton Key to Finnegan's Wake* in the library, and read it with concentrated enthusiasm. It was wonderful to finally learn what *Finnegan's Wake* was all about. A new edition of the *Wake* was published at about this time, and I lost no time in buying a copy. (I also bought Thomas Mann's *Doktor Faustus*, which was published at the same time.) I still have it, and the title page bears the date "August 26, 1959." And a few weeks later, when I went into the RAF, I took with me *Finnegan's Wake* and *Doktor Faustus*.

I have never ceased to be grateful to Joyce; *Ulysses* taught me more about writing than I learned from any other writer. But I have to admit that my opinion of Joyce is no longer as high as it was.

My initial doubts about his autobiographical obsession (which can be found even in *Finnegan's Wake*) were confirmed when I read Wyndham Lewis's *Time and Western Man*. It is clear that Lewis did not particularly like Joyce as a person and that he was probably envious of his success. But his comments about Joyce and his alter ego, Stephen Dedalus, go straight to the point. He refers to Stephen as "the irritating hero" and points out that he does everything "wearily" or "quietly"—Joyce is quite determined to portray him as superior to the shallow ignoramuses around him. He is, says Lewis, an infuriating prig, pompous, bad tempered, and conceited. And once this has been pointed out, it is impossible to read *Ulysses* without seeing it, in certain respects, as an act of personal revenge. Joyce felt that his genius had not been appreciated by his contemporaries, and he never ceased to bear a grudge. When he met Yeats—for the only time—all his wounded pride came out in the rude remark: "We have met too late—you are too old to be influenced by me." And when he came to write *Ulysses*, he set out to repay old debts.

All this reveals a certain lack of self-awareness. Joyce later tried to destroy the earliest version of the *Portrait of the Artist*, but a few hundred pages survived, and were posthumously published as *Stephen Hero*. And *Stephen Hero* is so badly and amateurishly written that any member of the Irish literary movement who saw it must have felt that Joyce was entirely without talent. It has no shape, no structure, and is written in a prose so devoid of tension that it sounds like a schoolboy essay on "What I did during the holiday." Nothing is more obvious than that Joyce's self-esteem far exceeded his talent.

His first book, *Dubliners*, is, of course, an entirely different matter. The physical observation is impressively exact, and the ear for dialogue is superb. Yet, even here, it is impossible not to feel that, as a writer, he had very little to "say." He has apparently determined to distinguish himself from the rest of the Celtic Twilight movement by shunning Romanticism and writing realistic sketches of Dublin life. They are bleak, gloomy little tales that usually center around weakness, meanness, and triviality. In "The Boarding House," for example, a landlady learns that her daughter Polly has given herself to one of the lodgers, a respectable clerk who works in a firm of wine merchants, and who cannot afford a scandal. So she tells him that she wants a talk with him. All his instincts are against marriage, and he finds Polly rather vulgar. But he goes down to her sitting room like a lamb to the slaughter—suspecting that all this has been deliberately arranged (as indeed it has—the daughter has virtually seduced him). And in due course, Polly is also called downstairs and told that the lodger wants to speak to her . . . .

After *Dubliners*, Joyce began to write *Portrait of the Artist*, a far more highly disciplined version of *Stephen Hero*. And in the end, Stephen decides to go abroad and "forge in the smithy of my soul the uncreated conscience of my race." What he did, in fact, was to write *Dubliners*, stories which have the quality of an Irish Chekhov. But Joyce lacked Chekhov's humanity—and his prodigious talent. His only subject was himself and his own past. He mined it carefully in *Dubliners* and *A Portrait of the Artist*. By that point, he had virtually run out of anything further to say. His solution was, in effect, to rewrite *Dubliners* on a larger scale.

Was *Ulysses*, as E.M. Forster once said, "a determined attempt to cover the universe in mud?" Joyce's admirers have made fun of the phrase, implying that Forster was an old fashioned Victorian who could not recognize genius when he saw it. But it is impossible not to realize that Joyce must have been fully aware of the shock effect of sentences like "the grey sunken cunt of the world," and of the controversy they were bound to cause. He was an admirer of Ibsen, who had achieved widespread fame through the scandal surrounding *A Doll's House* and *Ghosts*. And Bernard Shaw, another Ibsen admirer, had achieved celebrity by writing about prostitution in *Mrs. Warren's Profession*. It sounds as if Joyce muttered through his teeth: "I'll give them something to complain about," and wrote the violent phantasmagoria of the "Nighttown" scene, culminating in the stream of foul language from Private Carr as he knocks Stephen unconscious. And as he wrote Mrs. Bloom's monologue, with her frank reminiscences of her lovers, and Boylan's "big red brute of a thing" that made her feel full up, one suspects that he murmured: "This will either land me in jail or make me famous."

The scandal made him famous, and the obvious seriousness of *Ulysses* gave his admirers firm grounds for defending him from a charge of writing pornography. Yet, he had once again run out of subject matter. Where could he go from there? *Ulysses* is apparently plotless, but the real story is about how Stephen comes to terms with his guilt about refusing to pray by his mother's deathbed and achieves a kind of reconciliation. When Joyce left Dublin, he went abroad to write *Dubliners*. Obviously, there was no more plot to be got out of *Stephen Hero*.

I suspect that, rereading *Ulysses*, Joyce saw the solution. Although it begins realistically enough, the photographic realism comes to an end well before halfway through the book, with the pub scene in which the Citizen accuses Bloom of blaspheming and hurls a biscuit tin after him. Here the humor lies in the contrast between the realistic dialogue, and the long parodistic passages in mock-heroic style that sometimes go on for three or four pages. The same is true of the scene in the maternity hospital, where Joyce sets out to parody English literary styles from the *Anglo-Saxon Chronicle* to modern journalism. Finally, in the "question and answer" chapter, a single question can lead to long paragraphs of exposition that sound as if they might have been taken from an encyclopedia. And towards the end of the chapter, the question about Bloom's traveling companions is answered in a long paragraph that begins: "Sinbad the Sailor and Tinbad the Tailor and Jinbad the Jailer and Whinbad the Whaler," in which Joyce has simply gone through the alphabet and taken every word that rhymes with "sailor." Clearly, this does not mean anything—it is merely playing with words.

So why not, Joyce probably reasoned, write a whole book that simply plays with words? After all, *Ulysses* abandoned the usual novelistic form of plot and development and merely chronicled a day in the life of Dublin—rather like a documentary film. Why not chronicle a night in the life of the same city, a kind of vast "dream play" or dream novel?

On closer examination, the notion is seen to be illogical. The purpose of words is to describe facts, and, in describing facts, to communicate them. Even poetry describes facts; it conjures up a quite definite situation—as in a haiku.

Music, of course, is a different matter. For some reason no one has been able to fathom, human emotions respond to sounds. In the case of rain pattering on windows, or wind moaning in a chimney, those reasons are obviously associative. But it is hard to explain exactly why we respond to the sound of musical instruments playing in harmony.

Now in a great deal of *Ulysses*, Joyce writes "associatively." For example, in the pub scene, Little Alf remarks that he has just seen Paddy Dignam, and Joe tells him that Dignam was buried this morning. This realistic conversation, so accurate that it sounds as if it had been tape-recorded, is followed by a parody of "spiritualism" as practiced by the Dublin Theosophical Society, with a spirit asking the sitters to send a pair of boots to be soled, since they had "greatly perturbed his peace of mind in the other region."

The purpose of these slabs of high-flown parody, juxtaposed with passages of accurately reported pub conversation, seems to be to tell us something about Joyce's sense of reality—in this case he is simply satirizing spiritualism. The reader has no difficulty making the connection, and recognizing instinctively what Joyce is doing, just as he recognizes what Beethoven is doing in the parody of a village band in the Pastoral Symphony. So it might be said that, in *Ulysses*, Joyce often uses a musical technique.

Now, poetry has been defined as "verbal music." But this is only in a manner of speaking. A poet chooses words for their sound as well as their sense, but not (usually) for their sound alone. So the analogy between words and music is extremely dubious and misleading.

In *Finnegan's Wake*, Joyce has chosen to write as if words were music. And this frequently seems to work impressively. For example, the last section of the book is supposed to be a monologue of the river Liffey (personalized by Joyce as Anna Livia Plurabelle), as she flows to the sea in the dawn. It begins:

"Soft morning, city! I am leafy speafing. Lpf! Folty and folty all the nights have falled on to long my hair. Not a sound, falling. Lispn! No wind no word. Only a leaf, just a leaf, and then leaves . . . ."

Read aloud, this makes some beautiful noises, and it evokes silence, the fall of leaves into the stream, and the quiet flow of the river. But, as the passage continues, the mood is soon broken, for words cannot be used for their sound alone for more than a sentence or two.

Moreover, an earlier version of *Finnegan's Wake* shows that Joyce wrote far more simply, and that he later complexified the text with all kinds of puns and double meanings. This is not authentic literature—it is a word game like Scrabble. (In the British Museum there are six or seven versions, all on different colored paper, which become steadily more abstruse and laborious.)

The truth seems to be simply that Joyce started from a false premise and went on working with manic persistence, like the painter in Balzac's *Chef D'Oevre Inconnu*, who goes on elaborating a canvas until it is an incomprehensible tangle of brushstrokes.

In fact, there are obvious signs of this "manic" tendency in Joyce. In the schoolroom chapter of *Ulysses*, Stephen asks the pupil a "riddle."

> *The cock crew*
> *The sky was blue:*
> *The bells in heaven*
> *Were striking eleven.*
> *Tis time for this poor soul*
> *To go to heaven.*

This is clearly not a riddle, since it does not have the form of a question. And when the baffled pupils ask him the answer, Stephen replies "The fox burying his grandmother under a hollybush."

What does he think he is accomplishing? What seems clear is that he is so bored with his job as a schoolmaster that his meaningless "riddle" is a kind of act of rebellion, a gesture of defiance, in some way directed against his pupils. It is supposed to show Stephen as cryptic and incomprehensible. In fact, it is as much a meaningless act of rebellion as James Dean urinating on the film set.

The chapter in the newspaper office again reveals Joyce's "manic" side. One of the men present tells the story of the Phoenix Park murders, in which Irish patriots murdered British diplomats. Then, another quotes an impressive speech on the law of evidence by a Dublin barrister. Another goes on to quote "the finest display of oratory" he ever heard, from a speech made by the politician John F. Taylor, in which the British are likened to the Egyptians who kept the Israelites in bondage.

After this, Stephen remarks: "I have a vision too." Then he goes on to tell a story of two old ladies who make an excursion to Nelson's

Pillar in O'Connell Street, buy some plums, then go to the top of Nelson's Pillar and eat them, spitting the plumstones out between the railings. Like Stephen's riddle, the story is totally pointless.

Of course, Joyce did not see it as pointless. He felt that he was asserting his own view of reality, full of minute realistic detail, in contrast to the romantic rhetoric of the older generation. The problem is that, in this particular context, it does nothing of the sort—the other persons present probably felt he was simply wasting their time. Professor McHugh recognizes that Stephen's problem is boredom and frustration, and comments: "You remind me of Antisthenes, a disciple of Georgias, the sophist. It is said that none could tell whether he were bitterer against others or himself."

In the library scene, we have Joyce presenting himself as he wanted to see himself—arguing brilliantly and knowledgeably about Hamlet. But here Joyce's ear for dialogue fails him, and Stephen talks in sentences so long and complex that no one could possibly take them seriously as a spontaneous contribution to a discussion. Wyndham Lewis is obviously right: Joyce is simply out to impress. Thin-skinned, irritable, almost paranoid, he is determined to present himself as everything he is not: brilliant, witty, forceful. (Wyndham Lewis saw his weaknesses so well because he himself was that kind of person.) He wants us to see Stephen as an unrecognized man of genius among a crowd of intellectual and artistic mediocrities.

Ulysses is a deliberate reaction against the Irish literary movement, a rejection of romanticism and mysticism. Yet looking back on it from over the decades, we can see that it failed in its purpose: to win the argument against Yeats and Synge and Russell and the rest. For Joyce was also reacting against their interest in ideas and trying to insist that ideas were unimportant compared to reality. In this respect, he was replaying Kierkegaard's argument against Hegel: that "philosophy" is bound to be a travesty, since it attempts to reduce reality—which is too real to reduced. Yet, this misses the point. Ideas are the way in which human beings digest reality, and the fact that ideas can be shallow and half-baked is no argument against ideas in general. Whitehead points out that, if the human race had turned its back on ideas, we would still be living in caves.

So, on the whole, posterity is inclined to agree that Yeats and Shaw won that particular argument and that Joyce, by implication, lost it. We can see that Joyce's determination to be a writer of "lived experience" (i.e., a true existentialist) landed him in the cul-de-sac of *Finnegan's Wake*. In fact, *Ulysses* itself is a cul-de-sac; he was unable to develop beyond it, and he has had no followers.

We have only to imagine a "Joycian" novel about modern London or New York—a minute description of a day in the lives of a number of "ordinary" characters—to see that it would not work. No one would want to follow average Londoners or New Yorkers through an average day; it would bore us. In fact, it is surely obvious that *Ulysses* would be a long-forgotten curiosity of literature but for its "obscenity" and the controversy it aroused. If some British or American publisher had been the first to publish *Ulysses*, excising every passage that might have caused offense to middle class readers, it would probably have sunk without a trace.

As it is, it remains the kind of book that must be read while one is young and impressionable, and willing to take Stephen Joyce-Dedalus at his own valuation as a rebel who was determined to fly close to the sun. Once we begin to see him from the Wyndham Lewis point of view—as a rather tiresome young man clamoring for attention—it is difficult to read the book without impatience.

Even at the beginning, it is clear that Stephen is thin-skinned and paranoid. When Buck Mulligan asks him what he has against him, Stephen reminds him of how, when Mulligan's mother asked the name of his visitor, Mulligan answered: "Oh, it's only Dedalus, whose mother is beastly dead." Mulligan assumes that Stephen is objecting to the disrespectful reference to his mother's death, but Stephen explains: "I was not thinking of the offence to my mother (but) of the offence to me." And here, at the beginning of the book, Joyce has signaled one of his basic motivations: to be admired and respected. He is like a man who feels he has been insulted and who is determined to tell you about it at length, whether you like it or not.

After that, all Joyce's attempts to present Stephen in a good light only make the reader more skeptical. Joyce is even willing to show us Stephen's determination to impress other people. In the library scene, in the course of the argument about Hamlet, Stephen repeats what Professor McHugh has said to him earlier: "Antisthenes, pupil of Georgias, took the palm of beauty from Kyrios Menelaus's brooddam, Argive Helen, the wooden mare of Troy in whom a score of heroes slept, and handed it to poor Penelope." And again, the reader's reaction to that improbable clause about "Kyrios Menelaus's brooddam, Argive

Helen, the wooden mare in whom a score of heroes slept," is that he is trying just a little too hard to show us how clever he is—nobody really talks like that.

I am sad that, as I reread it, *Ulysses* no longer seems to me the masterpiece I thought it in my teens. Yet, I only have to read a few pages to realize how much I owe to Joyce. I turn the pages casually and read the description of a dog on the beach: "The dog ambled about a bank of dwindling sand, trotting, sniffing on all sides . . . Suddenly he made off like a bounding hare, ears flung back, chasing the shadow of a lowskimming gull. The man's shrieked whistle struck his limp ears. He turned, bounded back, came nearer, trotted on twinkling shanks . . . At the lacefringe of the tide, he halted with stiff forehoofs, seawardpointed ears. His snout lifted, barked at the wavenoise, herds of seahorse. They serpented towards his feet, curling, unfurling many crests, every ninth, breaking, plashing, from farther out, waves and waves."

It reminds me that Joyce taught himself to write by close observation, and that by the time I was eighteen, he had taught me the same important lesson.

15

ESCAPE FROM PERSONALITY—THE PUZZLE OF ERNEST HEMINGWAY

In Matthiessen's *Achievement of T. S. Eliot* I came upon Eliot's comment, "Mr. Hemingway is a writer for whom I have considerable respect; he seems to me to tell the truth about his own feelings at the moment when they exist." This startled me. I knew Hemingway's name because I had seen it in newspaper advertisements for films of *For Whom the Bell Tolls* and *The Killers*, and I had naturally assumed that he was a "popular" writer, like James Hadley Chase, who wrote *No Orchids for Miss Blandish*. I was surprised—and a little shocked—to see him praised by my latest literary hero.

In 1948, a new paperback firm called Pan republished Hemingway's *Fiesta* (*The Sun Also Rises*), and I bought it out of curiosity. The casual opening sentence, "Robert Cohn was once middleweight boxing champion of Princeton," led me to suspect that he was, after all, merely another "popular" writer. But his description of the Paris of the 1920s and the American expatriate crowd held me, and I read on. I could soon see why Eliot respected him; the tone was flat, unemotional, not unlike *The Waste Land*:

"After we finished the lunch we walked up to the Cafe de la Paris and had coffee. I could feel Cohn wanted to bring Brett up again, but I held him off it. We talked about one thing and another, and I left him to come over to the office."

When I realized that the subject of the book was the emotional frustration of a man who has been rendered sexually impotent by a war wound in the genitals, I was even more impressed. Eliot had written in his essay on Hamlet about the "objective correlative"—the need to find a plot and characters that will express the emotion the writer wants to express. Hamlet, said Eliot, was a baffling play because Shakespeare had not succeeded in finding the right "objective correlative" for what he wanted to express—that is, Hamlet's self-division about killing his stepfather.

It seemed to me that this was Hemingway's problem in *The Sun Also Rises*, and that his solution was ingenious. The surface of the book was about the surface of the life he lived in Paris, and about pointless conversations and drunken parties and superficial people, but since the reader knew that the hero, Jake Barnes, was in love with Lady Brett Ashley, and that she was in love with him, and that because they were unable to sleep together, she had affairs with other men, the whole book took on a deeper resonance. The overall technique was like *The Waste Land*: the contrast of meaning with meaninglessness.

But in the later bullfighting scenes in Pamplona, it becomes suddenly apparent that Hemingway does possess a set of basic values, and that these values are the mental states man achieves when he is in mortal danger, the states when, as Yeats says, "he completes his partial mind."

"Nobody but a bullfighter lives his life all the way up." Hemingway clearly had no patience with T. E. Lawrence's "thought-riddled nature," or the gloom of the Romantics, or the cerebral miseries of the heroes of Aldous Huxley. Like Van Gogh, he had learned that salvation can lie in the world of external objects—a vista of apple orchards, a starry night, even a pair of old boots. In his own curious, unintellectual way, Hemingway was a kind of mystic.

Not long after *The Sun Also Rises*, I found in the library a recently-published book called *The Essential Hemingway*. It contained *The Sun Also Rises*, and most of the short stories (which I liked less), and extracts from *A Farewell to Arms* and *For Whom the Bell Tolls*. I was unimpressed by the chapters from *A Farewell to Arms*. It struck me as good "war writing," but I was not particularly interested in war writing.

But the *El Sordo on the Hilltop* chapter from *For Whom the Bell Tolls* left me breathless. El Sordo ("the deaf one") has been driven to take refuge on the hilltop by fascist soldiers, who have surrounded his party. El Sordo knows that planes are coming to bomb them, and wants to take some of the fascists with him. So he fires five shots into the ground, to make them believe they have all killed themselves. One of the fascists, Captain Mora, is convinced that they are all dead, and orders a soldier to go and see. The soldier refuses, even when threatened with a pistol. Captain Mora stands up and shouts, "Shoot me! Kill me!" to convince the others that everyone is dead. Finally, disgusted with the cowardice of his own men, he strides towards the hilltop. Sordo waits until he is close, then kills him with a burst of automatic fire.

Now he waits for the captain's second-in-command to break cover from behind a rock, determined to get him too. Then the planes appear overhead, and as he looks up at them, the officer makes his break, and Sordo does not even see him go.

He orders his men to lie on their backs and fire on the three planes. He tells a man called Ignacio to hold the legs of a tripod while he fires. Someone begins to repeat a Hail Mary.

"Then there were the hammering explosions past his ears and the gun barrel hot against his shoulders. It was hammering now again, and his ears were deafened by the muzzle blast. Ignacio was pulling down hard on the tripod and the barrel was burning his back. It was hammering now in the roar and he could not remember the act of contrition.

"All he could remember was at the hour of our death. Amen. At the hour of our death. Amen. At the hour of our death. Amen. The others were all firing. Now and at the hour of our death. Amen.

"Then through the hammering of the gun, there was the whistle of the air splitting apart and then in the red black roar the earth rolled under his knees and then waved up to hit him in the face and then dirt and bits of rock were falling all over and Ignacio was lying on him and the gun was lying on him. But he was not dead because the whistle came again and the earth rolled under him with the roar. Then it came again and the earth lurched under his belly and one side of the hilltop rose into the air and then fell slowly over them where they lay.

"The planes came back three times and bombed the hilltop but no one on the hilltop knew it. Then the planes machine-gunned the hilltop and went away."

I found it stunning. I had never read a description with such an almost physical impact. This kind of writing had the power to blow away all the cobwebs of the mind and to confront a sense of reality. I still find it so powerful that, even copying it down on paper, I find myself overwhelmed with the same emotion I felt when I first read it. I would certainly not dare to try to read it aloud to someone else.

It was after I came out of the RAF that I read *A Farewell to Arms*, which was published in a cheap hardcover edition. Now, since I possessed my own copy, I summoned the patience to read it—otherwise, it would have been a waste of money.

It begins with one of Hemingway's typical "flat" descriptions: "In the late summer of that year we lived in a house in a village that looked across the river and plain to the mountains. In the bed of the river there were pebbles and boulders, dry and white in the sun, and the water was clear and swiftly moving and blue in the channels. Troops went by the house and down the road and the dust they raised powdered the leaves of the trees . . ."

It was in the third chapter, where the hero tries to make the regimental priest understand why he has not kept his promise to visit the priest's home in the Abruzzi, that I experienced that same glow of excitement that I had felt when reading the El Sordo chapter.

"I had wanted to go to the Abruzzi. I had gone to no place where the roads were frozen and hard as iron, where it was clear, cold and dry and the snow was dry and powdery and hare-tracks in the snow and the peasants took off their hats and called you Lord and there was good hunting. I had gone to no such place but to the smoke of cafes and nights when the room whirled and you needed to look at the wall to make it stop, nights in bed, drunk, when you knew that was all there was, and the strange excitement of waking and not knowing who it was with you, and the world all unreal in the dark and so exciting that you must resume again unknowing, and not caring in the night, sure that this was all and all and all and not caring . . ."

By this time I had also experienced getting drunk—in the RAF—and that feeling of the world rolling like a ship when you close your eyes, and the sheer truth of Hemingway's description filled me with astonished admiration. I was particularly struck by the phrase "nights in bed, drunk, when you knew that was all there was." This captures precisely the feeling of being drunk, and the odd sense that time has stopped. But of course, the feeling that "that was all there was" is a description of everyday human consciousness. In moments of happiness and intensity, we suddenly know that this is not all there is. Van Gogh knew it as he painted *The Starry Night*. But when he killed himself, he felt that that was all there was.

I was also glad to read Hemingway now that I was a civilian again, and was working as a clerk in a large steel factory, and hating every minute of it. Every time I sank into boredom, I felt that "that was all there was." Then I picked up Hemingway, and suddenly I knew that that was not all there was.

In the next chapter, the hero—Frederick Henry—goes with his friend Rinaldi to meet Miss Barkley, a nurse in the local hospital. Hemingway does not even bother to describe Miss Barkley. He merely says, "The British hospital was a big villa built by Germans before the war. Miss Barkley was in the garden. Another nurse was with her. We saw their white uniforms through the trees . . ."

The second time he meets Miss Barkley, he tries to kiss her, and she slaps his face. The sting makes tears come to his eyes, and she apologizes. He says, "I was angry and yet I was certain, seeing it all ahead like the moves in a chess game."

A moment later she says, "I'd be glad to kiss you if you don't mind." He kisses her, and she resists his attempt to open her lips. Then she begins to cry on his shoulder.

"Oh, darling," she said, "You will be good to me, won't you?"

"What the hell," I thought.

The next time they meet, he has been away on post, and she has been worried. She asks, "And do you love me?" He tells her he loves her. "I thought she was probably a little crazy. It was all right if she was. I did not care what I was getting into. This was better than going every evening to the house for officers where the girls climbed all over you and put your cap on backward as a sign of affection between their trips upstairs with brother officers. I knew I did not love Catherine Barkley nor had any idea of loving her. This was a game, like bridge, in which you said things instead of playing cards."

A moment later he says, "I wish there was some place we could go," and tells the reader, "I was experiencing the usual masculine difficulty of making love very long standing up."

The accuracy of the observation made me laugh out loud. By that time, after my affair with Sylvia, I knew exactly what he meant. I had also started to spend my evenings at the flat of the works nurse, who was nine years my senior; inevitably, she reminded me of Catherine Barkley.

Henry is surprised when Catherine suddenly says, "This is a rotten game we play, isn't it?" And when he protests, "You don't have to tell me you love me. That's over for the evening."

A few days later, Henry is wounded. His description of the event seems to indicate that Hemingway had an "out-of-the-body experience" when he was also wounded:

". . . then there was a flash, as a blast-furnace door is swung open, and a roar that started white and went red and on and on in a rushing wind. I tried to breathe but my breath would not come and I felt myself rush bodily out of myself and out and out and out and all the time bodily in the wind. I went out swiftly, all of myself and I knew I was dead and that it had all been a mistake to think you just died. Then I floated, and instead of going on I felt myself slide back. I breathed and I was back."

He is put into an ambulance with another man above him.

"As the ambulance climbed along the road, it was slow in the traffic, sometimes it stopped, sometimes it backed on a turn, then finally it climbed quite fast. I felt something dripping. At first it dropped slowly and regularly, then it pattered into a stream. I shouted to the driver. He stopped the car and looked in through the hole behind his seat.

'What is it?'

'The man on the stretcher above me has a hemorrhage.'

'We're not far from the top. I wouldn't be able to get the stretcher out alone.' He started the car. The stream kept on. In the dark I could not see where it came from the canvas overhead. I tried to move sideways so that it did not fall on me. Where it had run down my shirt it felt warm and sticky. I was cold and my leg hurt so that it made me feel sick. After a while the stream from the stretcher above lessened and started to drip again and I heard the canvas above move as the man on the stretcher settled more comfortably.

'How is he?' the Englishman called back. 'We're almost up.'

'He's dead I think,' I said.

"The drops fell very slowly, as they fall from an icicle after the sun has gone. It was cold in the car in the night as the road climbed. At the post on the top they took the stretcher out and put another in and we went on."

This passage contains the very essence of Hemingway at his best. The stream of blood is described factually, almost casually, entirely without any of the trappings of drama. It is the event itself that makes the impact, not the telling. Hemingway does not even bother to tell you if the man is dead when he is taken out.

This also explains why Hemingway declined as a writer. To make its full impact, his work needed events that "spoke for themselves." It so happens that the events of *A Farewell to Arms* speak for themselves so powerfully that "literary style" would only destroy their impact. But to reproduce that effect, Hemingway had to find yet more events brutal enough to "speak for themselves." And after *A Farewell to Arms*, he never quite succeeded—except in occasional passages, like the El Sordo episode.

In other words, Hemingway's "objective correlative" had to involve some purely physical event, preferably violent, that would produce an impact on the reader.

The events of *A Farewell to Arms* make an ideal objective correlative because they involve a love story as well as a tale of war. This is something I had failed to realize when I read the "Caporetto" passage in *The Essential Hemingway* where Henry is arrested during the retreat from Caporetto, almost shot as a deserter, and escapes by diving in the river. It was interesting enough, but I could not imagine anyone wanting to read a whole book of this kind of thing.

In fact, the love story resumes immediately after Henry is wounded. He is sent to hospital in Milan, and Catherine Barkley is there.

"I heard someone coming down the hallway. I looked towards the door. It was Catherine Barkley.

"She came in the room and over to the bed.

"'Hello, darling,' she said. She looked fresh and young and very beautiful. I thought I had near seen anyone so beautiful.

"'Hello,' I said. When I saw her I was in love with her."

I thought that one of the most effective sentences in all Hemingway. Not, "When I saw her I realized I was in love with her," not even, "When I saw her I fell in love with her," but simply, "When I saw her I was in love with her." That is masterly observation, the observation of a man who studies things carefully before he describes them.

A moment later he grabs her. "You mustn't," she said. "You're not well enough." And afterwards she says, "That was just madness. We can't do that again." I found the scene stunning, and could see why the book had become a bestseller. No one had ever described love and sex with that kind of truthfulness.

The following day, he has to have an operation to remove shrapnel. He and Catherine spend the night together. The next morning she comes in and they have a conversation—she asks him to try not to talk under the anesthetic in case he mentions her. Finally she says, "There, darling. Now you're all clean inside and out," and the reader realizes that she has been giving him an enema.

Before she goes, he asks her if she will be on duty after his operation. "I probably will. But you won't want me." "Yes I will." But after the operation he comments, "I was sick and Catherine was right. It did not make any difference who was on night duty."

They spend an idyllic summer, making love, taking drives in the park, even going to the races. Then he has to go back to his unit. There follows the description of the retreat from Caporetto—but after the interlude of the summer of lovemaking, it again makes a powerful impact of realism—that feeling that everyone knows, of having to leave some pleasant situation, and return to the dreariness of everyday work and life.

After his escape from the firing squad, Henry decides that it is time to leave the army—hence the book's title. He finds Catherine, who has gone on leave to a hotel in Stresa, and the two escape to Switzerland by rowing across the lake.(According to Edmund Wilson, this is one of the first of Hemingway's absurd feats of bravado, which become increasingly frequent in the later work; but I certainly found nothing unbelievable in it at the time.)

Catherine is pregnant, and the couple go to Lausanne to be near a hospital. Catherine has a long and painful delivery, and the baby is born dead. Henry goes and sits in front of the fire in another room, and reflects, "Now Catherine would die. That was what you did. You died. You did not know what it was all about. You never had time to learn. They threw you in and told you the rules and the first time they caught you off base they killed you. Or they killed you gratuitously like Aymo. Or they gave you syphilis like Rinaldi. But they killed you in the end. You could count on that. Stay around and they would kill you."

He goes on to describe how he once sat in front of a fire, watching ants trying to escape from a burning log. It is one of Hemingway's most effective and powerful images.

When he goes back, he learns that Catherine has had a hemorrhage. He is allowed to go in and hold her hand until he is told to leave the room. When she is unconscious he is allowed to go back and stay with her until she dies.

The ending is one of Hemingway's most effective pieces of writing. After talking to the doctor, he tries to go back into the room, but the nurse tells him he can't come in.

"Yes I can," I said.

"You can't come in yet."

"You get out," I said. "The other one too."

"But after I had got them out and shut the door and turned off the light it wasn't any good. It was like saying goodbye to a statue. After a while I went out and left the hospital and walked back to the hotel in the rain."

Earlier in the book, Catherine comments, "I don't like the rain. I see me dead in it."

A Farewell to Arms is undoubtedly Hemingway's masterpiece. When I was twenty, it seemed to me the greatest novel ever written. Now, as I reread it for the first time in more than thirty years, I become aware of the false notes. Catherine is too sugary, and often downright silly:

"Your temperature's always normal. You've such a lovely temperature."

"You've got a lovely everything."

"Oh, no. You have the lovely temperature. I'm awfully proud of your temperature."

"Maybe all our children will have fine temperatures."

"Our children will probably have beastly temperatures."

There is far too much of this kind of thing. And Catherine simply gushes too much. "'I'll just say what you wish and I'll do what you wish and then you will never want any other girls, will you?' She looked at me very happily 'I'll do what you want and say what you want and then I'll be a great success, won't I?'"

In fact, Catherine is so submissive and so adoring that she is unreal; you do not have to sympathize with women's lib to find her nauseating. But I certainly failed to notice this the first time I read the book; its total truth seemed so impressive that I ignored such minor points.

On rereading Hemingway, I notice many "false notes." Even Jake Barnes in *The Sun Also Rises* acts a little too tough and says "Go to hell" too many times. But it was *For Whom the Bell Tolls* that made me aware of the basic Hemingway problem. It was obvious that Hemingway felt that the Spanish Civil War was the perfect subject, with its incredible violence and bitterness, and that it would provide an opportunity to write another *Farewell to Arms* on an even bigger scale. Yet this time it simply fails to work. There are two reasons; the first, that Hemingway has become just a little too self-conscious about his literary art, a little too preoccupied with telling "the truth" in simple and transparent language; second, that he simply goes on far too long.

The book would be better cut by a half. No one wants to listen to so much conversation between characters sitting around a campfire, particularly when so much of it strikes the wrong note: ". . . we blow up an obscene bridge and then have to obscenely well obscenity ourselves off out of these mountains." Hemingway could not have dreamed that within a few years it would be possible to print "fuck" or "fucking," but even so, "obscenity" somehow creates an effect of bathos.

Even the story of the love affair with the girl Maria has a kind of self-consciousness that spoils it.

"Am I thy woman now?"

"Yes, Maria. Yes, my little rabbit."

"She held herself tight to him and her lips looked for his and then found them and were against them and he felt her, fresh, new and smooth and young and lovely with the warm, scalding coolness and unbelievable to be there in the robe that was as familiar as his clothes, or his shoes, or his duty . . ."

Somehow, Hemingway is trying too hard. And this is even more embarrassingly true of the sex scene in chapter 13, where Jordan makes love to Maria in the heather. "For in it was a dark passage that led to nowhere, then to nowhere, then again to nowhere, once again to nowhere, always and forever to nowhere, heavy on the elbows in the earth to nowhere, dark, never any end to nowhere, hung on all time always to unknowing nowhere, this time and again for always to nowhere, now not to be borne once again always and to nowhere, now beyond all bearing up, up, up and into nowhere, suddenly, scaldingly, holdingly all nowhere gone and time absolutely still and they were both there, time having stopped and he felt the earth move out and away from under them."

This reads like a parody of Hemingway by his worst enemy.

How is it possible for a writer as intelligent and sensitive as Hemingway to write so badly?

To begin with, because Hemingway was taken in by his own legend. As a human being, Hemingway was shy, sensitive and vulnerable. His mother was a highly dominant woman of powerful religious convictions. In becoming a journalist, then traveling abroad, Hemingway was doing his best to leave her behind. Even so, she reacted violently against his writing, which she found anti-Christian and obscene. Hemingway badly needed to get away from home—the respectable, puritanical middle-class suburb called Oak Park, Illinois, where he had been born in 1899. He was running away from himself as much as from his mother; he wanted to be a completely different kind of person—someone more like the Jake Barnes of *The Sun Also Rises*—tough, sophisticated, self-controlled, well-traveled. And he set out with determination to turn himself into the kind of character he wanted to become.

As odd as it sounds, this Hemingway alter-ego had something in common with James Joyce. He wanted to be known as a realist, a man who was not afraid to tell the truth. And this in turn involved a rejection of ideas. Ideas were the province of constipated intellectuals—who, by definition, were completely out of touch with reality. *Ulysses* and *A Farewell to Arms* were both anti-intellectual manifestos.

According to Hemingway, a truly healthy human being knows reality through its touch and its taste—in that respect he is a direct descendant (perhaps the only literary descendant) of Walt Whitman. He does not need to lie to himself about religious "otherworlds;" he accepts this world.

After the worldwide success of *A Farewell to Arms* in 1929, Hemingway did his best to live out his fantasy as the tough, sophisticated realist, the man who never lies to himself. But in trying to live up to his fantasy, he became a kind of actor, a man with a continual need to inflate his own ego. He says things like "When I am writing I am as proud as a goddam lion." And to make it worse, this comment was made apropos his worst book, *Across the River and Into the Trees*, which he firmly believed was better than *A Farewell to Arms*.

The passage about the ants on the log provides the real clue to Hemingway's decline. "Now Catherine would die. That was what you did. You died. You did not know what it was all about. You never had time to learn . . ."

Is this passage intended simply to express Henry's state of mind after the death of the baby? If so, it would be quite understandable. But it is not. It is intended to express Hemingway's basic philosophy of life: that it can be very beautiful, very enjoyable, but that it is fundamentally tragic; ". . . they killed you in the end."

Hemingway is in such deep and powerful reaction against the puritanical religion of his childhood that he is determined not to make the slightest concession to the notion that life might have a meaning. This is his way of asserting his independence. (Once again, we are reminded of Stephen Dedalus and his refusal to pray beside his dying mother.) So he embraces a stoic philosophy of meaninglessness not unlike that of Sartre, Camus and Heidegger. Man is thrown into the world and he never finds out what it is all about.

The problem with such a philosophy is that it leaves no room for personal development. After *A Farewell to Arms*, Hemingway had, in effect, lost his subject. Where could he go from there? His attempts at a solution involved writing a book on bullfighting, *Death in the Afternoon* (1932), and a book on big game hunting, *The Green Hills of Africa* (1935.) Both celebrate the physical world as if "that is all there is." The only value left in Hemingway's nihilistic world is courage. And he, of course, had to epitomize courage—so that one sarcastic reviewer asked when Mr. Hemingway was going to come out from behind the hairs on his chest. After that, Hemingway discovered humanitarianism, the religion of man. He never became a Marxist, but his craving for some kind of intellectual position led him to the crypto-leftism that is expressed in the title of *To Have and Have Not* (1937), and the "religion of humanity" of *For Whom the Bell Tolls* (1940). But stoicism returns in *Across the River and Into the Trees*, in which an aging war hero has a love affair with a young Italian countess, and then dies stoically. The "message" is the same as in *A Farewell to Arms*, but there is a grotesque underlying element of self-praise. This can be found again in the novel *Islands in the Stream*, written immediately after *Across the River*, but only published after Hemingway's death. It is about an artist, based on Hemingway, and is once again full of self-glorification. But there is another element: guilt about the women he has betrayed, and about how badly he has behaved.

The last novel published in Hemingway's lifetime, *The Old Man and the Sea*, won him the Nobel Prize, but did not deserve to; it is as bad as anything he ever wrote. The attacks on *Across the River* had made Hemingway aware that the critics regarded him as a kind of poseur, and that another novel in which he was obviously the hero would bring another chorus of jeers. So instead, he wrote a novel in which he is disguised as an old fisherman, who displays the kind of courage in adversity that Hemingway admired so much. The critics at the time were taken in—I can recall its enthusiastic reception, and how much I disliked the book when I finally managed to borrow it from the library. For all its attempt to maintain a calm, objective voice, it has as many false notes as *Across the River*. After that, Hemingway published no more before his suicide in 1961, just before he reached the age of sixty.

His autobiography, *A Moveable Feast*, published three years after his death, shows what is wrong with Hemingway. He cannot stop being Ernest Hemingway. Autobiography calls for a straightforward, unpretentious style. But Hemingway was a slave of the Hemingway style, whose pseudosimplicity had become as pretentious as the most overblown Victorian poet. Instead of beginning, "When I was in Paris . . . ," he writes, "Then there was the bad weather. It would come in one day when the fall was over . . ." It is obvious that he thinks he is still writing *A Farewell to Arms*, incredibly unaware that the style of a novel is completely unsuitable for an autobiographical memoir. "When we came back to Paris it was clear and cold and lovely" is, in its way, as pretentious as "It was a truly magnificent red-gold autumn of overwhelming sunsets . . ."

So Hemingway became the victim of the Hemingway personality he had fabricated so carefully. And, like every egomaniac, he blamed everyone else for his problems. Yet he was too intelligent not to be instinctively aware of what had happened, and it may have been in some unbearable moment of truth that, on July 2, 1961, he decided to blow out his brains.

As to myself, I have no doubt that, in spite of the fact that I find virtually all of his work after *A Farewell to Arms* false and unreadable, Hemingway was one of the great writers of the twentieth century. His style has influenced every writer since, including myself. The lesson to be learned from Hemingway's fiction is to keep your eye carefully focused on what you are trying to describe, like an artist painting a portrait.

The lesson to be learned from his life is, in its way, even more interesting. When I was a teenager, I became utterly sick of the person labeled "Colin Wilson," for I was aware that it was not me. Inside the skin of this awkward, clumsy, easily-embarrassed teenager, I felt like someone trapped inside a pantomime horse. When I became absorbed in poetry, or when I went for a bicycle ride on a bright spring morning, I seemed to slip out of my personality as Hemingway felt himself slip out of his body when he was wounded. So when I began keeping a diary, at about the age of sixteen, I entitled it "Escape from Personality."

It seemed clear to me that escape from personality is the basic aim of the human race—not merely of "intellectuals" trapped in their own sense of inadequacy, but all human beings: the farmer ploughing a field, the mechanic repairing a car, even the politician carried away by his own rhetoric. Insofar as we are aware of ourselves as "persons," we are trapped in personality—this is what Eliot meant by, "We each think of the key, each in his prison."

One of the most subtle forms of entrapment comes with celebrity. For, as Sartre pointed out, our sense of ourselves is due largely to "the gaze of others." It was "the gaze of others," in combination with his own pessimistic personal philosophy, that destroyed Ernest Hemingway.

16

DAVID LINDSAY AND A
VOYAGE TO ARCTURUS

In the late 1950s, when I had first moved down to Cornwall, a friend who lived in a nearby cottage asked me if I had read *A Voyage to Arcturus*. I did not consider him a particularly good literary critic—he regarded Samuel Beckett as the greatest living writer—but he was certainly intelligent. So when I saw that my publisher, Gollancz, had reissued *Arcturus* in his series of Rare Works of Imaginative Fiction, I hastened to buy it.

I read it throughout a hot summer afternoon, lying out on the lawn. The beginning disappointed me, for the style is crude. But by the sixth chapter—when the hero arrives on the planet Tormance, a satellite of Arcturus—I was totally gripped. Lindsay had an incredible capacity for creating the strange and unexpected. Yet by the time I finished the book, I felt oddly frustrated; the ending simply failed to make sense.

I wrote to Lindsay's old friend E. H. Visiak, who introduced the Gollancz volume (and whose own *Medusa* was one of the other Rare Works), but although he replied at some length, it was obvious that he did not really understand Arcturus. I had to finally work it out for myself.

And work it out I did, for Arcturus stuck in my mind. One day, when I was on holiday in Blackpool with my wife Joy and my old friend Bill Hopkins, I began outlining the plot of Arcturus as an example of the ability to create a wholly nonterrestrial environment, and this aroused so many interesting memories of the book that I read it again as soon as I returned to Cornwall. This time, I suddenly understood what Lindsay was saying, and what the ending meant.

Since then, I have read it half a dozen times, and when I was writer-in-residence at a women's college in Virginia, I set Arcturus as one of the class books. It was a considerable success—my students obviously found this mixture of fairy tale and parable as exciting as Tolkien—who was then at the height of his fame on American campuses.

It seems odd that one of the most strange and exciting British masterpieces of the twentieth century should be almost unknown outside the British Isles; but what is even more odd is that even in England, it has virtually been forgotten. Its title—*A Voyage to Arcturus*—makes it sound like science fiction. In fact, it was written immediately after the First World War, eight years before the earliest "science fiction" stories were published in the magazine *Amazing Stories*. As the reader soon discovers, *A Voyage to Arcturus* cannot be described as science fiction, or fantasy, or even allegory. It is, quite simply, one of the greatest works of imagination of the twentieth century. For sheer inventiveness, it can only be compared to Tolkien's *Lord of the Rings*. But it is, as we shall see, a far more profound and serious work.

Its author, David Lindsay, was born at Blackheath, a suburb of London, in 1878. His father, a Scotsman, deserted the family when David was a child, and his mother had a painful struggle to raise three children. At school, Lindsay showed remarkable brilliance, and could easily have obtained a scholarship to a university. To his intense disappointment, his grandmother decided he should go into business. So Lindsay became an insurance clerk in Lloyds of London, and was so hardworking and conscientious that he was offered a partnership at the age of forty. But Lindsay was tired of business, and took the bold and risky decision to become a writer. It was even more risky because he had recently married—an attractive, vivacious girl who was eighteen years his junior—and he did not possess a private income. He used his savings—and his pension—to buy a house in Cornwall. There, in a few months, he wrote *A Voyage to Arcturus*. The book was accepted immediately by the first publisher he sent it to, and appeared in the following year, 1920. It looked as if Lindsay had justified his decision to abandon the insurance business, and achieved his goal with remarkable ease.

In fact, publication of *A Voyage to Arcturus* was the beginning of a long-drawn-out tragedy that would continue until the time of his death, twenty-five years later. His extraordinary masterpiece received appallingly bad reviews, and sold only 596 copies. His second novel, *The Haunted Woman*, was not even attacked; it was ignored by the critics, and also failed to sell. His third novel, *Sphinx*, found a publisher after many rejections, but was also received with complete indifference. His next novel, *The Violet Apple*, could not even find a publisher, and remained in manuscript until long after his death. Finally, the novel he considered his masterpiece, *Devil's Tor*, was published in 1932 to the same bored indifference as the others. His last novel, *The Witch*, was never completed.

Meanwhile, Lindsay's relations with his wife deteriorated; understandably, she felt that she had married a self-deluded failure. She was forced to run a boardinghouse in Brighton to support them, and she did this throughout the Second World War. It was typical of Lindsay's bad luck that the first bomb that fell on Brighton actually fell through the boardinghouse roof while he was taking a bath. Luckily the bomb failed to explode. Finally, a few weeks after the end of the war, he died of blood poisoning, a bitter and frustrated man. Yet in the following year, a publisher reissued *A Voyage to Arcturus*, and since that time, all Lindsay's novels—even the unfinished *Witch*—have been published.

Any reader who begins reading *A Voyage to Arcturus* can see immediately why it was a failure. The brutal truth is that the style is amateurish. Lindsay began writing too late to learn to sound like a professional. And the first six chapters of the novel, which take place on earth, are so stylistically awkward that it is not surprising that many readers fail to get beyond them. Yet when the hero—a huge, bearded man called Maskull—arrives on the planet Tormance, everything changes. The quality of imagination is so tremendous that it becomes impossible to doubt that David Lindsay is a man of extraordinary genius. From then until the end of the novel, the fantastic invention grips us with hypnotic force, until the reader closes the book with a feeling that he has been on a long journey, and is surprised to find himself back in his armchair.

It is necessary to repeat that David Lindsay is a far more serious writer than Tolkien, with whom he invites comparison. His mother, a deeply religious woman, brought him up in the tradition of gloomy

Scottish Presbyterianism, and although he revolted against it, his basic outlook remained that of a mystic. In this respect he bears a close resemblance to Nietzsche, the son of a clergyman, who was also brought up by his mother, and who, in spite of his avowed atheism, remained a kind of inverted religious mystic.

Lindsay is a typical example of what I have called an "outsider." He is revolted by the triviality of human beings ("human all-too human," Nietzsche called them), and his basic vision is of some tremendous sublimity that calls out to the human spirit, and makes man aware that he is really a god. Lindsay was particularly obsessed by the opening of Beethoven's Seventh Symphony, those magnificent chords that mount upward like some gigantic flight of steps cut out of the side of a mountain. This is Lindsay's basic message—that there is a sublime greatness that lies beyond the triviality of everyday life, and which beckons human beings to mount the giant stairway to reality.

According to Lindsay, the enemy of this sublime reality is the sugary, sentimental notion of "beauty," which mediocre human beings regard as the highest good. In fact, says Lindsay, this "beauty" is as dangerous as sweet, sugary cakes that cause the teeth to decay.

The original reviewers of *A Voyage to Arcturus* found the book bewildering and incomprehensible, and many modern readers will feel the same. Yet as soon as we possess the key—Lindsay's hatred of mere "beauty" and his obsession with "the sublime"—it suddenly becomes easy to understand. Like Bunyan's *Pilgrim's Progress*, *A Voyage to Arcturus* consists of a series of encounters and adventures. But while Bunyan's characters are allegories of "worldliness"—Mr. Worldly Wiseman, Giant Despair, and so on—Lindsay's are symbols of philosophical ideas. It sounds boring, yet the sheer power of Lindsay's imagination transforms it into a masterpiece.

The novel opens with a strange scene at a spiritualist seance, in the course of which the medium causes a beautiful and mysterious youth to materialize. His "sitters" are charmed and intrigued. Then the door bursts open, and a powerful, vulgar-looking man called Krag seizes the youth's neck and snaps it. Immediately, the face ceases to be beautiful and mysterious, and dissolves into a "vulgar, sordid, bestial grin, which cast a cold shadow of moral nastiness into every heart."

The reader has probably guessed already that the beautiful, mysterious youth represents Lindsay's idea of trivial "beauty," while the vulgar and demonic Krag is a kind of Beethoven who enjoys shocking the sentimentalists with his own superhuman "sublimity." But what is so interesting about this scene is that the reader is at first taken in by the fascination of the beautiful and mysterious youth, just as the audience is, and is shocked by Krag's brutality. And throughout the book, Lindsay continues to repeat this situation with interesting variants. Just as the reader is convinced that someone is expressing a philosophy of existence that surely must be true, the philosopher is killed and the face dissolves into the disgusting "Crystalman grin." The irony, of course, is that Krag is what human beings call "the Devil," whereas in reality, it is the beautiful and mysterious Crystalman who is the real Devil, the Deceiver who tries to lure humankind into laziness and complacency (which, for Lindsay, is the same thing as damnation).

It would be impossible to summarize the incredible adventures that Maskull encounters on Arcturus—the weird creatures and unearthly scenery. C. S. Lewis attempted something of the sort in *Out of the Silent Planet* and *Voyage to Venus*, but compared to Lindsay, his imagination is feeble and conventional.

Briefly, then, Maskull's first encounter on Arcturus is with a beautiful and gentle girl called Joiwind, who gives him some of her blood to revive him, and shows tenderness and love to all living creatures. Surely she is intended as a real heroine? No. According to Lindsay, she is sentimental and brainless. (If he had been alive today he might have added, "Like many modern liberals.") The same is true of her husband, a poet and mystic: when he is overwhelmed by beauty, crystal eggs fall out of his mouth. But when Joiwind tells Maskull that Crystalman is the great architect of the universe, we begin to suspect that she is a symbol of the "human all-too human," a victim of the deceptions of Crystalman.

Maskull's next encounter is with a savage, sensual woman called Oceaxe, who quickly destroys the effect of Joiwind's teaching by making him eat fish, which she cooks by concentrating her will on it. She can also knock savage vampire-birds out of the sky with her willpower. But Oceaxe herself is killed by a rival female, a gentle and feminine creature called Tydomin, who deceives her into walking over a cliff by filling her mind with delusions. Tydomin convinces Maskull that the answer to life lies in self-sacrifice. And yet, once again, Maskull "wakes up" to realize that he is being deceived by her hypnotic powers and by the delusions of Crystalman. When Maskull eventually kills her, her face turns into the idiotic Crystalman grin.

And so it goes on—mighty forests, strange oceans, incredible mountain landscapes, bizarre and wonderful characters, all created with tremendous power and authority. So far, we are less than halfway through the novel, and Lindsay's amazing invention never seems to flag. In the overwhelming climax of the book, Maskull himself dies—only to realize that he is not dead at all—that "Maskull" was yet another of the delusions of Crystalman. He then turns into his true self—a being called Nightspore (meaning "seed of the night"), and once again encounters Krag, whom he now recognizes as the only force in the universe powerful enough to resist the delusions of Crystalman. Krag tells him, "On earth I am called pain"—the pain which saints and ascetics accept willingly to rise above their own human limitations.

It is impossible to summarize *A Voyage to Arcturus* in a short chapter. It is enough to say that it leaves the reader with a conviction that Lindsay was one of the great minds of his time. It is true that the philosophy has some resemblance to Buddhism; but *A Voyage to Arcturus* resembles no other novel of the twentieth century.

Yet when Lindsay tried to project this "sublime" vision into other books, he failed. Why? I suspect because he chose to set them on earth—like the beginning of *A Voyage to Arcturus*—and, like his own hero Maskull, he feels strangely out of place on earth, a typical "outsider." It is as if the powerful gravity of earth refused to allow Lindsay's imagination to leave the ground. And, as Baudelaire said of the poet, "His giant wings prevent him from walking." All the later novels have magnificent pages, even chapters, and the ideas are invariably fascinating—for example, *Sphinx* is about a man who invents a machine that can record dreams—yet in the last analysis, they lack genuine unity. Lindsay obviously found it difficult to finish them, and the reader feels the same.

Yet in his second novel, *A Haunted Woman* (1922), Lindsay at least found a magnificent symbol of the artist's basic problem. It is a novel about the "reality" glimpsed by great artists and mystics, and the world of "the triviality of everydayness" (Heidegger's phrase) in which we find ourselves trapped.

The heroine, Isbel, is a young woman who is engaged to be married. Yet she feels vaguely discontented with her life, as if it is somehow a second best. Listening to the ascending scales of a passage in the first movement of Beethoven's Seventh Symphony, she experiences an intuition of some other reality.

Together with her fiance, she goes to look at a house that they are thinking of buying. This house is associated with a peculiar legend. It was built in the time of the Saxon invasion by a man called Ulf, and the land it was built on was reputedly haunted by trolls, who had raised the hillside from flat earth. But one day, the upper part of the house vanished, together with Ulf. Through the centuries, many people claim to have seen the house as it was when Ulf first built it.

The present owner of the house is a middle-aged man named Judge, and he and Isbel meet without feeling any particular interest in one another. As Isbel is wandering alone around the house, she finds a flight of stairs that leads to an upper story. Judge has also found a similar flight of stairs at the other end of the house, and the two meet in a room above. There is something strange about this upper story. It seems to be a part of a far older house, and the scene outside the windows is quite different from the scene out of the ground floor windows: it seems to be an ancient landscape, which is bathed in spring sunshine—while in the "downstairs" world it is autumn. Outside the window is a gaily-dressed musician, lying asleep on the hillside, with a fiddle lying beside him.

When Isbel and Judge meet one another in this upper room, they know they are meant for one another. Judge is somehow younger, more authoritative. And when Isbel glimpses her own face in a mirror, she also seems a different person—somehow far more mature and fulfilled. Normally she is a rather prim, restrained young lady; now she feels herself throbbing with a strange vitality that is partly sexual.

The problem is that when they descend to the lower story, both immediately lose all memory of the upper room. They once again meet as strangers. But when, later in the novel, they meet once more in the upper story, they are chagrined at their former amnesia. They try to devise means of reminding themselves of their "other selves" who are meant for one another; they write themselves notes that they place in their pockets. But when they are downstairs again, and find the notes, they find them incomprehensible, and throw them away.

The novel ends frustratingly. The last time they meet is on the lawn. But Judge has climbed out of the window of the upper story, and is in the spring sunshine. Isbel, who has entered through the gate, is surrounded by autumn mists. To her, Judge is still a relative stranger, and she is offended when he calls her by her first name.

Judge begs her to wait, and leaves her. He borrows the musician's violin, and plays. As he does so, Isbel finds herself standing in spring sunshine, and the house has vanished. Judge has succeeded in making her see the world with transformed vision. He returns and takes her in his arms. For a few minutes they are triumphant—they have found one another again. Then, for Isbel, the autumn mists begin to return, and the sun vanishes. She tells him miserably, "I'm returning to the old state." A few minutes later, her amnesia is back, and she is addressing him formally as "Mr. Judge."

In a final effort to bring her back to him, Judge picks up the musician's instrument again and plays. For a moment, the spring sunshine comes back. Then the musician wakes up. Isbel sees Judge staring into his face, looking as if he is seeing "some appalling vision." Then Judge collapses with a heart attack, and the autumn mists return.

The Haunted Woman expresses a theme to which Lindsay returned in all his novels: the feeling that social relations turn us into mechanical dolls, and separate us from reality. (Lindsay, an extremely formal and awkward man, undoubtedly felt this strongly.) The "upper story" of the house is the state of mind we achieve when, as Yeats says, we "complete the partial mind." Then, suddenly, we understand what life can be, what it ought to be. For a moment we are in spring sunshine, suddenly swept away by the feeling of "absurd good news." Then the autumn mists return. And, what is worse, we have lost all memory of the spring sunshine and the "upper story" of the mind.

In spite of the odd clumsiness of his prose, there can be no doubt that Lindsay was a great writer, with much in common with Nietzsche and Schopenhauer. It is true that his central idea—that the Devil is cloying, sentimental and rather nauseating—is shared by Bernard Shaw in the third act of *Man and Superman*. But Shaw treats the idea as comedy, while Lindsay rises to something like the sublimity of the "step" passage in Beethoven's Seventh Symphony.

Lindsay himself was a victim of that social formality that entraps Isbel Loment and so many other of his heroes and heroines. Even his prose is formal and oddly inelegant, forming a kind of barrier between the writer and his readers. Yet Lindsay's vision is so remarkable that no one can read even his worst novels—like *Devil's Tor*—without receiving a powerful impression of his genius.

Oddly enough, I can think of only one other writer of the twentieth century who once expressed a vision of "sublimity" that would have appealed to Lindsay—I say "oddly enough" because the writer is Bertrand Russell, a philosopher Lindsay probably detested as a shallow rationalist. In a letter to his mistress, Lady Constance Malleson, Russell wrote, "I must, I must, before I die, find some way to say the essential thing that is in me, that I have never said yet—a thing that is not love or hate or pity or scorn, but the very breath of life, fierce and coming from far away, bringing into human life the vastness and the fearful passionless force of non-human things." This is the essence of David Lindsay, and if his critics had been intelligent enough to understand it, he might have learned to create more masterpieces instead of dying of discouragement, neglect and frustration.

It would be a pity to conclude this chapter without some mention of Lindsay's friend E. H. Visiak, who wrote the introduction to the Gollancz reissue of *Arcturus*, and who is the author of an equally strange and baffling book.

As I have said, I wrote to Visiak soon after reading *Arcturus* for the first time, to see if he could throw more light on it. He replied at length, in a crabbed, precise handwriting, but what he had to say left me as much in the dark as ever.

However, we continued to correspond. I learned that he was almost ninety years old, and that he lived in a nursing home in Hove. It was soon obvious that he was a rather lonely old man, and that he was glad to correspond with another writer, particularly one of the younger generation. Soon he was addressing me as Colin, and inviting me to call him Harold.

Eventually, I went to see him in Hove, near Brighton—he occupied a fairly large bedroom in a boardinghouse close to the sea. He was very thin, with an interesting, sensitive face. When I asked him to what he attributed his great age, he replied briefly, "Worry."

I learned that Harold Visiak had led a quiet, bookish existence, and had never married. He had always been fascinated by the sea, which touched his romantic imagination. He had published a few volumes of poems, three novels, and books on Milton and Conrad; he was regarded as a more-than-competent Milton scholar, and had edited the Nonesuch works of Milton in one volume.

It was obvious to me that he was dying of boredom; he felt that his life had finished many years ago. His first novel, *The Haunted Island*, had appeared in 1908; *Medusa*, his best known novel, came out in 1929, but a subsequent novel had been rejected, leaving him shattered and depressed; as a consequence, he had simply stopped writing—thirty five years before I met him.

163

Now, as he talked to me about his life—particularly his early days—I urged him to write it down. Some of it, it seemed, was already written, and he sent me a dog-eared typescript. He wrote extremely well, and I urged him to go on with it. I also persuaded a publisher to accept a book about David Lindsay by myself and Visiak (another writer, J. B. Pick, would also join us), and the result was *The Strange Genius of David Lindsay*. The autobiography was published in 1968 as *Life's Morning Hour*.

Now the truth is that I did not think *Medusa* a very good book. It was written in a style reminiscent of R. L. Stevenson or Arthur Machen—definitely late Victorian. It is narrated by a young boy who goes to sea in the company of middle-aged man named Huxtable, who is in search of his lost son, and has hired a ship and its crew.

The events of the novel are obscure, and involve the discovery of a deserted ship, and of a strange, mute little man, who produces a mysterious manuscript which refers to a "rock pillar." There is also a curious man-like sea creature with webbed feet, who proves to have been smuggled on board by one of the sailors. Mr. Huxtable now tells the captain that they are to go in search of the rock pillar, which he seems to feel will offer some clue to his son's disappearance.

Later, Mr. Huxtable tells the narrator a strange legend of an island off the coast of Ceylon, whose inhabitants were once prosperous and wise, but who, like the Atlanteans in Plato's *Timaeus*, gradually declined to a lower moral level. An old philosopher tries to recall them to their former virtue, but a tempter arises who tells them that this is unnecessary. He has discovered some strange form of light that can transform human beings and bring them to a higher state of awareness. In fact, this magical light only increases their degradation, until the island sinks, leaving only a pillar of rock projecting above the waves.

In the next chapter, they draw near the rock pillar, and the cabin is suddenly filled with the strange light, which causes the narrator to feel "a sweet rapture, an enthralling, enchanting joy" which seems to set his spirit free from his flesh.

Then, suddenly, web-footed sea creatures invade the ship, and the narrator is seized. He is carried on deck, and sees close to the ship a cylindrical pillar of black rock. The sea creatures have kidnapped the sailors from the ship, and are swimming with them to the pillar.

The narrator himself is taken there, and thrown down through a kind of square hatch cut in the rock. He lands on a ledge, where a sailor is lying. The man seems at first to be dead, but when the narrator looks into his face, he is smiling with "some wicked, impetuous joy." Then he sees a kind of dark red tentacle, covered in suckers, rising out of the depths below him, groping along the ledge. He manages to evade it. But when he looks down into the depth, he sees the captain held in the tentacle of a kind of giant squid. Then he glimpses the captain's face, and is shocked to see that he is wearing an expression of ecstasy.

Soon after, someone calls down from above and throws a rope; he is rescued and taken back on board the ship. And the greatly-reduced crew (including Mr. Huxtable, who now appears to think that the narrator is his long-lost son) sails the ship back to England.

I found it all totally baffling and, to my great regret, never asked Visiak to explain just what he meant. But I doubt whether he could have told me. And it was only many years later—long after his death in his mid-90s—that I suddenly caught a glimpse of the meaning. I suspect that the octopus-like creature was Visiak's own symbol for the "sexual illusion," which grips men and fills them with ecstasy. As someone whose practical knowledge of sex was minimal, I believe that Visiak, with a poet's intuition, grasped that sex is an illusion, designed to persuade animals to perpetuate the species, and filling them with a sense of mystical purpose which, when analyzed closely, is seen to be a kind of confidence trick.

This also appears in a peculiar dream the narrator experiences as he lies on the ledge. He dreams of a boat or ship, oval in shape, sailing over the sea. It seems to be made of a kind of flesh, of "alluring strange softness." It is, he says, feminine but not human. "It was enchanting beyond utterance; than any mortal woman, though it were Helen or Cleopatra, more seductively and ravishingly fair."

Clearly, this is Visiak's own symbol of Woman, shaped like female genitals, although he has declared that its color is bluish green, as if suggesting decay. It is after this dream that he wakes up and sees the captain gripped by the tentacle, wearing an ecstatic expression on his face.

Again, when the narrator looks back at the pillar, he describes it as tall and cylindrical, with a hole near its top—again, obviously a sex symbol; its blackness once more suggests darkness and evil.

I suspect that any Freudian psychiatrist, reading *Medusa*, would have declared unhesitatingly that it was a kind of dream-novel symbolizing Visiak's own fear of sex. And I suspect he would be right.

Yet it also seems to me that in his symbol of the flesh-colored octopus, gripping a man whose face wears an expression of ecstasy, Visiak had hit upon an overwhelming symbol of the power of sex. At the time I read it—in my early thirties—I had not yet clearly formulated the notion that sex is basically an illusion, that it fills us with a sense of magic that makes it seem a gateway to some higher state of consciousness, then dissolves away, leaving us as bewildered as some hypnotic subject who is galvanized into wakefulness by a snap of the hypnotist's fingers.

Now, in retrospect, it seems to me ironic that Visiak, who regarded sex with such deep alarm, should have produced one of the most memorable symbols of its power in the twentieth century.

17

DOSTOEVSKY

In 1906, the London publisher J. M. Dent decided to launch a series of inexpensive reprints of classics called Everyman's Library—the first attempt to publish low-cost books for a mass audience. Dent chose a good time—when improvements in education had created an enormous appetite for "serious reading"—and Everyman's Library was an instant success. Its range was enormous: a fiction list of hundreds of titles, from Jane Austen to Zola, poetry from Chaucer to Browning, Greek and Roman classics, history, science, philosophy and even theology.

Each volume ended with a classified catalogue of all 934 titles, and, as an obsessive reader (I used to describe myself as a bibliomaniac), one of my greatest pleasures was to browse through this list to see how many new authors I could discover.

One of the authors of whom I had never heard was Dostoevsky. He had no less than seven entries, so was obviously an important writer. I asked a master at school what kind of books Dostoevsky wrote. He told me they were gloomy and morbid, and somehow gave me the impression that Dostoevsky was a kind of Russian Poe.

I loved Poe, so the next time I was in the library, I looked at *Notes from Underground* (called in the Everyman edition *Letters from the Underworld*), and was puzzled and disappointed by it. "I am a sick man, I am a spiteful man," it begins, and then rambles on for page after page without even trying to tell a story. I finally threw it down in disgust without getting to the story. I decided that Dostoevsky was not for me, and gave it up.

This was, I think, about 1944, when I was thirteen. In the following year, Heinemann publishers began to reissue their translation of Dostoevsky by Constance Garnett, with striking red dust jackets. I had heard that *Crime and Punishment* was supposed to be his greatest novel, and bought it. (In those days I still delivered newspapers every evening and greengroceries every Saturday afternoon, to make pocket money, most of which was spent on books.)

The translator's preface, only two pages long, contained a sketch of Dostoevsky's life.

It seemed that Dostoevsky's parents were so poor that they lived with five children in two rooms. His father, an impoverished nobleman, was a doctor. Dostoevsky's mother died when he was sixteen; his father was subsequently murdered by his own peasants, whom he had treated brutally.

While at engineering school, Dostoevsky wrote his first novel, *Poor Folk*, the story of a miserable clerk who is in love with an unhappy young girl who has been deserted by her lover. In the end he loses her. Dostoevsky handed the manuscript to his friend Grigorovich, who took it along to the poet Nekrasov. The two of them began to read it aloud, and found themselves unable to stop. Finally, both had tears running down their cheeks. They rushed around in the dawn to awaken Dostoevsky and tell him they thought it a masterpiece. Published in Nekrasov's magazine, it made Dostoevsky famous.

But Fedora Mikhailovich Dostoevsky was a touchy, irritable person, with a low opinion of himself, and more than a touch of paranoia; success did him no good at all. His pessimism was increased by the fact that subsequent stories were attacked by critics. He overreacted, and allowed the attacks to drive him frantic. In his misery, he lost all sense of proportion. And at this point, Dostoevsky was arrested for being part of a group who met to read revolutionary literature.

"After eight months in prison," says Constance Garnett, "he was taken out to the Semyonovsky Square to be shot. Writing to his brother Mihail, Dostoevsky says, 'They barked words over our heads, and they made us put on the white shirts worn by people condemned to death. Thereupon we were bound in threes to stakes, to suffer execution. Being the third in the row, I concluded I only had a few minutes of life before me. I thought of you and your dear ones, and I contrived to kiss

Plestcheiev and Dourov, who were next to me, and bid them farewell. Suddenly the troops beat a tattoo, we were unbound, brought back upon the scaffold, and informed that his Majesty had spared our lives.' . . . One of the prisoners, Grigoriev, went mad as soon as he was untied, and never regained his sanity."

That scene made a tremendous impact on me. I could imagine that, after Dostoevsky was taken back to his cell, every brick in the wall must have seemed to him fascinating and worthy of deep attention.

After his reprieve, Dostoevsky was sent to Siberia, where he served four years in a penal settlement, then another four in the army. Back in St. Petersburg, married to a consumptive widow, he wrote his account of the penal settlement in *The House of the Dead*, one of his most powerful books, and a classic of criminology. It brought him new fame, and two years later—and twenty years after *Poor Folk*—he established himself as a great novelist with *Crime and Punishment*. By that time his wife had died.

Dostoevsky was always under financial pressure, and wrote at incredible speed to stave off his creditors. (After the death of his brother Mihail, he undertook to pay his debts and support his family.)

In 1866, while *Crime and Punishment* was still unfinished, Dostoevsky was so pressed for money—and time—that he decided to dictate his novel *The Gambler* to a stenographer. A crooked publisher had forced him to sign a contract agreeing that unless he delivered a new novel by a certain time, all his work for the next nine years could be published without him receiving a penny. With less than a month to go, he began dictating to a twenty-year-old girl, Anna Snitkina—Dostoevsky was then forty-five. Twenty-six days later, the book was finished—with one day to spare. When Dostoevsky tried to deliver it, the publisher was out of town, and his office refused to accept the manuscript. With only hours to go, Dostoevsky succeeded in persuading the local police station to accept it and give him a receipt.

Dostoevsky decided that he liked dictating novels, and asked Anna to continue working for him. Seven days after delivering *The Gambler*, she came to his flat, and he told her that he was working on the plot of a new novel, about "an artist who is no longer young," and a young girl he falls in love with. But, Dostoevsky admitted, he needed advice. What might a young, exuberant girl see in an elderly, sick, debt-ridden man? "Put yourself in her place," said Dostoevsky, "Imagine that this artist is me, and that I have confessed my love for you and asked you to be my wife. What would you answer?"

"I would answer that I love you and will love you all my life."

They fell into one another's arms. When Dostoevsky asked her her opinion about his plans for the future, she answered, "How can I make up my mind about anything when I'm so horribly happy?"

Anna brought order into his life, cured him of gambling, and even became his publisher, so that he at last achieved freedom from debt. They were to be together for only fourteen years. But by the time of his death, at the age of fifty-nine, Dostoevsky had achieved widespread recognition, and his speech at the unveiling of a memorial to Pushkin, in June 1880, was received with almost hysterical acclaim. His funeral was followed by thousands of mourners.

Reading *Crime and Punishment* was an extraordinary experience. I had become accustomed to the notion that most "classic" novels require considerable stamina on the part of the reader. But with *Crime and Punishment* I was gripped from the first page, with its description of a young man—Raskolnikov—tiptoeing down the stairs to avoid meeting his landlady, to whom he owes money. And the description of the stifling heat of summer, the stench of St. Petersburg, the drunks staggering along the streets, the scaffolding, bricks and dust, has an overwhelming realism. Dostoevsky possessed a marvelous eye for detail.

"The master of the tavern was in another room, but he frequently came down some steps into the main room, his jaunty, tarred boots with red turn-over tops coming into view each time before the rest of his person. He wore a full coat and horribly greasy black satin waistcoat, with no cravat, and his whole face smeared with oil like an iron lock."

Dostoevsky seems to want to create grotesques, like the figures of Heironymus Bosch.

It is in this tavern that Raskolnikov, meets the drunk Marmeladov, whose face, "bloated from continuous drinking, was of a yellow, even greenish, tinge, with swollen eyelids, out of which keen, reddish eyes gleamed like little chinks." He owes something to Dickens' Micawber, but is far more degraded than Micawber. Marmeladov is consumed with guilt about his family—his wife has been beaten by their landlord, and his daughter has been forced into prostitution.

Waking up the next morning from an unrefreshing sleep, Raskolnikov receives a letter from his mother, which describes how his sister

Dounia's employer has tried to seduce her, and how the would-be seducer's wife has thrown her out into the street, believing her to be the guilty party. Then, just as the family has reached the depths of despair and humiliation, the seducer's wife has learned the truth, and has called on them to beg their forgiveness, then gone round the whole town telling the story. Now Dounia is about to make a loveless marriage with a rich lawyer who is many years her senior—obviously for the sake of her poverty-stricken brother. Raskolnikov rushes out of the house in torment, determined that he must not allow this to happen.

Dostoevsky continues to turn the screw. Out in the street, Raskolnikov sees a girl of sixteen walking unsteadily, with a torn dress. She has obviously been made drunk and then seduced; even now, another well-dressed man is watching her with interest, anxious to take advantage of her. Raskolnikov calls a policeman, who agrees to make sure that the girl does not fall into the hands of yet another seducer.

As I read these opening chapters again, half a century after the first time, I must admit that they no longer affect me so powerfully. It now seems to me that Dostoevsky is "laying it on too thick"—that he is a little too determined to try to wring the last drop of emotion out of every scene. I realize, of course, that this kind of thing really happens, that drunken men allow their daughters to become prostitutes, that virtuous girls are forced to marry older men for money, that teenage girls are made drunk and then raped. But it also seems clear to me that Dostoevsky has a strong tendency to masochism which grates on my nerves. In my teens I found it powerful and moving; now I find it unconvincing.

Raskolnikov's solution, of course, is to kill an old pawnbrokress with an axe; he is also forced to kill her mentally-retarded stepsister. He has convinced himself that a hero like Napoleon would not hesitate to commit murder if it would enable him to escape from an intolerable situation. But the murder fails in its purpose. He is immediately suspected by the police. The detective Porfiry plays a cat-and-mouse game with him, more interested, apparently, in his soul than in ensuring a conviction. Finally, Raskolnikov confesses, and is sentenced to eight years in Siberia. Sonia, the drunken Marmeladov's daughter, accompanies him—her father has been killed in a street accident. And so Raskolnikov's rehabilitation begins.

I was stunned by the novel's power, yet at the same time, far from convinced by its savage pessimism. The truth was that, as a person,

Dostoevsky was far more neurotic than I was, far more inclined to self-contempt and paranoia. Freud once remarked that any child who has received the undivided love of his mother goes through the rest of life feeling curiously confident and invulnerable. Well, I had been the first born of my family, and had certainly received a great deal of maternal love. I had also been regarded as "clever" and interesting by grandparents and aunts and uncles. That meant that even when I was feeling most depressed, in my mid-teens, I was never much inclined to self-pity or self-abasement. So while I found Dostoevsky by far the most powerful and impressive novelist I had ever read, I found many of his characters rather irritating and offputting. If people were really as miserable as Marmeladov, and as wracked by guilt about the misery they were inflicting on their families, why didn't they do something about it? Why, in *A Gentle Spirit*, does the wife only realize that her husband loves her as she is committing suicide? Why couldn't the idiot tell her so earlier, and so avoid an unhappy ending? I felt that Dostoevsky rather enjoyed wallowing in unhappiness. Shaw was far more naturally suited to my basically optimistic temperament.

At about this time, I began reading *Dostoevsky, The Man and his Work* by the Dutch writer Julius Meier-Graefe, whose book on Van Gogh I greatly admired. (I had discovered the paintings of Van Gogh through a friend who was widely acquainted with the visual arts, and had begun reading books on painting and sculpture.) I enjoyed Meier-Graefe's book because he includes lengthy plot summaries of the major works. More than fifty pages is devoted to *The Idiot*, which Meier-Graefe considers Dostoevsky's masterpiece.

I settled down to reading *The Idiot*, and persisted until I was about halfway through. But compared to *Crime and Punishment*, it seemed to ramble and lack direction. Besides, I found Prince Myshkin, Dostoevsky's attempt at a Christ-like hero, unconvincing. Could he not see that a "good man" makes a very dull hero? For the only way to make the reader admire a good man is to contrast him with people who are not good, and demonstrate his superiority. In fact, Myshkin is so passive that he never succeeds in arousing the reader's interest.

I was particularly irritated by the party scene in which everyone is asked to describe the most despicable thing they have ever done. It seemed to me that Dostoevsky was simply wasting too much time on past sins and weaknesses, and that he would have done better to devote his mind to something more sensible and constructive.

So I gave up *The Idiot*, and have not finished it to this day.

The Possessed I found altogether more readable, in spite of the irritating device of a narrator who claims to know every single thought and action of all his characters. It is, of course, based on the Netchaev murder case, in which a ruthless young revolutionary tried to bind together a group of conspirators by getting them to participate in a pointless murder. The revolutionaries bored me. But I was fascinated by two of the characters: Stavrogin, the spoiled, Byronic playboy who suffers from a sense of futility, and Kirilov, the mystic who has decided to commit suicide to prove that man is a kind of god with the right of ultimate choice. Having myself been so close to suicide, I could understand Kirilov's reasoning. But I also understood Stavrogin's boredom and sense of futility. I was still struggling with the same feeling of meaninglessness, and Dostoevsky was the only novelist who seemed to understand it. Yet it also seemed perfectly clear to me that suicide—the solution chosen by Stavrogin—is not the answer.

My feeling that Dostoevsky was one of the greatest of all novelists was confirmed when I read the book on Dostoevsky by the philosopher Nicholas Berdyaev. He suggests that Dostoevsky is the greatest writer of ideas that the world has ever known, that ideas form the backbone of his work, and that it is his passion for ideas that makes his works enduring masterpieces.

It was also a passage in Berdyaev's own autobiography, *Dream and Reality*, that underlines why I regarded Dostoevsky as so superior to all other novelists except Tolstoy. Berdyaev tells how he and a group of other intellectuals had spent the whole night talking and arguing. And when someone finally yawned and said it was time to go home, someone else replied, "No, we can't go yet—we haven't decided whether God exists." This was the reason I admired Dostoevsky. It had always seemed to me that the British are basically trivial-minded, and that none of our major novelists—Richardson, Fielding, Scott, Dickens, Thackeray, Hardy—have ever expressed a single important idea. But Dostoevsky, like Tolstoy, was willing to confront the question of why we are alive. So in spite of my irritation with his masochism, I was more than willing to regard him as the world's greatest novelist.

Yet when I came to read the novel that is regarded as Dostoevsky's masterpiece, *The Brothers Karamazov*, I found that view more difficult to sustain. It seemed to me that this vast work, nearly half a million words long, rambles intolerably. Just as in *The Idiot*, we get a sense that Dostoevsky has no idea of where he is going. The book is a series of conversations and meetings that seem to have no particular point.

Of course, where Dostoevsky was concerned, they do have a kind of point. Dostoevsky wants to write about atheism and belief in God, about debauchery and man's natural longing for goodness. So old Karamazov is a disgusting lecher, while his youngest son, Alyosha, is a novice in a monastery, and his second son, Ivan, is an atheist who is tormented by the world's misery.

The most powerful scenes, of course, are Ivan's long discussion with Alyosha, and his parable of the Grand Inquisitor. Certainly, it is in these scenes that Dostoevsky comes closest to expressing his lifelong torment. Ivan explains that he cannot accept the notion that life is good, and that God is all-powerful, because there is so much misery in the world that it is impossible to feel that, "placed in perspective," it can all be recognized as part of the Grand Design.

Certainly, Dostoevsky is here expressing one of the most important of all philosophical or theological arguments—the argument that Kierkegaard expressed when he objected to Hegel's great system on the grounds that it is like trying to find your way around Copenhagen with a map of Denmark on which Copenhagen appears the size of a pinhead. Confronted with individual misery, reason often falls silent.

Yet this does not mean that Ivan's objections are unanswerable. This is what Alyosha should have replied to his brother:

"The problem is that, whether we like it or not, we all have to live on the assumption that effort is worthwhile. Yet I agree with you that it is only necessary to read of some appalling tragedy, from the misery of earthquake survivors to man's crimes against his fellow man, to feel that our optimism is based on a kind of short-sightedness. We have only to read a newspaper item about cruelty to children—or for that matter, to the old—to feel that life can be appallingly brutal.

"Yet the people who actually allow themselves to be depressed and traumatized by such considerations often have mental breakdowns or commit suicide. In fact, the logical response to your ideas is to cease making all effort, to become completely passive. Is that what you are suggesting—that we should all sit down in the corner and gaze blankly in front of us?

"Is it not far better to do what we can to fight against the evil in the world, and to get on with the business of living?

"In fact, there are certain moments when we seem to be filled with an enormous strength and optimism—for example, on spring mornings, or at night, staring up at the sky, with its millions of worlds.

"We all have to fight this battle from moment to moment. One day life seems wonderful, the next day it is so painfully difficult that we wonder if we can carry on. Yet we are clearly not intended to surrender, as your philosophy would seem to suggest. In fact, your philosophy is like a cup filled with poison. My own moments of optimism seem to suggest that we are far stronger than we realize, and that our own strength is often hidden from us by self-pity and lack of self-belief. So while I cannot help admiring your intellect, I feel instinctively that your gloomy view of human existence is some kind of a miscalculation . . ."

To which Ivan would probably reply, "And what about my Grand Inquisitor? How can you answer that?"

Now I must admit that I have always felt the argument of the Grand Inquisitor is also a great deal less profound than it looks. In essence it is an attack on the Catholic Church and the practice of confession. Ivan describes how, when Christ returns to Seville, he is thrown into prison, and there the Grand Inquisitor visits him, and warns him that he must die. The monologue that follows is basically an attack on the notion that man can be "saved." "Men are mere cattle," says the Grand Inquisitor. "All they want is food and security. Don't tell them the kingdom of God is within them—they don't want to know. Don't tell them they possess freedom—they don't want freedom. We have taken away their freedom, and turned them into slaves of the Catholic Church. We tell them what to do if they want to escape damnation, and they obey us and drop money into our collection plates. Why do you want to come and interfere? Don't you know they are lazy and stupid, and only want to be told what to do?"

As an attack on Catholicism—or perhaps the Church in general—this might be regarded as fair comment. Luther would certainly have approved. But the argument between Luther and the Catholic Church is almost five centuries old; why drag it all up again? As far as our century is concerned, it is irrelevant. "Outsiders" do want freedom, and they do feel an obscure need to struggle for "salvation"—and this is common to every religion in the world. It may be true that the great mass of people are spiritually lazy, and glad enough to swallow a religion of pure dogma. But that fails to prove anything for or against religion in itself.

In short, the Grand Inquisitor argument simply misses the point, and it is hard to see how it has acquired its reputation as a profound piece of literature. And since neither Dostoevsky nor most of his readers were Roman Catholics, it is also hard to see why he bothered to write it.

The Grand Inquisitor story does have one extremely powerful moment—at the very end, when, instead of replying, Jesus simply kisses the old man on the lips. The Inquisitor shudders, then opens the door and says, "Go, and never come back." Jesus has reminded him that Christianity is about love. Yet, as Dostoevsky acknowledges, the Inquisitor also loves mankind in his own way, and so hardly needs the reminder. Possibly the kiss is intended to symbolize a love so transcendent that it can even forgive the old man as he delivers the death sentence. It is a deeply moving gesture; yet it is also irrelevant to the argument of the Grand Inquisitor, and to Dostoevsky's attack on the Church.

Vladimir Nabokov once confessed that he was unable to abide Dostoevsky. At the time, this seemed to me an admission of stupidity and shallowness. Yet in retrospect, I find myself sympathizing with Nabokov. If I was stranded on a desert island with a complete set of Dostoevsky, it is conceivable that I would read him again. But recent attempts have been a failure. I can no longer put up with the masochism, self-pity, and hysteria. There was a time when I was willing to swallow these—although even then they bored and irritated me—but I now find that they form too much of an obstacle. Dostoevsky is regarded, quite rightly, as one of the first existentialist philosophers. And I feel that, like Sartre and Camus and Heidegger, his philosophy is so riddled with errors that I grow impatient.

What are these "errors?" Here I can only say that the errors of philosophers spring from what William James called "a certain blindness in human beings." James tells a story of how he was driving through a backwoods region of America, and was appalled by the ugliness of the clearings, where the settlers had hacked down trees and built themselves log cabins. And at that moment, his driver suddenly commented approvingly on all the wonderful things that these settlers had accomplished, and James realized that for them, these clearings were not in the least ugly; they represented the result of human effort in its struggle against chaos.

All philosophers allow their own temperament to intrude into their beliefs. This is why Edmund Husserl felt the need to create a truly "scientific" philosophy, which he called phenomenology.

Dostoevsky's problem as a writer was that he was so sensitive to criticism, so inclined to fits of petulance and resentment, that he was always picking his scabs and licking his wounds. If he had not been arrested for "revolutionary activities," he would probably have turned into a petty, resentful egoist. His near-execution and the years in Siberia saved him from this. Yet to the end of his days he nursed an oversensitive ego that tormented him like a bad toothache.

Seen purely objectively, Dostoevsky's achievement is extraordinary. His family was poverty stricken, even though his father was an "aristocrat." His gentle, frail mother put up with her violent and neurotic husband until she died of consumption in her thirties; Dostoevsky's father's murder followed. For most of his life, Dostoevsky fought poverty, and lived in slums, surrounded by human misery. Yet although he wrote so powerfully of human misery, he was also able to achieve moments of total affirmation—like Alyosha's ecstasy as he looks at the night sky. He surmounted his suffering to become a great writer.

This is what I would have said to Nabokov if I had met him face-to-face.

Yet I can now see that there is another side to the argument. Dostoevsky was always slightly paranoid. Even as a cadet, he was disliked because he was so thin-skinned, and took offense too easily. *Poor Folk* was a success because he grafted the subject matter of Dickens—with a touch of Balzac—on to Gogol's *Overcoat*. The mixture was highly original—hence its impact on his contemporaries.

The problem is that it does seem to be influenced by the worst of Dickens—for example, those gloomy and lachrymose stories in *Pickwick Papers*, full of dying children and starving mothers. Nekrasov sobbed at the scene where the father of the poor student, Pokrovsky, is so distracted by his son's death that he drops a paper trail of his books at the funeral. But this kind of thing, intended to bring a tear to the eye and a sob to the throat, is a little too calculated.

The other major feature of Dostoevsky's work is the strange, hysterical characters who seem to wallow in their own weakness and self-contempt. Their line runs from Golyadkin in *The Double*—the oppressed little clerk who goes mad—through Marmeladov in *Crime and Punishment*, down to old Karamazov, with his silly chatter and his debauchery. Such characters obviously sprang out of Dostoevsky's own self-division and hysteria. Not unnaturally, they strike most normal people as thoroughly irritating. So when Dostoevsky tried to combine his two favorite themes—misery and hysteria—in *The Double*, it provoked some harsh criticism, which led Dostoevsky to new heights of misery and hysteria.

It seems to me that what Matthew Arnold said about poetry is also true of the novel—that it is a "criticism of life." Its aim, like that of a computer manual, is to teach us to master a difficult and complex subject. It also seems to me incumbent on the critic to make a powerful effort to be detached and fair. And since Dostoevsky is quite obviously biased and unfair, his "criticism" is going to be as misleading as a computer manual that continually contradicts itself.

It seems to me that the answer to the basic problem of human existence is fairly straightforward. Doctor Johnson said, "The thought that he is to be hanged in a fortnight concentrates a man's mind wonderfully." Most of our human problems arise from the fact that our minds are so unconcentrated. And when the mind is unconcentrated, the will fails to do its proper work—of recharging our vital batteries, and keeping us at a high level of drive and purpose.

In most twentieth-century literature, there is a continual emphasis on the superficiality of modern life, on the lack of challenge that stifles the will. This is very obviously the theme of *The Waste Land*, and of Hemingway's *The Sun Also Rises*, and it runs through the novels of D. H. Lawrence. Yet when we examine this "criticism" more closely, we see that it is largely the fault of the writers themselves. Whenever we are faced with some crisis, it has the effect of galvanizing the will, and filling us with a desire to return to the state of affairs before the crisis loomed on the horizon. In other words, a desire for a quiet life, which is precisely what Eliot and Hemingway and Lawrence are criticizing.

Yet when we are facing crisis, we feel that if only it would go away, life would be delightful. We can see that all we have to do is to recall this crisis to feel delighted and relieved that it has gone away. In other words, we merely have to draw upon the power of imagination. In fact, we ought to be able to feel delighted with the present by merely imagining some potential problem, and realizing how lucky we are that it has not materialized.

Crises have the power of arousing what might be called the "deep will," as opposed to the "superficial will" that we exert upon trivial problems. Modern writers, from Dostoevsky onward, complain that our lives themselves are so devoid of real challenge that we only exercise the "superficial will," which fails to recharge our vital batteries. But implicit in this comment is the assumption that we can only arouse "deep will" by facing some deep crisis. And this is clearly not true. Human beings differ from animals because they possess imagination, a mental life apart from the physical. I can, for example, awaken my "deep will" by reading Hemingway's *El Sordo on the Hilltop*, or by reading Dostoevsky's *House of the Dead*, with its account of criminals and their crimes. In fact, I can stir myself out of my sloth by merely imagining some crisis that will never happen.

This ability to arouse the "deep will" by the use of imagination is one of the most remarkable faculties that man possesses. Dostoevsky certainly ought to have grasped this, having stood in front of a firing squad. And indeed, to some extent he did—but by no means enough. The "problems" of most of his characters are not real problems. If Marmeladov is really so conscience-stricken about his wife and daughter, he would stop drinking away his wages, and set out to give them a better life. Sonia's naive faith in the Bible is no answer—merely comforting herself with fairy stories. And Dostoevsky's appeal to religious faith is also no answer. He has stacked the cards unfairly against his characters—by presenting their stupidity and ineptitude as a part of the problem—that the only solution would appear to lie in the grace of God; in fact, a little common sense would go a long way towards solving it.

18

NIETZSCHE

I have already described how, at the age of twelve or thirteen, reading Einstein had plunged me into a state I called "nihilism"—belief in nothing. I knew, of course, that Einstein had not intended his work to have "moral" implications, for an essay by Einstein in a book called *I Believe* indicated that his views were fairly (as it seemed to me then) conventional.

My problem was that I craved some kind of certainty, and felt that everything was uncertain. At that age, you badly want someone to admire, but all the adults around me seemed fools. One vicar with whom I got into an argument told me I was suffering from "intellectual indigestion." To me, he seemed simply another fool who had decided to make his living by telling lies.

The problem, as far as I could see, is that human beings do not want truth; they merely want some comforting lie that will satisfy their emotions. It seemed to me that people who believed that Jesus had "saved" them must know that this was almost certainly untrue.

What really troubled me was that I could see why people were content to accept a "truth" without examining it. Why should they? I had imbibed my idea of truth from science—the notion that the universe was basically rational, and that it ought to be possible to understand it. But why should ordinary people bother to understand it? What would they have to gain? The answer, it seemed to me, was obvious: nothing. On the contrary, they would have a great deal to lose by destroying their comforting illusions.

Moreover, what did I have to gain? The answer again was: nothing. My determination to try to understand "truth" brought me nothing but misery and depression. On the whole, stupid people seemed far happier than intelligent ones—they went to their football matches, and sang their sentimental songs in pubs, and never asked themselves uncomfortable questions.

Like T. E. Lawrence, I often found myself envying a soldier with his girl, or a man patting his dog, because they were simple and undivided.

If most human beings were not interested in "truth," what were they interested in? The answer seemed obvious: self-esteem. Everybody wanted to have a reason for feeling "superior" to others. If my father spoke of his boss at work, it was always in a slightly patronizing tone. And although my mother was an ardent film fan, she often remarked that Hollywood stars were not really happy—the fact that they divorced and remarried so often proved it.

What really drove people, I concluded, was a will to power. Everyone would like to be the most powerful individual on earth—or, in the case of women, the most beautiful and alluring.

So when, one day, I saw a book in the library called *The Will to Power*, I retreated to the nearest table, and began to read.

This book, it explained in the translator's preface, was intended to be Nietzsche's "greatest theoretical and philosophical prose work." His *Thus Spake Zarathustra* had caused such misunderstandings that he saw the necessity for some major work that would make his meanings quite clear. Unfortunately, he had gone insane before it could be finished, and even the present edition, in two volumes, was incomplete.

I was fascinated by the account of how Nietzsche had first decided that the "will to power" was the basic human impulse. According to Frau Forster-Nietzsche, the idea had "first occurred to her brother in the year 1870 . . . while he was serving as a volunteer in a German Army Ambulance Unit" in the Franco-Prussian war.

"On one occasion, at the close of a very heavy day with the wounded, he happened to enter a small town which lay on one of the chief military roads. He was wandering through it in a leisurely fashion when, suddenly, as he turned the corner of a street that was protected by lofty stone walls, he heard a roaring noise, like thunder, which seemed to come from the immediate neighborhood. He hurried forward a step or to, and what should he see but a magnificent cavalry regiment . . . ride past him like a luminous storm cloud. The thundering din became louder and louder, and, lo and behold, his own beloved cavalry regiment of field artillery dashed forward at full speed . . . and sped westward amid an uproar of clattering chains and galloping steeds. A minute or two elapsed, and then a column of infantry appeared, advancing at the double—the men's eyes were aflame, their feet struck the hard road like mighty hammer strokes, and their accoutrements glistened through the haze. While this procession passed before him, on its way to war, and perhaps to death . . . Nietzsche was struck with the thought that the highest will to live could not find its expression in a miserable 'struggle for existence,' but in will to war, a Will to Power, a will to overpower."

The translator—Anthony Ludovici—goes on to say that twelve years later, Nietzsche put the concept into *Thus Spake Zarathustra*:

"Whenever I found a living thing, there I found a Will to Power, and even in the will of the servant found I the will to be master."

I was excited to find someone whose thought was so close to my own, and even more excited to find that the opening chapter was called *Nihilism*, the word I used to describe my own sense of lack of belief in anything. Nietzsche wrote, "What does Nihilism mean? That the highest values are losing their value. There is no refuge. There is no answer to the question: To what purpose?"

Yet as I read on, I found myself baffled and disappointed. Nietzsche went on to talk about Christianity, and seemed to be obsessed by morality, and something he called "metaphysics." I think I was hoping for something more akin to Schopenhauer (who, of course, I had never read), with a denunciation of all human values as illusions. It was hard to see what Nietzsche was driving at.

I took *Thus Spake Zarathustra* off the shelf, and read its opening section—how Zarathustra came down from the mountains, and met an old saint, who spoke to him of God. And as they separated, Zarathustra said to himself, "Has he not heard that God is dead?" Then followed the passage in which Zarathustra goes into the marketplace and tells the people, "I teach you the Superman. Man is something that has to be surpassed . . ."

I saw his point: man was something that had to be surpassed. Yet what difference would that make if truth remained unattainable?

At this point I saw another Nietzsche title on the shelf: *Human, All Too Human*, that expressed my own basic feeling about my fellow men. But a glance inside the book convinced me that there was nothing here for me. It began with a long discussion of the shortcomings of philosophers, and was beyond my understanding. I closed it and put it back.

It was about a year later, when I had discovered Shaw's *Man and Superman*, that I went back to *Zarathustra*, this time with more understanding. When I read the eighth chapter, *The Tree on the Hillside*, I recognized my own problem. A young man who has always avoided Zarathustra admits, "I no longer trust myself since I aspired to the heights, and no one trusts me any more . . . I change too fast; my today contradicts my yesterday . . . When I am at the top I find myself alone. . . . The frost of loneliness makes me shiver."

But I could see that Zarathustra was speaking common sense when he replied, "You are not free—you still search for freedom. You are exhausted from your search and overtired."

I also knew what he meant when he said, "Your soul thirsts for the stars. But your wicked instincts too want freedom." For by this time I was experiencing a continual sexual fever. It seemed to me that if I could undress a girl and make love to her, the ecstasy would be so great that it would transform me. It seemed unfair that the world should be so full of attractive schoolgirls, all looking for boyfriends, and yet that there should be no one for me. And the contrast between my obsession with truth, and my desire for a girl—any girl—made me feel a kind of freak, almost a monster.

I was also amazed to discover, in Yeats' autobiography, a passage in which he admitted that, as a young man, he had indulged in masturbation to the point of exhaustion. That seemed to me an incredibly courageous admission, and one that would have cost me an agony of shame. (I failed to note that Yeats had written this in later life.)

It was four or five years more, after I had been in the RAF, that I finally began to achieve something of the sense of affirmation that Nietzsche wrote about in *Zarathustra*.

I had enjoyed my early days of National Service in the RAF—where I had to spend eighteen months—with their "square bashing" and hard work. As a civilian, I had grown into too much of a recluse, and it was a relief to fall into bed at nine o'clock so exhausted that I immediately fell asleep, no matter how much noise there was going on around me. But when I had finished this basic training, I was posted to a camp near Nottingham—twenty-eight miles from Leicester—and set to work as a clerk in an office. I had wanted to work as a medical orderly—I had spent a week in a hospital with muscular strain, and decided that being a male nurse was the kind of job I would enjoy. I had spent more than a year in the Civil Service, and had come to hate offices. Now I was bored, angry, and inefficient. The only consolation was that I had plenty of time to read. I was one of the few regular members of staff on an Auxiliary Anti-Aircraft unit, and most of the other airmen arrived only on weekends.

Unfortunately, my boredom showed, and the adjutant became increasingly hostile and bad-tempered. Under his barrage of criticism, I became resentful—what right had this brainless idiot to lord it over me? One evening, I had to stay late to type a letter. The next morning, he waved it under my nose, saying it was a disgraceful mess, and asking me if I wasn't ashamed of myself. That was too much, and I snapped, "No." He looked astonished and told me to wait in the next room. I contemplated throwing a bottle of ink at him as he came in, but fortunately decided against it, for he was astonishingly reasonable. He asked me what was the matter, and I told him I was sick of being a clerk—that I wanted to become a medical orderly. He told me to go and see the Medical Officer, and that if he would certify that I was temperamentally unsuited to being a clerk, then I could be transferred.

Sitting opposite the M.O., I had a sudden inspiration—I told him I was homosexual, and that my nervous tension was due to being in a billet with so many attractive males.

As it happened, I knew all about homosexuality, because for the past two years, my closest friend in Leicester had been a homosexual. The friendship was based on the fact that he was virtually the only well-read person I knew in my hometown, and that he, like me, was determined to become a writer. He had read Proust so many times that he knew it by heart. Inevitably, he had told me he loved me, and that he felt I could be his inspiration; I replied, with the unconscious cruelty of a totally heterosexual male, that I saw myself as Dante, not as Beatrice.

But now I used Alan's case history to convince the M.O. that I was homosexual, and that the sight of muscular males undressing at night was giving me a nervous breakdown.

My intention was only to get myself transferred to the medical branch. But to my astonishment, I was out of the RAF within a few weeks.

I was determined not to return to the Civil Service. And when my RAF pay ceased, I began taking laboring jobs on building sites. It was—as I have already described—while working on a fairground that I met Sylvia, and this first experience of sex confirmed in me the new sense of optimism that drove me.

Suddenly, it seemed quite clear to me that I had wasted most of my teens in a sterile intellectualism. In retrospect, I can see that I was failing to grasp what was happening. Throughout my early teens I had felt an awkward adolescent, trapped in my own immaturity. I had become accustomed to a sense of frustration and futility—two words that ran like a refrain through my journals. Now, suddenly, I had decided to stop being passive. Allowing my frustration to explode at the adjutant had changed my life. I recalled the sudden realization of H. G. Wells' Mr. Polly, "If you don't like your life you can change it." I determined that never again would I work at some job I hated. I would rather, like Mr. Polly, become a tramp.

What had happened, in effect, was that I had come to accept myself as an "outsider"—but had suddenly realized that there was no need to be an unhappy outsider. In the Middle Ages, outsiders found refuge in the Church. In India, they became religious wanderers. I resolved that, if necessary, I would also become a "wanderer."

The decision marked a fundamental change in my attitude to myself. I felt like a chrysalis that has suddenly changed into a butterfly.

My father had been baffled and upset when I told him that I had resigned from the Civil Service. He could simply not understand why the "clever" one of the family wanted to work on building sites. He grew so embarrassed when his friends in the pub asked him what his son was doing that he finally ordered me to leave home. I set off with a few pounds in my pocket—borrowed from my mother and grand-mother—and hitchhiked down to Kent, where I took a job potato picking, then sorting apples—the farmer allowed me to sleep in a ruined cottage. I crossed the Channel to France, and in Paris, stayed for a while at the "Academe" run by Raymond Duncan, the brother of the famous dancer Isadora. Then, driven on as usual by deep-seated dissatisfaction, I went on to Strasbourg, and stayed for a while with a pen friend. His parents soon grew tired of my presence, and after two weeks I borrowed the fare from the British consulate and returned to England.

During all that time I had carried in my knapsack a copy of the *Bhagavad Gita*, and *Thus Spake Zarathustra*, in the Everyman edition (I have it beside me on the table as I write, roughly bound in leather).

Now, at last, I had come to understand the book—that Nietzsche was speaking about great health. I no longer saw myself as a tormented romantic misfit, doomed to die in misery and frustration. If the worst came to the worst, I would enter a monastery. (But when, as a preliminary step, I went for instruction to a Catholic priest, I soon came to the conclusion that Catholic dogma was nonsense, and gave it up.)

Now, at last, I began to see the true significance of Nietzsche. During the nineteenth century, dozens of men of genius had been destroyed by that problem of "outsiderism"—the sudden glimpses of ecstasy and intensity, followed by entrapment in the "triviality of everydayness." Van Gogh had committed suicide leaving a note that read, "Misery will never end." So many had committed suicide or died in despair. They suspected that the "real world," and the world they glimpsed in moments of ecstasy, were separated by a great gulf. Plato was partly responsible, for making Socrates declare—on his death-bed—that since the philosopher spends his life trying to separate body and soul, death is a consummation. Nietzsche was the first to see that he was talking nonsense.

Nietzsche had recognized, in effect, that the man of genius must stop regarding himself as a misfit, a victim. His genius qualifies him to be a pathfinder. This was why I was fascinated by figures like George Fox and John Bunyan; they had recognized that their religious despair was due to the frustration of their impulse to "say what was in them." Once they began to say it, they were accepted as teachers instead of social misfits.

Now, in retrospect, I can see that Nietzsche followed a path that was very like my own. His father had been a minister, but reading Schopenhauer cured Nietzsche of the last vestiges of Christianity. He plunged into pessimism, the conviction that all human effort is futile, based on illusions. Then, one day, in the depth of his despair, he saw the answer. He had gone to climb a nearby hill, and a rainstorm forced him to take shelter in a hut in which a shepherd was killing young goats. At that moment, the storm broke with a tremendous crash, and rain battered down on the roof. Nietzsche would normally have been disgusted with the smell of blood and the sight of the slaughter, but the thunder and lightning caused a surge of exultation that filled him with a sense of total affirmation. He described the experience in a letter to a friend, and wrote, "Will, pure will, without the troubles and perplexities of intellect—how happy, how free!"

He became the youngest professor of philology in Germany. When he heard the music of Wagner, he was carried away, as he had been by the storm. For a while he became an ardent Wagnerite, and expressed his admiration in a long essay in his *Thoughts Out of Season*, and in *The Birth of Tragedy from the Spirit of Music*, which glorifies Dionysian ecstasy.

All this gave him a completely new perspective on Germany and German culture and philosophy; it also led to a decisive rejection of Christianity, with its glorification of meekness and surrender. He must have felt that he was the only person in Germany who saw things clearly.

This emerges in *Human, All Too Human*, which had baffled me so much at the age of thirteen. Now, as I reread it, I could see why Nietzsche felt so impatient. He said that philosophers seem to regard man as fixed and unchangeable, failing to grasp how much he has evolved over dozens of millennia, and how much, therefore, he can evolve. Philosophers, he said, sit in front of their lives and experience them as if sitting in front of a picture in an art gallery. But this is a failure to recognize the dynamic nature of reality.

In any case, says Nietzsche, the philosopher is not seeing "reality;" "we have surfeited ourselves on the vices of illogical thought," and we are seeing meanings that we have put there. The phenomenon (he uses the word in Kant's sense of the world we see around us) is largely a product of human emotions, human needs.

Now the obvious next step would be to try to create a method of philosophizing that would do its best to try to filter out this "human" element. But it would be more than thirty years before one of the greatest philosophers of the twentieth century, Edmund Husserl, set out to create such a method—an attempt to "pull back," to see things coolly and without prejudice. Nietzsche was not yet ready for this. He could merely see that modern philosophy and modern culture are ninety percent prejudice, and wanted to take a hammer to it. So his books are explosions of impatience; he sets out to offend and outrage. He succeeded all too well, and during his most important creative period, was attacked and misunderstood. Ironically, his contemporaries only began to understand his greatness after he had lost his mind.

From the point of view of the history of philosophy and western culture, this was fortunate. If Nietzsche had set out to create a method, as Husserl did, no one would have been interested—except a few academic philosophers. By stating his opinions in such impatient and defiant terms, he attracted other rebels, and became the most influential thinker since Hegel.

At the time I wrote of Nietzsche, in *The Outsider*, no "respectable" philosopher took him seriously; Bertrand Russell's sneering attack in *The History of Western Philosophy* is typical. And there is a sense in which this suspicion of Nietzsche is not entirely unjustified. *A Genealogy of Morals* is a very dangerous book, for it formulates the idea of what he calls "master and slave morality"—the notion that the "good" is identical with the noble, the aristocratic, and that the bad is identified with the plebeian, the stupid. It is easy to see how convenient the Nazis found this philosophy in justifying their own brutality—although, as Nietzsche would have pointed out, they were fundamentally un-Nietzschean in that they were stupid.

In fact, the real problem with the thesis of *A Genealogy of Morals* is that the noble and the aristocrat are just as likely to be stupid as the plebeian. I had noted in my teens that major writers are usually those who have had to struggle against the odds—to "pull their cart out of the mud," as I put it—while writers who have had an easy start in life are usually second-rate—or at least, not quite first-rate. Dickens, Balzac, Dostoevsky, Shaw, H. G. Wells, are examples of the first kind; in the twentieth century, John Galsworthy, Graham Greene, Evelyn Waugh, and Samuel Beckett are examples of the second kind. They are far from being mediocre writers; yet they tend to be tinged with a certain pessimism that arises from never having achieved a certain resistance against problems.

The problem, quite simply, is that human beings are slaves to the force of habit, and it is habit that tends to confine us in our laziness. If a Martian psychologist wrote a book about human beings, it would probably have a title like *The Pessimistic Animal*. For left to itself, without external stimulus, human consciousness tends inevitably to degenerate into depression and pessimism. This is because when we are not involved in some kind of action, consciousness tends to get stuck in boredom, and a boring palace is no better than a boring hovel.

When I was a child, one of the first fairy stories I learned was the tale of the old woman in the vinegar bottle. A good fairy, flying above a ditch, hears a voice complaining, "Oh dear, oh dear!" and finds a little old woman who is so poor that she is forced to live in a vinegar bottle. With a wave of her hand, the fairy changes it into a pretty cottage. But when she passes by a few weeks later, the old woman is still moaning, "Oh dear, oh dear." The cottage is damp and the well too far down the garden. So the fairy changes the cottage into a house. Weeks later, the old woman is still complaining—it is too drafty, too hard to keep clean. The fairy changes it into a palace with servants. A few weeks later the old woman is still complaining—the servants are dishonest and lazy. This time, the fairy changes it back into a vinegar bottle.

My own observation of human beings is, that while they hate inconveniences and difficulties, they quickly become accustomed to a life without problems, and feel bored. The mind seems to collapse under its own weight. People living in the most delightful circumstances can be bored and unhappy.

This observation means that Nietzsche's distinction between "noble" and "plebeian" loses most of its force in the real world. On this point, Nietzsche was, quite simply, too simplistic. What human beings need, quite clearly, is a sense of reality—what the psychologist Janet calls "the reality function." Nietzsche's heroes—Cesare Borgia, Machiavelli and the rest—are tiresome bores. We have to recognize that Nietzsche himself was a sick man and a poor man; when he retired from academic life—through ill health—he spent most of his days in a cold room, with a blanket round his knees, writing these works that hurl defiance at the world.

Whether or not Nietzsche became insane through syphilitic infection, it is certain that his loneliness, and the total hostility with which his works were received, were enough to have affected his mind.

I can sympathize, because after *The Outsider*, reaction to my own books was hostile. Because of the accident of being associated with the playwright John Osborne and the "Angry Young Men," I received far more publicity than is good—or useful—for any young writer, and the result was a violent reaction in England. One newspaper editor told a friend of mine, who wanted to review one of my books, "I hope never to print the name of Colin Wilson again."

But at least I had a wife and family, and a happy domestic background—even if a book had been savaged by the critics, I could relax in the evening with a glass of wine, telling my children a fairy story. One day in the early 1960s, my publisher wrote me a letter suggesting that perhaps I should give up trying to write for a living, and instead take a "regular job" with a newspaper, or in a publisher's office, and write books as a spare-time occupation. For a few minutes, I was plunged into total depression—when suddenly, my small daughter Sally laughed in the next bedroom, and my misery vanished as abruptly as a bursting bubble.

Without a wife and children, Nietzsche lacked this counterweight to depression. In theory, Nietzsche knew the answer to the romantic pessimism of his age:

"The psychology of the orgiastic as an overflowing feeling of life and strength, where even pain still has the effect of a stimulus, gave me the key to the concept of tragic feeling . . . Tragedy is so far from proving anything about the pessimism of the Hellenes . . . that it may, on the contrary, be considered its decisive repudiation and counter-instance. Saying Yes to life, even in its strangest and hardest problems, the will to life rejoicing over its own inexhaustibility, even in the very sacrifice of its highest types—that is what I called Dionysian, that is what I guessed to be the bridge to the psychology of the tragic poet."

This was written in 1888, the year before he became insane. He is probably wrong about Greek tragedy; yet this passage reveals the essence of Nietzsche, and the reason for his violent reaction against what he called the "slave morality" of his time, whether it appeared as Christianity or communism. He experienced occasionally that overwhelming sense of sheer vitality and ecstasy that Dostoevsky experienced just before an epileptic attack.

Now in fact, Nietzsche is simply expressing the point of view that has traditionally been expressed by the poet. For example, Rupert Brooke writes about being *In Examination*:

> *Lo! from quiet skies*
> *In through the window my Lord the Sun!*
> *And my eyes*
> *Were dazzled and drunk with the misty gold,*
> *The golden glory that drowned and crowned me*
> *Eddied and swayed through the room . . .*
> > *Around me,*
> *To left and to right*
> *Hunched figures and old,*
> *Dull blear-eyed scribbling fools, grew fair*
> *Ringed round and haloed with holy light . . .*

Yeats makes the same point in *The Scholars*:

Bald heads forgetful of their sins,
Old, learned, respectable bald heads
Edit and annotate the lines
That young men, tossing on their beds,
Rhymed out in love's despair
To flatter beauty's ignorant ear.

This is why Nietzsche has been regarded as one of the first existentialists; he is judging philosophy by the living reality it attempts to circumscribe, and finding it wanting. He is determined to create a philosophy that keeps its feet in the living reality.

But in doing so, Nietzsche is himself inclined to be unreasonable. He chooses Christianity as one of his main opponents because he feels that it is based on "slave morality." Yet if Nietzsche had been able to wave a magic wand, and transform the world into whatever he wanted, would he actually have destroyed Christianity? Would he have made all copies of the Bible and the Christian hymnal disappear into thin air, and be replaced by *Thus Spake Zarathustra* and his hymns of Dionysus? The answer is obviously no, for if we actually envisage this situation, we can see that this would fail to bring about the kind of change that Nietzsche has in mind.

Nietzsche's critics might suggest that what he would really like to see is something like the Third Reich, with its policy of extermination of the weak. But that is clearly a mistake—Nietzsche would have hated the Nazi thugs, just as his spiritual descendant Spengler hated them. (Even Heidegger, who agreed to serve under the Nazis, quickly realized his mistake and backed out.)

The truth was that what Nietzsche wanted was the secret of maintaining a high level of affirmation and vitality—what Abraham Maslow calls the "peak experience." He could see that his rather dull, scholarly life was not the solution. He admired the "bluestocking" Lou Salome enough to propose to her, but was certainly lucky that she turned him down—the marriage would have been a disaster.

In fact, it has to be admitted that, where his reputation was concerned, what actually happened to Nietzsche was probably the best thing that could have happened. To die insane stamped his life with tragedy—the suggestion that he became insane because he was the archetypal "outsider," living alone with his thoughts on a kind of spiritual mountaintop. It is almost impossible to imagine a "successful" Nietzsche, wealthy from the proceeds of his books, and surrounded by disciples. It is almost as if Nietzsche chose the manner of his own death, preferring to slip away just as his name was about to become famous.

Perhaps the strangest irony is that after a century of being a philosophical "outsider," sneered at by every academic philosopher, Nietzsche has once again come into his own, until he is today as respectable as Kant or Hegel.

This came about in a curiously roundabout manner. Husserl's disciple, Heidegger, was anxious to establish his own identity. He began as a typical nineteenth-century Romantic, denouncing technology and its effect on modern life—at this stage he sounds a little like the Eliot of *The Waste Land*. Then he announced that all philosophy since Plato has been a blind alley. In pondering about the meaning of the universe—a practice known as metaphysics—philosophers have simply imposed their own emotions on it, and lost sight of the miraculous fact that it actually exists. It is this "forgetfulness of existence"—encouraged by technology—that has entrapped us in "the triviality of everydayness." Philosophy, declared Heidegger, must return to the contemplation of existence—and specifically, human existence. From then on, Heidegger's philosophy became a study of man's "mode of being" in the world, with pessimistic overtones reminiscent of Schopenhauer.

In saying that man has imposed his own emotions on existence, Heidegger is repeating what Nietzsche said. So Heidegger claimed Nietzsche as an important forebear.

It is true that Heidegger himself was not really respectable, particularly after his flirtation with Nazism. I once spent an afternoon with the philosopher Karl Popper, and I commented that it seemed to me a pity that Heidegger had not been included in Northwestern University's Library of Living Philosophers. Popper replied indignantly that if the editors had contemplated including Heidegger, he—Popper—would have refused to allow himself to be included.

But whether or not tainted with Nazism, it was a reading of Heidegger's *Being and Time* that stunned Sartre in the 1930s, and that led Sartre to try and outdo him in *Being and Nothingness*.

The new generation of French philosophers saw it as their business to outdo Sartre, and Gilles Deleuze wrote a remarkable and perceptive little book on Nietzsche in 1962. It must be admitted that Deleuze's style is dull and academic, suggesting that the same is true of his mind. This impression is false. Moreover, Deleuze was wryly aware of his own tendency to academicism, and his later work (with Felix Guattari) has been a flight from it. So his admiration of Nietzsche was, so to speak, an attempt to unite with his opposite. His book was quickly recognized as a classic, and did a great deal to make Nietzsche respectable in France—whose rationalistic philosophy Nietzsche had detested.

Then came Jacques Derrida, prophet of "deconstruction," who was heavily influenced by Husserl and Heidegger, and later (regrettably) by Saussure. He began by taking it for granted that all "metaphysics" is self-delusion. But this extremism placed him in the same position as Heidegger, who had never written the second volume of *Being and Time*, because a philosophy based on rejection of metaphysics—and therefore of reason—is bound to end by swallowing its own tail.

This had been the great dilemma of existentialism ever since Kierkegaard. Kierkegaard had attacked Hegel (without actually reading him) on the same grounds that Ivan Karamazov wanted to give God back his entrance ticket—that no assurance that "everything is for the best in this best of all possible worlds" can somehow make sense of the sufferings of a child. Kierkegaard objected that Hegel was too abstract and failed to take account of the sufferings of real life. He used the word "existential" (which he virtually coined) as a contrast to unrealistic abstraction. But if a philosopher is not allowed to be abstract, then he is not allowed to philosophize, for philosophy is an abstraction from real life. A century after Kierkegaard, Ernest Hemingway found himself in exactly the same double bind, and died as an artist long before his suicide.

The problem with rejecting metaphysics is that it always lands the philosopher in a kind of materialism. In fact, it is just a rerun of the old medieval dispute between nominalists and realists. The "realists" were, oddly enough, not materialists; they agreed with Plato that ideas are real, existing independently of real things. For example, the notion of a circle is a reality, even if it could be proved that every actual circle in the world is not quite round. Nominalists disagreed. They said that the word circle is not an idea—merely a name for a real thing.

It seems to me that realists, including Plato, are plainly correct, and that nominalists are wrong. Hemingway is actually a nominalist. He insists that we are living in a purely material world, that death is the end, and refuses to have anything to do with ideas. And, as we have seen, Hemingway's philosophy drained his work of all possibility of development. This is always true of nominalism as a philosophy.

Now Derrida claims that he is not actually a philosopher. Just as Nietzsche claimed to be a philosopher with a hammer, so Derrida could be compared to a man with a rifle, shooting down balloons. What he likes to do is to show that philosophers are introducing metaphysical concepts, and to shoot them down. Rousseau, for example, declared that he preferred masturbation to real sex, and referred to it as "the supplement," obviously feeling that "real sex" is the substance of which masturbation is only the shadow. Derrida points out that "real sex" involves a mental element, and is therefore a kind of masturbation. He is obviously correct.

But then sex, as I have argued elsewhere in this book, is a special case. It is in the interests of nature to make us believe that when a female gives herself to a male, something tremendous and momentous has taken place. This is why Othello kills Desdemona, and why Tarquin rapes Lucrece. Derrida is "deconstructing" the sexual illusion, which is not hard to do.

On the other hand, D. H. Lawrence insists that something momentous has taken place when a man and a woman make love, and calls the penis "the rod that connects man with the stars." He insists that the reality of sex brings us back to the reality of the universe—in other words, that it awakens us from Heidegger's "forgetfulness of existence." So Lawrence would accuse Derrida of being the "abstract" thinker who has lost sight of reality.

I personally reject Derrida because he seems to me to be thinking about the wrong things—the same grounds on which Nietzsche rejected rationalistic philosophers. Nietzsche felt that truth lies in the "overflowing feeling of life and strength," and that we ought to be thinking about that and how to achieve it. He would reject Derrida's balloon-shooting as a kind of game.

Now it seems to me that this criticism of Derrida is correct, and that, like Ernest Hemingway, he is subject to a kind of law of diminishing returns because he is a "nominalist." But I am inclined to feel that the same applies to Nietzsche, and to his philosophizing with a hammer. He may have made some bad cracks in Christian morality and the western philosophical tradition. But if we ask, "Then what is your solution?" he can offer us no answer. His emphasis on the

Dionysian feeling could certainly be interpreted as a defense of war, but war is clearly no answer either. A sex murderer might argue that Nietzsche justifies him in pursuing sexual ecstasy through "sex with the stranger," but again, it is quite clearly no solution to the basic problem of human existence—sex killers tend to end empty-handed, with a sense of futility. (The absurd mistakes that often lead to their capture look oddly like an unconscious desire to be caught.)

I would suggest that the person who came closest to seeing the answer was Dostoevsky when he stood in front of a firing squad, and when he made Raskolnikov declare that if he had to stand on a narrow ledge forever and ever, in eternal darkness and tempest, he would rather do that than die at once.

Doctor Johnson also saw the answer when he remarked—as quoted in an earlier chapter—that when a man knows he is to be hanged in a fortnight, it concentrates his mind wonderfully.

This concentration of mind, of attention, is clearly the road to a new phase of human evolution. This, I believe, is what Nietzsche meant by the superman. Nietzsche attempted to show such a type in Zarathustra—a man who has taught himself mental concentration that makes him stronger and healthier than most human beings.

It seems to me that this vision constitutes Nietzsche's greatness. And the fact that he was the first Romantic to see the errors of romanticism, and to see clearly beyond it, makes him one of the most important philosophers of the past two centuries.

19

THE JAMES BROTHERS

W hen I was in my late teens, I regarded Henry James as the greatest novelist in the world, and his *Art of the Novel*—his collected prefaces—as a kind of bible.

I had come across James' *Daisy Miller* in a volume of classic short stories, borrowed from our school library, and found it incredibly difficult to read.

It is, of course, a kind of love story. A young American student in Switzerland meets an extremely pretty American girl in a hotel garden, and is puzzled and amused by her directness and naiveté; it never seems to enter her head to flirt or do the things pretty young ladies normally do. Neither does she seem in the least troubled to be seen with him without a chaperone. Later, in Rome, her honesty and naiveté are misunderstood as wantonness, and she becomes something of a social outcast. Then, just as I was expecting the hero to propose to her, she dies of malaria. It all seemed rather pointless, and I was puzzled and disappointed.

I learned later that Henry James was regarded as a "difficult" writer, and this acted as a challenge. I found another of his stories—*Pandora*—and read it carefully and slowly. It was harder to read than *Daisy Miller*, and James was inclined to engage his characters in long conversations that seemed to get nowhere very slowly. The story also gets nowhere as the young German count, who has been fascinated by the American girl on a ship crossing the Atlantic, discovers that she is what is called "the self-made American girl," who dominates her parents, and virtually bullies the president of the United States into giving her fiancé a diplomatic post. I could not quite see why James had bothered to tell the story; it seemed like a joke without a punch line. Now, of course, I can see that it was not intended to be a story, but a sketch of a new type of woman. As it was, I felt somehow cheated. I decided that James demands an effort out of all proportion to what he is saying.

My next encounter with his work confirmed this. In an introduction to a volume of ghost stories, the editor regretted that there was not space to include the greatest ghost story of all time, James' *Turn of the Screw*. He went on to say that he would not like to read a ghost story by candlelight, underneath a gibbet with a swinging corpse, but that he would prefer to do this rather than read *The Turn of the Screw* again.

Naturally, I rushed to buy a copy—the Everyman edition which also contained *The Aspern Papers*. I began to read breathlessly, prepared to be thrilled. But I found the style oddly irritating. "The story had held us, round the fire, sufficiently breathless . . ." What does he mean "sufficiently breathless?" And when the governess comes to tell her story of the two children and the two ghosts who have "corrupted" them, James indulges in his most affected mannerisms. "She broke into a breathlessly affirmative groan." "She seemed to square herself, to plant herself more firmly to utter the wonder of it. 'Yes, Mr. Quint is dead.'" This language actually forms a barrier between the reader and the story. The impression that comes over is that if the governess had to tell the story in this absurdly complicated manner, then she was a fool. I persevered to the end, but thought it was one of the silliest novels I had ever read. As far as I was concerned, if I never read James again, it would be too soon.

But when I read F. O. Matthiessen's *Achievement of T. S. Eliot*, and learned that Eliot thought James "the most intelligent man of his generation," my interest revived. I regarded Eliot as the most intelligent man of his generation, and if he held James in high esteem, then I was willing to do the same.

James' *Portrait of a Lady* was issued in the World Classics, in an India paper edition, and I bought it. This was not as mannered as *The Turn of the Screw*, although the length finally defeated me. Then I came upon the short novel, *The Europeans*, about the impact made by two rather bohemian Europeans on their puritanical Boston cousins, and found it delightful. I also read James' first novel, *Roderick Hudson*, about a poverty-stricken young American sculptor who is taken under the wing of a wealthy patron, and goes to Rome. Yet what happens from then on was, for me, a disappointment. I identified entirely with Roderick; there was nothing I would have loved more than to find a wealthy patron and go to Rome. But Roderick, instead of finding fame and fortune, simply has a romance with a silly girl, and ends by falling to his death from a mountain. It was as if James was unwilling—or unable—to make the effort of imagination to offer Roderick real freedom.

I felt just as dissatisfied with *Portrait of a Lady*. Like Roderick Hudson, Isabel Archer is spirited out of a dull American background by a rich aunt, and taken to Europe. An English lord immediately proposes to her, but she turns him down, feeling that life is so full of rich possibilities that it would be a pity to settle down before she has sampled them. Her uncle leaves her half his fortune, and she goes to Italy, having turned down yet another suitor. But in Rome, she decides to marry a cultured and charming artistic dilettante, who proves to be interested only in her money. The marriage is unhappy, but at the end of the novel she returns to Italy—and her husband—with the feeling that she has made her bed and she has to lie on it.

It was obvious that James was preoccupied by the problem of how life could be lived fully, yet seemed—in his novels—unable to meet the challenge.

In 1948, Everyman's Library published *The Ambassadors*, and I hastened to buy it. This is written in James' later style, which I had found very irritating, but which I was now willing to accept because Eliot regarded him so highly. (Naturally, it affected my own style in the stories I wrote.) Once again, the theme was how to live fully. Lambert Strether, engaged to a rich widow, is sent by her to Paris to persuade her son, Chad, to return to America and take over his father's business. But Strether is so charmed by Europe, as well as by Chad's aristocratic mistress, that he now advises Chad against returning to America. "Live, live all you can—it's a mistake not to." He himself is finally forced to return, more or less in disgrace, no longer engaged to Chad's mother, and with uncertain prospects for the future.

Although I found the style tiresome, I read the book with absorption and admiration, for that "Live all you can" was exactly what I intended to do. But it seemed to me that, once again, James had given the book a disappointing ending. It was as if he did not believe that human beings could live fully.

By now I was a James enthusiast. When I left the tax office in Leicester to take up my first permanent post in Rugby, my colleagues took up a collection for me, and I devoted the money to buying James' last novel, *The Golden Bowl*, in two volumes, and getting everyone in the office to sign it. But I never succeeded in reading it from beginning to end.

The same was true of *The Wings of the Dove*, the last novel but one, based on James' cousin Minnie Temple, who had died young. Millie Theale is also dying when she falls in love with a penniless young journalist, Merton Densher. Densher is in love with an equally penniless woman, Kate Croy, who persuades him to get engaged to the wealthy Millie, who cannot live long. But after Millie's death, Densher realizes that he cannot marry Kate and live on Millie's money—his deceit would haunt him for the rest of his life. He gives the money to Kate, and remains penniless.

But what moved me about the book was James' comment about Millie. "In the end, death was terrible to her. She would have given anything to live." It was Dostoevsky's theme again, the recognition that life is infinitely valuable. It was for this reason that, although I never succeeded in finishing it, *The Wings of the Dove* struck me as James' most important novel.

When, after my RAF period, I hitchhiked to France, I took in my haversack F. O. Matthiessen's *Henry James, The Major Phase*, about the last three novels. (A library stamp in my copy reminds me that—I regret to confess—I stole it from the Canterbury public library; in those days I had virtually no conscience where books were concerned, although I would not have dreamed of stealing anything else.) And I wrote in the front of it, "To go through life as an observer is, after all, the Ideal." It seemed to me that Henry James was immensely lucky—to have enough money to be able to spend his days studying other people's lives and noting down his observations. I was not sufficiently realistic to see that life as a solitary bachelor was no more pleasant for James than it had been for Nietzsche.

So for years I continued to read James with admiration—but an admiration that was based on the idea that he was the most intelligent man of his age rather than on any real enjoyment of the novels. In 1952, when I was married and living in Wimbledon, south London, I saw an omnibus volume of James' American novels in a Stockwell bookshop; unfortunately, it was Sunday and the shop was closed. I seethed with impatience until I could return the next day and buy it. For years it remained a treasured possession. Yet I have to admit that I have never read it from beginning to end.

Again, after *The Outsider* came out, I bought virtually all of James, including Edel's set of the complete short stories, as well as his four-volume biography. Yet many of them have never been opened. I bought James as a kind of nostalgic gesture to my past rather than because I still wanted to read him.

The nostalgia is real enough. In my teens and early twenties, I often thought that, if some genie of the lamp would offer me the opportunity to meet some author of the past, I would choose Henry James without hesitation. It seemed to me that there could be no greater pleasure than spending hour after hour with James, asking him questions about the structure of his novels, and making him aware that, for at least one person, he was the world's greatest novelist.

Why did I cease to read Henry James? For the same reason we all cease to admire things we have admired in the past: I outgrew him. His sheltered life prevented him from maturing emotionally or intellectually and, like all old bachelors, he grew increasingly fussy and finicky—particularly in his style. It now seems incredible that he could have rewritten so much of his early work for the New York edition in the over-complex later style, failing to recognize that the early, more direct style was far more effective.

It was experience that changed Dostoevsky from the irritable, self-conscious dilettante of *Poor Folk* and *The Double* to the great novelist of *Crime and Punishment*. But James never had any experience, and so remained the victim of his own immaturity. The later work makes it clear that he has simply lost touch with life. It now seems obvious to me that James was never a great writer—although the young James has freshness and charm.

Yet Eliot was not entirely wrong; James was formidably intelligent. And it was his intelligence that made him long for psychological realism—to express fine nuances of psychological response in his dialogue. What remains astonishing is that he did not recognize that he was overdoing it, and becoming so subtle and allusive that he was simply asking too much of the reader.

His brother William deplored the later style, and this was one reason that, in the days when I admired Henry James so much, I was inclined to underrate William. Nevertheless, it was through Henry that I came to William, for in Matthiessen's *Henry James, The Major Phase*, I read of the appalling experience that had brought William James to the point of mental breakdown, and which James had cited in *The Varieties of Religious Experience.*

James describes how, in a state of anxiety about his future prospects, he entered a room at twilight, and suddenly recalled vividly the face of a patient he had seen in a lunatic asylum; the man was suffering from catatonia, and his eyes stared blankly from his green-colored face. "There but the grace of God go I," James thought. "If the hour should strike for me as it struck for him, nothing could save me from his fate." He says that he felt something "collapse inside him," and he was suddenly plunged into a state of profound gloom. For week after week after this experience, he would wake up with a sinking feeling in his stomach. He found it incomprehensible that his mother, a cheerful person, could be so happy when human life was so uncertain and fraught with dangers.

It seemed to him then that life was a purely mechanical process, and that we are mistaken to believe we possess free will. This conviction, of course, robbed him of all incentive to effort, and the lack of incentive seemed to confirm that life is meaningless.

He was finally rescued from this state of pessimism and depression by reading the French philosopher Charles Renouvier. Renouvier had commented that we know we possess free will because we can think one thing rather than another. I may feel that all my other actions can be explained away as mechanical stimulus and response. But there can be no doubt that I can turn my thoughts from one thing to another as often and as arbitrarily as I like. Hume was obviously wrong; our thought is not mere "association of ideas."

As soon as James became intellectually convinced that he possessed free will, his sense of futility and meaninglessness gradually dissolved away.

I borrowed *The Varieties of Religious Experience* from the library, and found it one of the most important and absorbing books I ever read. Years later, when asked by an interviewer what I regarded as the most important book ever published in America, I replied, *"The Varieties of Religious Experience."*

Yet even in this book, which I am inclined to regard as James' masterpiece, there are signs that he has failed to grasp the true meaning of his triumph over despair. He writes, "Unsuspectedly from the bottom of every fountain of pleasure . . . something bitter rises up: a touch of nausea, a falling dead of the delight, a whiff of melancholy, things that sound a knell, for fugitive as they may be, they bring a feeling of coming from a deeper region and often have an appalling convincingness."

It seems strange that James should fail to recognize that these "touches of nausea" (a remarkable anticipation of Sartre's use of the term) are merely due to a failure of energy. When we do things with purpose and conviction, we recharge our vital batteries, and the sudden flash of "life failure" never occurs. But when we begin to live mechanically, performing our everyday tasks as a mere habit, this robotic activity fails to recharge our vital batteries; then, suddenly, our inner resources are inadequate to meet some sudden challenge. Moreover, if we allow ourselves to be bullied and taken in by this feeling that something is not worth the effort, the boredom gains a foothold, and we can easily fall into the bad habit of trying to avoid effort.

Yet, as we shall see, James' essay *On Vital Reserves* makes it clear that this talk of nausea coming from "a deeper region" is a momentary aberration.

In those early days, a further incentive to read William James came from Whitehead—whom I came to admire more than any philosopher except Husserl; in *Science and the Modern World* he refers to James as "that adorable genius."

After *The Varieties of Religious Experience*, I next came upon James' essay *On a Certain Blindness in Human Beings*, in which he points out how our feelings can blind us to reality. This is the essay in which he describes driving through the mountains in North Carolina—I have mentioned it earlier, but it is so important that I will do so again—looking at the newly-cultivated patches of land (called "coves") covered with stumps of trees, which gave him an impression of "unmitigated squalor." He asked his driver what kind of people lived here, and the driver replied cheerfully, "We ain't happy here unless we're getting one of these coves under cultivation." And suddenly, James realized that he had been blind to the fact that these farmers regarded each "cove" as a personal victory, and saw them as beautiful.

James comments, "Wherever a process of life communicates an eagerness to him who lives it, there the life becomes genuinely significant"—summarizing also what is wrong with his brother's later novels. He quotes Stevenson, who has described the joy felt by boys in bulls-eye lanterns made out of an old tin, and smelling of heated metal, "For to miss the joy is to miss all." He speaks of the "mystic sense of hidden meaning" to be found in poets like Wordsworth and Walt Whitman, and prose writers like W. H. Hudson. The essay is a celebration of what the playwright Granville Barker calls "the secret life," the glow of meaning and purpose hidden inside everyone.

He continues the theme in his next lecture, *What Makes a Life Significant*? And in this he describes how he spent a week in the Chautauqua Community, a kind of utopian paradise on the shores of a lake in New York State, a place full of "sobriety and industry, intelligence and goodness, orderliness and ideality, prosperity and cheerfulness." There was a college, a fine concert hall, a gymnasium, churches, clubhouses and lecture halls—in short, everything to make man happy.

"And yet," says James, "what was my own astonishment, on emerging into the dark and wicked world again, to catch myself quite unexpectedly and involuntarily saying, 'Ouf! what a relief! Now for something primordial and savage, even though it were as bad as an Armenian massacre, to set the balance straight again. This order is too tame, this culture too second-rate, this goodness too uninspiring.'" And as he saw from the train a workman poised on the scaffolding of a high building, he realized that what human beings crave is the heroic.

Now this, of course, is precisely what Nietzsche is saying. It is also what Kierkegaard is saying when he objects to Hegel's "system," and what Dostoevsky's underground man is saying when he objects to a world in which everything is ordered and controlled. This is what Shaw's Captain Shotover means when he tells Ellie, "You are seeking a rich husband. At your age I sought horror, hardship, danger and death, that I might feel the life in me more intensely." Here once again we glimpse this basic existential problem that has been the subject of all my work. Lack of willed effort puts us into an odd state of separation from reality.

Now Nietzsche had made the mistake of thinking that "the will to war is higher than the will to peace," and that therefore what we need is war. James does not make the same mistake; he recognizes that what is needed is "the moral equivalent of war" (the title of another essay)—some sense of inner purpose that can create the exultation of war.

When I was on Long Island in the late summer of 1967, staying with my friend Pat Murphy, a professor of philosophy, I found in a secondhand bookshop a copy of a first edition of James' essay, *On Vital Reserves*. Its opening paragraphs filled me with immediate excitement:

"Everyone knows what it is to start a piece of work, either intellectual or muscular, feeling stale . . . And everybody knows what it is to 'warm up' to his job. The process of warming up gets particularly striking in the phenomenon known as 'second wind.' On usual occasions, we make a practice of stopping an occupation as soon as we meet the first effective layer (so to call it) of fatigue. We have then walked, played, or worked 'enough,' so we desist. That amount of fatigue is an efficacious obstruction on this side of which our usual life is cast. But if an unusual necessity forces us to press onward, a surprising thing occurs. The fatigue gets worse up to a certain critical point, when gradually or suddenly it passes away, and we are fresher than before. We have evidently tapped a level of new energy, masked until then by the fatigue-obstacle usually obeyed. There may be layer after layer of this experience; a third and forth 'wind' may supervene. Mental activity shows the phenomenon as well as physical, and in exceptional cases we may find, beyond the very extremity of fatigue-distress, amounts of ease and power that we never dreamed ourselves to own—sources of strength habitually not taxed at all, because habitually we never push through the obstruction, never pass those early critical points."

He goes on, "Everyone is familiar with the phenomenon of feeling more or less alive on different days. Anyone knows on any given day, that there are energies slumbering in him that the incitements of that day do not call forth, but which he might display if these were greater. Most of us feel as if a sort of cloud weighed upon us, keeping us below our highest notch of clearness in discernment, sureness in reasoning, or firmness in deciding. Compared with what we ought to be, we are only half awake. Our fires are damped, our drafts are checked. We are making use of only a small part of our possible mental and physical resources. In some persons this sense of being cut off from their rightful resources is extreme, and we get the formidable neurasthenic and psychasthenic conditions, with life grown into one tissue of impossibilities, that so many medical books describe.

"Stating the thing broadly, the human individual thus lives far within his limits; he possesses powers of various sorts which he habitually fails to use. He energizes below his maximum, and he behaves below his optimum. In elementary faculty, in coordination, in power of inhibition and control, in every conceivable way, his life is contracted like the field of vision of an hysteric subject—but with less excuse, for the poor hysteric is diseased, while in the rest of us it is only an inveterate habit—the habit of inferiority to our full self—that is bad."

What excited me so much is obvious. Abraham Maslow's work had introduced me to the concept of the peak experience—the bubbling experience of sudden happiness. J. B. Priestley called it "delight" or "magic." Maslow had noted that all healthy people seem to have it with a fair degree of frequency. And the reason is obvious. Healthy people tend to be well motivated; they hurl themselves into things with a sense of purpose. And this sense of purpose induces the sense of movement that Nietzsche experienced as he watched his old regiment marching past him on the Strasbourg road. A racing driver must experience the same thing as he makes an attempt on the world speed record.

Now James was suggesting that a man who was able to make use of these powers that are normally suppressed and forgotten would be quite different from the rest of us—a kind of Zarathustra—perhaps even what Nietzsche called the superman. In other words, we all have a kind of sleeping superman inside us.

But what James says has another important implication. Consider that "nihilism" that made Dostoevsky's Stavrogin and Svidrigailov commit suicide, the feeling that life is meaningless. Svidrigailov tells Raskolnikov that he dreamed of eternity, and that it was like a small, dusty room full of cobwebs.

This is one of the most dangerous feelings we can experience. It is what Eliot means when he says, "We each think of the key, each in his prison." And this seems so obviously true: that each of us spends a lifetime trapped inside ourselves. We accept it as an inevitable part of the human condition. But while this may, in the narrowest sense, be true, it vanishes every time we experience the "spring morning" feeling, as it vanished for Nietzsche on the Strasbourg road, or during the storm in the shepherd's hut. Perhaps our moments of "delight" are not a genuine release from the prison, but they certainly release us from Svidrigailov's feeling that we are trapped in a small dusty room.

Now this, it seems to me, is one of the most fundamental conflicts of human existence—between the "dusty room" feeling and the "spring morning" feeling. When Van Gogh committed suicide, he was overwhelmed by the dusty room feeling; but when he painted his greatest pictures, he knew that the truth is in the spring morning feeling.

This is something that has preoccupied me all my life: the problem of how to maintain a memory of the spring morning feeling (or the Christmas feeling) when life has become a burden. My own method was to provide myself with a series of mnemonics: Hemingway's El Sordo episode, Raskolnikov's comment about preferring to live on a narrow ledge rather than die at once, Yeats' line "He completes his partial mind," Chesterton's phrase "absurd good news," Proust's feeling as he tastes the madeleine dipped in tea: "I had ceased to feel mediocre, accidental, mortal." The problem is that when we are feeling bored and tired, even Van Gogh's *Starry Night* can arouse a sense of "So what?"

Now I am suggesting that William James provides an interesting alternative. If we can grasp intellectually that "in every conceivable way," our lives are contracted like the field of vision of a hysteric subject, and that our problem is "a habit of inferiority to our full self," it can become something more than a mere mnemonic. After all, when you have learned to change gears in a car, this is not a mnemonic, but a practical way of getting up hills. If you did not know about changing gear, your car would stall on hills—as human beings often stall when facing problems. Moreover, you would regard it as an inevitable inconvenience that applies to all cars. But the simple practical knowledge of how to change gear causes the whole problem to evaporate.

What is so dangerous about the dusty room feeling is that we are taken in by it. It convinces us that life is narrow and dull and boring. And that feeling can quickly lead to the "negative feedback" that leaves us depressed, exhausted and—at the worst—suicidal. This is the state—in Eliot's words—of "not knowing what to feel, or if I understand." It is essentially a lack of perspective.

We can quickly dispel the darkness in a room by switching on the light, provided we know where the light switch is. James' insight provides that light switch. It offers us a sudden sense of perspective: "Don't be taken in by the dusty room feeling—it's a confidence trick." The dusty room feeling is a swindler who intends to dupe you out of your vitality and confidence, and perhaps even your life. But provided a friendly policeman mutters in your ear, "Don't trust him—he has a criminal record as long as your arm," then you are in no danger of being duped. William James is the friendly policeman.

He goes on to ask: what is it that gives some men far more energy than others?

His answer is: Either some unusual stimulus fills them with emotional excitement, or some unusual idea of necessity induces them to make an extra effort of will. Excitement, ideas and efforts, in a word, are what carry us over the dam.

Here James' use of the word "ideas" underlines my point. Ideas can save us from being taken in by the con man.

He goes on to point out, "In those 'hyperesthetic' conditions which chronic invalidism so often brings in its train, the dam has changed its normal place. The slightest functional exercise gives a distress which the patient yields to and stops. In such cases of 'habit-neurosis', a new range of power often comes in consequence of the 'bullying treatment,' of efforts which the doctor obliges the patient, much against his will, to make. First comes the very extremity of distress, then follows unexpected relief. There seems no doubt that we are each and all of us to some extent victims of habit-neurosis. . . . We live subject to degrees of fatigue which we have come only from habit to obey. Most of us may learn to push the barrier farther off, and to live in perfect comfort on much higher levels of power."

James is obviously right. In fact, it is habit-neurosis that normally kills us. In *Back to Methuselah*, Shaw suggests that human beings could quite easily live to be three hundred. He thought that, sooner or later, this would "just happen." I suspect he was unaware of the exact nature of the problem. We summon vitality from hidden depths when we urgently need it—this, as I say, is Granville Barker's "secret life." Human beings are capable of tremendous efforts—as James points out—when some "unusual idea of necessity" galvanizes them. He gives an example of a colonel named Baird-Smith, during the siege of Delhi, upon whom the lives of the whole garrison—including women and children—depended. With a sprained arm, a festering wound, and mouth ulcers, he lived for weeks on opium and brandy, without feeling any need for food (which in any case he could not swallow), and without becoming even slightly drunk. In such extreme emergency, his body used the brandy as food.

What had happened is—in James' phrase—that his dam had moved upriver. On the other hand, in the case of a man who has worked hard all his life, and dies soon after retirement, the reverse has happened—the dam has moved downriver. His unconscious mind receives a signal telling him that he can now relax—and he finds himself suddenly bereft of all energy and purpose.

For humans to live a great deal longer than at present, they would simply need a stronger "sense of necessity," and an ability to refuse to be taken in by the confidence trickster.

But Shaw is undoubtedly correct about one thing: his assertion in *Man and Superman* that the path to human evolution lies in consciousness of its necessity. Evolution has so far been a matter of instinct and a kind of blind groping. As often as not it defeats itself by drifting and forgetting its own aim. To recognize consciously that our main problem is our "habit of inferiority to our full self" is to recognize that we can combat the habit, just as we can combat any habit that poses a serious threat to our well-being.

We can grasp the actual mechanism of the process by considering again James' recovery from his nervous breakdown. Absurdly enough, it was an idea that started the recovery—the recognition that we can think one thing rather than another: that we possess the power of choice.

This I would regard as the very essence of my work, the most important thing I have to say. The twentieth century has been inclined to belittle intellect, to regard it as second in importance to intuition and instinct, and perhaps to action. I have always believed that the solution to our deepest problems lies in knowledge, and therefore in the powers of the mind. Intellect is the most powerful instrument we possess. And the next stage of our evolution will be brought about by a brilliant flash of insight, when we shall suddenly grasp what we already know, see it from above in a "bird's-eye view." This means that stating things clearly and incisively is the most important means to this end. And in our century, no one has epitomized this ideal more powerfully than William James.

20

ERNST CASSIRER

E rnst Cassirer was once regarded as one of the great thinkers of the twentieth century; now his name is virtually unknown, except to students of philosophy.

This is a pity, for Cassirer is a thinker of extraordinary range—his mind resembles, in many ways, that of Whitehead, who is perfectly capable of quoting Einstein and Wordsworth on the same page. But in spite of a rather Germanic mode of expression, Cassirer is far more readable than Whitehead. And this is partly because Whitehead, except in *Science and the Modern World*, is concerned with expressing his own philosophical ideas, while Cassirer, who began as a brilliant historian of ideas, enjoys expounding other people's. He once remarked, "The custom . . . of hurling one's ideas into empty space, as it were, without enquiring into the general development of scientific philosophy, has never struck me as fruitful"—a sentence I might well quote as a defense of my own method, from *The Outsider* onward.

Cassirer was also one of the cleverest men of the century. His memory was phenomenal, and one of his professors recollected that he could quote page after page of poetry. The range of his knowledge was so enormous that he gave the impression that he remembered every book he had ever read.

Typical of his brilliance is the fact that when he became a professor at Oxford in 1933, he had to teach for the first term in German. After that, he taught in English, which he had learned during the first term.

And in his later years—he died in 1945, at the age of seventy—he always wrote in English.

The reason that Cassirer has been half-forgotten is simple. Look him up in any dictionary of philosophy, and you will learn that he is regarded as a member of the Marburg school of neo-Kantian philosophers. Most people are not even quite sure what a Kantian philosopher is, except that it sounds irrelevant to the twentieth century, and a neo-Kantian sounds doubly irrelevant.

Let me explain briefly.

Descartes, as everyone knows, tried to create a new kind of philosophy based on "doubting everything"—that is, anything that could be doubted. Anything that was left standing was beyond doubt—like, as we know, Descartes' famous, "I think, therefore I am."

John Locke turned to the senses in his quest for certainty. The mind, he said, is a kind of empty blackboard—tabula rasa—and our experience gradually fills it. So "you" are merely the sum of your experiences. There is nothing in the mind, said Locke, that was not first in the senses. Descartes had already concluded that animals are robots; Locke came close to regarding man as a robot.

Bishop Berkeley turned Locke's empiricism inside out. "Very well," he said, "it is true that I know the world through my senses. But many things change according to the state of my senses—for example, when I have a fever, my food may taste extremely odd. So how can I say that the 'normal' taste of food is the way it really tastes?"

He then took a controversial—and to us absurd—step. If things change according to the state of my senses, then would it not be true to say that my senses create taste and smell and color? The answer, of course, is no—if that were true, then your senses might arbitrarily make a banana taste like an orange. But if, for the sake of argument, we leave Berkeley's point unchallenged, then his next step follows logically: that it is possible that our senses create the outside world. Perhaps when you walk into a room, it suddenly pops into being—rather like a television set that switches itself on as you open the door.

Berkeley probably had his tongue in his cheek—after all, he was a bishop, and would hardly dare to doubt God's creation —but his basic purpose was serious: to suggest that reality is mental or spiritual in nature. But David Hume was a more combative type; he felt that a great deal of religious belief is nonsense, and he managed to doubt more than Descartes would have thought possible. For example, he doubted that we have a real "self" inside us. He said that when he looked inside himself for the real David Hume, he just saw a lot of ideas and impressions, whirling around like autumn leaves. According to Hume, "thinking" is a mere association of ideas. He even doubted whether there is any necessary connection between cause and effect.

Kant was deeply shaken by Hume's trenchant skepticism. Yet it seemed to him obvious that we see a certain order in the world, and this order is not an illusion. If I comb my hair, I make it neat and tidy by making its strands run parallel. And we make the universe neat and tidy by imposing certain forms of understanding (concepts) on it—for example, we distinguish between liquids, solids and gases. We impose order on events by the use of clocks, which gives them an arrangement in time, and by maps, which gives them an arrangement in space. Perhaps the simplest example is the way we impose order on things by giving them names. That four-legged creature is called a cat, and that one a dog, and that one a cow. We know that these are not really their names, but it simplifies things to behave as if they were.

All these things—liquids, solids, gases, space, time, cats, dogs and cows, are examples of "combs" that make reality neat and tidy. Kant called these combs "categories" (although concepts would have been a better word), and agreed that we create them with our minds. They might also be compared to colored spectacles through which we see reality.

One further thing must be said about Kant. Recognizing that our senses and our assumptions (concepts) change what we see, he concluded that the "true reality" that lies behind these—the "thing in itself" or "ding an sich"—is unknowable. This doctrine led some of his distinguished contemporaries to despair—for obvious reasons. If reality is unknowable, then we are living in a kind of shadow house of illusions. And nineteenth-century poets had enough problems without this. (Kant's views were instrumental in driving one of them, Heinrich von Kleist, to suicide.)

One of the chiefs of the neo-Kantians, Hermann Cohen, had the good sense to reject this aspect of Kant. He felt that when you look at the moon in the sky, what you are seeing is really the moon. It is true that you do not know the moon as you know your own backyard; but that is only because you do not know enough about it. In theory, there is nothing to stop you knowing the moon as well as you know your own backyard. The "ding an sich" is not, as Kant believed, "unknowable."

There is another central difference between Kant and the neo-Kantians. Kant thought of his categories as permanent—they do not change their nature from age to age, because human beings do not change their nature But it struck Cassirer one day—as he was sitting on a bus—that many categories do change. For example, what would Kant have made of Einstein's strange view of space and time, or of Riemann's spherical geometry?

This insight did not bother Cassirer. For he suddenly saw that a great many human creations—language and myth and religion and art—are also spectacles through which we see reality. Human beings are fundamentally creative; we possess imagination and freedom.

What happens when you look at a painting, or read a novel, or listen to a symphony? You appreciate what the artist or novelist or composer is "saying," although you may see the world in quite a different way. This is because all creators use symbols, and we have created a common language of symbols.

Animals seem to be quite different from humans. When an animal receives a stimulus, it simply responds directly to it, like a penny-in-the-slot machine. But when you drop a penny into a human being, his response is not at all direct; it has to be filtered through a world of symbols. In fact, the penny falls into a whirlpool of symbols, and is spun around as if in a washing machine, before producing a response. "Man," says Cassirer, "lives in a symbolic universe."

It is a pity that Cassirer never wrote about the one subject that would have made his meaning clear to all—sex. The male response to a female is, as we have seen earlier, almost entirely symbolic. This can be clearly seen in a recent case of a Roman Catholic priest who was found guilty of pedophile offenses against boys. There were found in his possession around thirty thousand items of child pornography. It would seem that he spent most of his life in a state of sexual arousal at the thought of sex with children—not a particular child, but virtually any child. The fact that he was a Catholic priest underlines the point; this was not simply a kind of animal innocence, like the fox's predilection for chickens. He must have been fully aware of the conflict between his symbolic response to the image of a child, and the teachings of his church, which declared pedophilia contrary to moral law. The case enables us to understand not merely the power of the symbol, but of man's slavery to the symbol.

The book that gives the clearest idea of Cassirer's remarkable mind is probably the late *Essay on Man* (1944), written in the year before his death in an attempt to provide a straightforward summary of his "philosophy of symbolic forms." It is full of fascinating examples of what he means. To illustrate how an individual can pass from the "practical attitude" to the "symbolic attitude," he cites the case of the blind and deaf girl Helen Keller. Her teacher, Mrs. Sullivan, had somehow taught her to spell and to understand words by writing on her hand. But the child must have felt she was living in a confusing and chaotic universe. For example, she was not quite clear about the difference between "mug" and "milk."

Then one day, her teacher taught her the word "water," and later, as they stood in the pump house, Helen held her mug under the pump. As cold water rushed over Helen's hand, Mrs. Sullivan once again spelled "water." For the first time, Helen grasped that "water" was this cold stuff pouring over her hand, and had nothing to do with the mug from which she drank it.

"She dropped the mug and stood as one transfixed. A new light came into her face. She spelled 'water' several times. Then she dropped on the ground, and asked for its name and pointed to the pump and the trellis. . . . in a few hours she had added thirty new words to her vocabulary."

This knowledge—that each thing has a name—excited her so much because it offered a method of getting to understand her world, of simplifying it, and ultimately of controlling it. This is what Kant meant—that we achieve mastery over the world by classifying things—like "mug" and "milk"—under concepts.

Helen Keller is, incidentally, the ultimate refutation of Locke's view that there is nothing in the mind that was not first in the senses. She ended with a great deal in her mind that was not first in her senses.

In a central chapter called *Facts and Ideals*, Cassirer speaks of the problems that arise when our symbolic function is impaired. Patients who were suffering from aphasia (defective power of speech) lost the power to think abstractly about certain things. For example, a patient who was suffering from paralysis of the right hand could not even say, "I can write with my right hand." Laura Bridgman, a deaf and dumb girl who was not as intelligent as Helen Keller, had the utmost difficulty grasping abstract ideas. When her teacher read her a sum from an arithmetic book, she asked, "How did the man who wrote that book know I was here?" When asked a sum involving the cost of barrels of cider, she replied,

"I wouldn't give much for cider, because it's very sour."

The rest of us are so accustomed to the idea that a problem in arithmetic is not "real" that we fail to grasp that, for Laura Bridgman, it seemed as abstract as the page of algebraic symbols that baffles many of us.

But this also makes us aware that the process of evolution must involve an increasing capacity for abstraction—that is, for grasping the world in terms of symbols rather than "facts." And it also makes us aware that most of us spend our lives trapped and surrounded by mere facts, which enmesh us like a spider's web. The stupidest—and most malicious—people have no capacity to see beyond facts. They are trapped in a "worm's-eye view," what another writer, Ayn Rand, calls "the anti-conceptual mentality." And the problem of becoming truly human depends on our developing the capacity to see the world from a bird's-eye view.

I must admit that when I first came upon Cassirer, I was inclined to think of him as a kind of inferior version of Edmund Husserl. (I still feel much the same about Kant.) Husserl wanted, like Kant, to create a truly scientific philosophy, which he called phenomenology. His major step in that direction was to recognize that all perception is intentional. Things do not walk in through my eyes and implant themselves on my brain; I have to pay attention. If I look at my watch without paying attention, I do not see the time. If I read a paragraph without attention, I have to reread it.

Intentionality can also have physical effects. If someone talks about itching, I often begin to itch; it would seem that itching is, to some extent, intentional. So is being ticklish. If you reach out to tickle a child, he is screaming with laughter before your hands reach him. If someone talks about something disgusting while you are eating, you feel sick. And if you are feeling low and depressed, you may actually become sick, by a form of hidden intentionality.

When you see a conductor directing an orchestra, you can see that he is imposing his intentions on the orchestra. But when you walk about on a spring morning, and feel that the whole world is wonderful, you fail to recognize that a kind of invisible inner conductor is orchestrating your sense impressions into a kind of symphony. Husserl called this invisible conductor the "transcendental ego," and used the interesting phrase, "the hidden achievements of the transcendental ego." (The transcendental ego was Kant's term for the "real you.")

In other words, Husserl's basic insight was that we transform our world by a kind of unconscious intentionality. And this is identical with Kant's basic insight—that our minds impose order on the world we see. If someone had drawn his attention to it, Kant would undoubtedly have recognized that intentionality is the ultimate category.

Cohen, as we have seen, disagreed with Kant about the "thing in itself," insisting that we know something by acquiring knowledge about it. This again is a basic tenet of phenomenology. It is basically a form of "realism;" it rejects Berkeley's "idealism"—the notion that our minds create the world—and insists, for example, that it is quite meaningless to say that grass is not "really" green.

This is why, to begin with, I was inclined to dismiss Cassirer as a kind of less perceptive Husserl. Even now, I can see that there is an element of truth in this view. But then, Cassirer has certain definite advantages over Husserl. To begin with, he is far more readable. Second, his omnivorous interest in physics, biology, psychology, history, art, language, and myth, means that his work is a kind of plum pudding, full of fascinating insights and anecdotes. He loves citing examples to reinforce his facts, and these examples—like the story of Helen Keller and the pump—give his work a resonance that is associated with art rather than philosophy. (I particularly recommend the chapter on history in the *Essay on Man*, and its discussion of the two different accounts of why Cleopatra fled from the battle of Actium.)

Cassirer seems to me to epitomize what he is saying about symbolic forms—art, myth, language. His basic insight is that they are dynamic expressions of the human spirit, and he quotes Kant to the effect that any intelligent person can learn to grasp what Newton said in the *Principia*, but that no matter how much he knows about poetry, he cannot write good poetry on command. In other words, art is an expression of freedom. And as we read Cassirer, we feel what it means to be a dynamic thinker, swinging daringly from concept to concept.

This means that it does not matter too much when Cassirer is occasionally wrong. Giorgio de Santillana attacks his concept of myth in *Hamlet's Mill*, and it is true that *Hamlet's Mill* has a brilliance and audacity that gives Santillana the right to criticize Cassirer. Similarly, we could criticize Cassirer's comment—at the end of the *Essay on Man*—that there is no genetic inheritance of acquired characteristics; since Cassirer's death, an increasing amount of evidence for such transmission has accumulated. It is true that Cassirer is making the valid point that man has discovered another method of transmission of his "spiritual acquisitions." But it seems to me that the statement that there is no transmission of acquired characteristics runs counter to Cassirer's basic insight—that the spirit of man is essentially dynamic and creative.

The point might be expressed like this. If we look at a candle flame burning on a perfectly still night, its lack of motion gives an impression that it is solid; it might be an illuminated jewel. But we only have to place a hand above it to realize that the stillness is an illusion; the flame is actually a mass of seething energy. Similarly, if a child goes into a library, he feels overawed and oppressed by the sheer number of books; they seem to be so much dead paper covered with printer's ink. Yet for a scholar, or a philosopher like Cassirer, each of them burns with a living flame. Moreover, the knowledge that they epitomize is not dead knowledge; it is in a continual process of transformation.

In *The Occult*, I have devoted two pages to examples that seem to contradict "Darwinism" (although it must be remembered that Darwin himself was willing to concede that there might be inheritance of acquired characteristics). One of the oddest examples is a flatworm called microstomus, which gobbles up a polyp called hydra, which has stinging capsules to which the flatworm is immune. But when the polyp has been digested, the hydra's stinging cells are picked up in the lining of the flatworm's stomach, and passed on to other cells that carry them, in the way that builder's laborers carry bricks, through to the flatworm's skin, where they are mounted like gun turrets pointing outward, to discourage predators. Once the flatworm has a full set of these gun turrets, it will no longer eat hydra—in other words, it eats the polyp solely to steal its defense system. Sir Alister Hardy, who cites the case, quotes a zoologist as saying that such behavior can only be explained by some kind of "group mind" among the flatworm's cells.

The same seems to apply to a tiny creature called the flattid bug, which combines with hundreds of its kind to form a kind of coral-colored lilac, green at the tip and changing color with subtle gradations. Here again, the only possible explanation for its evolution seems to be some kind of "group mind."

Darwinism attempts to "staticise" nature, to explain it as a mechanical process, but the microstomus worm and the flattid bug seem to suggest that there is a far more dynamic mode of evolution. Cassirer sensed this mode in his "symbolic forms," but failed to see that it ought to apply elsewhere in nature.

All this makes no difference to the dynamism of Cassirer's work, just as it makes no difference to the greatness of William James' that psychology has changed unrecognizably since he wrote *The Principles of Psychology*. Like James, Cassirer is so readable because his brilliant mind is always throwing off new ideas.

Husserl remarked that the calling of the philosopher is so important because it "is linked with the 'possibility of a radical transformation of humanity,' and not only with a radical transformation of humanity but also a 'liberation,' and this possibility makes the calling of the philosopher unique..." This quotation again emphasizes the similarity between the basic visions of Husserl and Cassirer, and makes us aware that Cassirer's work could be labeled a phenomenology of culture.

But it is probably just as well that Cassirer failed to recognize this. The thought of playing second fiddle to Husserl might have discouraged him from pursuing his own remarkable course, and robbed us of some of the most stimulating philosophical writing of the twentieth century.

21

SARTRE

My attitude to Sartre has always been a strange mixture of admiration and exasperation. His philosophy has always struck me as basically flawed—in fact, riddled with schoolboy howlers that completely invalidate his basic position. Yet he is also one of the most interesting and successful examples of what Shaw called the "artist-philosopher"—a philosopher who was also a playwright, novelist and political activist.

I became aware of Sartre soon after the Second World War, when his name was frequently mentioned on the BBC as the chief proponent of a philosophy called "existentialism." And when the BBC presented his play, *Crime Passionnel* (*Les Mains Sales*), on its "Saturday Night Theatre," I listened eagerly, and was deeply impressed.

It is, in fact, Sartre's most powerful play. Hugo, a young left-wing intellectual, is sent by the Communist Party to assassinate the Communist politician Hoederer, who is about to form an "alliance of convenience" with political opponents. Hugo is to take the post of Hoederer's secretary. He arrives in his house with his wife Jessica, and while Hugo is out of the room, she finds that he has packed a revolver. Hugo then admits that he intends to kill Hoederer, although his wife finds it hard to believe.

Hoederer's bodyguards announce their intention of searching Hugo's belongings—although their true motive is a desire to humiliate him because they regard him as a bourgeois intellectual. Hugo, terrified that they will find the revolver, refuses to let them search. Hoederer is summoned, and supports Hugo—he says he prefers to trust people. Then Jessica seems to throw away the advantage when she invites the bodyguards to search after all. They do, and find nothing—Jessica later reveals that she had the revolver tucked in her dress all the time. Hoederer is led to believe that the reason Hugo refused to be searched is that he has a photograph of himself as a child in his suitcase, and is afraid of ridicule.

Hugo finds he likes Hoederer more and more, and cannot bring himself to kill him. Finally, the two of them have a philosophical discussion about politics, and Hoederer's pragmatism triumphs over Hugo's idealism—Hoederer tells Hugo that all politicians must be prepared to plunge their hands in shit up to the elbows (hence the play's title, *Dirty Hands*).

Finally, warned by Jessica that Hugo is supposed to assassinate him, Hoederer confronts him, and when it becomes clear that Hugo is not prepared to kill him, takes away the revolver. But while Hugo is in the garden, Jessica flirts with Hoederer—it is clear from the beginning that she finds him attractive—and he kisses her. At that moment, Hugo comes in, and thinks he understands why Hoederer has been so friendly and protective—because he intends seducing Jessica; he snatches up the revolver and shoots Hoederer. As the bodyguards rush in, the dying Hoederer tells them not to harm Hugo—that Hugo killed him because he has been sleeping with Jessica.

In a final scene, Hugo—now out of prison—learns that the Party now intends to kill him. The Party line has changed, and Hoederer's compromise with the right is regarded as politically correct. Hoederer has become a hero. No one, of course, knows that the Party was behind his murder.

But Hugo still has a chance to save his life. The Party wants to know if he is "salvageable," and asks the woman behind the assassination plot to ask Hugo why he did it. When Hugo confesses that he does not know, she decides that he can still be useful. But Hugo has to agree to be silent about the Party's role in the assassination, for that would reflect badly on those who ordered it, since everyone has been told that Hoederer was killed by a reactionary spy. So if he is to be spared, Hugo must stick to the story that his murder of Hoederer was a crime passionnel.

At this point, Hugo decides that he cannot keep silent. He dislikes the Party's dishonesty, and his self-respect demands that he should believe he killed Hoederer out of political idealism, not jealousy. So he declines to be "salvaged," and walks out, to face his assassins.

I found the play totally absorbing, but could not quite understand why Sartre was regarded as a philosopher. To me it seemed merely a political thriller. It was only later, when I read Sartre's first play, *The Flies*, that I understood what he was saying. *The Flies* is a kind of "dummy run" for *Crime Passionnel*, the story of the murder of Clytemnestra and her lover by her children Electra and Orestes—and therefore has the same kind of tension as *Crime Passionnel*.

It is Electra who urges her brother to murder Clytemnestra, in revenge for the murder of their father Agamemnon. When the queen and her lover have been killed, Orestes and Electra are pursued by furies in the shape of flies. But in the temple of Apollo—where they have taken refuge—Zeus appears, and calls them to account. Orestes is defiant, but Electra is relieved and delighted to be assured that she never really intended to kill her mother—that it was merely a vengeful daydream that got out of hand. She embraces forgiveness with enthusiasm.

Orestes remains defiant—even when Zeus causes the walls of the temple to open, revealing the stars in their courses. Orestes insists that the murder of Clytemnestra and Aegisthus was his own deliberate act, an act freely chosen, and that if he repudiates it, he repudiates his freedom. When Zeus asks angrily, "Who created you?" Orestes replies, "You did. But you made one mistake—you created me free."

And so Orestes rejects "mercy" and leaves the temple, pursued by the flies.

Hugo has made precisely the same decision as Orestes—to embrace his own act. The irony, of course, is that Hugo killed Hoederer out of jealousy, not political idealism. So his death might be seen as a form of self-deception.

Of course, what made *Crime Passionnel* so popular—it ran for eighteen months in Paris, and the printed version sold 140,000 copies—was its political realism, which flattered its audiences into feeling that they were being treated as intelligent adults. It made Sartre immensely unpopular with the French Communist Party, although he always insisted that it was not intended as an anti-Communist play. Nevertheless, he suppressed it in 1952 in deference to the Soviet Union and his own Communist alliances—adding one more twist to its meaning.

Sartre's post-war success is a kind of fairy tale. And there is a sense in which no one was better qualified for success. He was obviously no flash in the pan. He had behind him an impressive body of philosophical work, including the vast *Being and Nothingness*, and some remarkable novels. Sartre was just what the French needed in 1945—a new literary hero, with an impeccable background as a Resistance fighter.

Jean-Paul Sartre was born in Paris in 1905, an ugly, cross-eyed child who was half Jewish. His father died when he was two, and Sartre was brought up in the household of his dominant and flamboyant grandfather, Charles Schweitzer (uncle of Albert Schweitzer.) Sartre tells in his autobiography, *Words*, how he spent his childhood daydreaming of greatness and heroism. He was clever and spoiled, but his ugliness gave him an inferiority complex, which in turn led him to work tirelessly at his studies. When he went to college he knew ten times as much as the other students, and was greatly admired. In due course, a pretty girl called Simone de Beauvoir became his mistress.

Sartre became a schoolmaster in Le Havre, and discovered the philosophy of Edmund Husserl. Simone de Beauvoir tells in her autobiography how Sartre and his friend Raymond Aron were sitting outside a Paris cafe, and how Aron pointed to Sartre's glass and said, "If you were a phenomenologist, you would be able to philosophize about that cocktail." Simone de Beauvoir said that Sartre went pale with emotion, and lost no time in rushing to the nearest bookstore to buy anything by Husserl.

Since I have already discussed Husserl in the Cassirer chapter, I shall not repeat myself here. Suffice it to say that the starting point of his phenomenology is the recognition that all perception is intentional—that when we look at something, we fire our attention at it, like an arrow. The further we pull back the bowstring—that is, the harder we concentrate—the more clearly we perceive. Seeing is noticing.

Now this obviously raises an interesting question. If perception is an "arrow," who is the archer? David Hume said that when he looked inside himself for the essential David Hume, he only saw a lot of impressions and sensations. And thereafter, philosophers were inclined to agree that we do not possess an "essential self," only a personality created by our experience. Kant disagreed, for the essence of his philosophy is that we impose concepts on our experience—in which case, there must obviously be a "you" who does the imposing; Kant called this the transcendental ego, and Husserl borrowed the word.

Now Sartre was naturally gloomy by temperament, a kind of French Graham Greene. As a philosopher, his outlook was close to David

Hume. He spent most of his time stranded in a world of boredom. And his first book—a slight work called *The Transcendence of the Ego*—is a Humeian attack on the idea of the transcendental ego. According to Sartre, Husserl is correct in stating that all consciousness is intentional—it comes into being only when it is directed at an object. But Husserl, says Sartre, is incorrect in assuming that we therefore have a "real self."

But if consciousness is intentional, who fires the arrow of perception? The answer, says Sartre, is that the arrow is not "fired." The objects of consciousness attract our attention, so to speak, like someone shouting, "Hey, you." The modern American colloquialism "grab your attention" catches it precisely. Males know the sensation of having their attention "grabbed" by a pretty girl. According to Sartre, our attention is always being seized by external objects. The world "pulls" our attention as the moon pulls the tides.

This, clearly, is a highly mechanistic view, for it seems to mean that we can only respond to stimuli—that we are basically penny-in-the-slot machines. Such a view obviously leads naturally to the notion that we have no free will—and in the section on William James, we have seen how dangerous that can be. In a time of depression and discouragement, James—we may recall—collapsed into deep pessimism that brought him close to total breakdown. And it was only when he suddenly became convinced that Renouvier's argument for free will was correct—that I can pay attention to one thing rather than another—that he began to recover.

Sartre went on to create an equally pessimistic and mechanistic theory of the emotions—that our emotions are a form of self-deception (or "magic," as he called it.) When the fox convinces itself that the grapes are sour, it has escaped the discomfort of unsatisfied desire by deceiving itself, by choosing to believe a lie. Similarly, a criminal justifies himself by telling himself that society is rotten anyway, and that politicians and judges are all thoroughly corrupt. So his own criminality is turned into a "norm."

In 1936 Sartre was persuaded by a former student, now a doctor, to try the hallucinogenic drug mescalin. He hoped for marvelous visions; in fact, he experienced a classic "bad trip," in which umbrellas turned into vultures, clock faces leered at him, and he believed he was being followed by a giant lobster. (He hated shellfish.)

This experience had much the same kind of sequel as William James' inner collapse; he was plunged into depression. This manifested itself as frequent attacks of what Sartre called "nausea," a sudden sense of meaninglessness, in which things seem to become detached from their names, and to become simply grotesque objects. This is accompanied by a feeling of "what am I doing here?"

Now "nausea" is obviously due to lack of energy. When I feel low and miserable, my mood affects everything I look at. If someone is telling me a joke, it seems unfunny or pointless—just as, when I feel like vomiting, all food seems self-evidently nauseating. When I am full of energy, the world seems to sparkle with hidden meanings. "Nausea," on the other hand, makes me feel that, if there are any hidden meanings, they are menacing or unpleasant.

The odd thing is that Sartre came to feel that "nausea" is a truthful perception of reality—that things are really like that, and that we disguise this with unjustified optimism. This, of course, is in line with Sartre's theory of the emotions—which was published soon after the novel *Nausea* (1938), which dramatizes Sartre's depression in a tale of a historian named Roquentin, for whom it suddenly becomes clear that history is a meaningless concept because "there's no adventure."

We only have to consider this for a moment to see that Sartre was revealing an appalling lack of the logic for which the French are supposed to be famous. According to Sartre, seeing things with "nausea" is to see them truly; nausea is the basic truth of existence, the reality behind human delusions. Nausea is to see the reality of things, when intentionality has broken down. What Sartre has failed to recognize is that this is a contradiction of his Husserlian faith that all perception is intentional—in which case, nausea is also intentional, and not some intuitive perception of the "thing in itself."

The point emerges even more clearly in Camus' book, *The Myth of Sisyphus*, where he speaks of nausea as "the absurd." We go to work, Camus says, and we come home again, Monday, Tuesday, Wednesday, Thursday . . . Then one day we ask, "Why?" and suddenly we become aware of "the absurd." Once again, we can see that he is talking about a collapse of energy. If you are enjoying your job, or feel highly motivated because you wish to provide the best possible life for your family, you get a certain pleasure from routine, as you do from eating when you are hungry. If your motivation is minimal—you are working merely to stay alive—then you perform your duty with a low level of "intentionality," and it becomes boring. But this is, after all, simply a failure of imagination. A half-starved refugee who has spent his life in poverty would regard any paid employment as a gift from heaven.

Now amusingly enough, Sartre himself soon came to recognize this. For at this point, the Nazis invaded France, and Sartre spent nine months in a prisoner-of-war camp. When he returned to Paris, he joined the French Resistance (although, as a Paris litterateur, it seems doubtful that he played an active role). And he was to remark that he had never felt so free as during this period, when he might be arrested and tortured at any moment. In other words, he was paying attention, and preventing his energies from leaking away in a kind of boredom.

Now Sartre found himself confronted by a paradox. He had never denied freedom, since boredom is in itself a recognition of freedom (you feel free to follow any direction you choose, but feel no motivation to choose any one of them). He had once said, "We are as free as you like, but helpless . . . " But this philosophy hardly suited a patriot who wished to see the defeat of Nazism. Sartre had an obvious choice. He could either refuse to be moved by patriotism, regarding it as yet another form of self-deception (or, as he called it, "bad faith"), or he could decide to justify it philosophically, and leave himself open to the accusation of "bad faith."

Yet his recognition that he had never felt so free as when he might be arrested and shot any moment provided a philosophical rationale for his decision to place freedom at the center of his philosophy. Of course, it made nonsense of all his earlier work, with its deep pessimism, but if he realized this, Sartre probably reasoned that the philosophical obscurity of his books on imagination and intentionality would cover his trail.

And yet at this point, he began his largest philosophical enterprise, his own attempt to create a kind of phenomenology of human existence, *Being and Nothingness*.

It needs to be explained that *Being and Nothingness* is Sartre's own attempt to outdo Heidegger's *Being and Time* (1927), which had deeply influenced him. Martin Heidegger had begun as a disciple—and pupil—of Husserl, and had decided to make his own contribution to phenomenology, by applying the phenomenological method to man himself—what he called Dasein (or "human being").

This was obviously a risky enterprise, since phenomenology usually restricts itself to precise descriptions of our inner states, in an attempt to "root out prejudice." I might, for example, decide to attempt a "phenomenology of love," in an attempt to define the precise nature of falling in love, or a phenomenology of sexual attraction, trying to explain how and why we come to experience sexual desire. But to attempt a phenomenology of man himself—the human condition—is obviously going to run the risk of being heavily influenced by the temperamental prejudices of the philosopher in question. We might compare it to a deeply-convinced Christian who sets out to perform a phenomenological analysis of Christianity; obviously, he will have immense difficulty treating Christianity as if it is merely one among many religions. Phenomenology begins by placing "in suspension" the truth of what it is studying, and attempts a simple and unprejudiced description. So an attempt at a phenomenology of the human condition will obviously run into all kinds of inbuilt prejudices.

That is why Husserl himself had strong reservations about *Being and Time*. He felt that it was simply untrue to the phenomenological method. A glance at almost any page of *Being and Time* makes us understand why. For example, in Chapter Five (section twenty-nine), Heidegger attempts a phenomenological analysis of human moods, and remarks casually that "a mood of elation can alleviate the manifest burden of Being; that such a mood is possible also discloses the burdensome character of Dasein, even while it alleviates the burden."

Here, like Sartre, Heidegger assumes that his own pessimistic view of existence as a "burden" is universal, and so can be admitted as a "fact." He is ignoring what William James called "the religion of healthy mindedness," shared by millions of human beings: that is, that although life has its problems, it is basically wonderful. This is, for example, the view that can be found in all the books of G. K. Chesterton. To say, "We all agree that life is burdensome," is rather like saying, "We all agree that suicide is a permanent temptation."

With a mentor like Heidegger, it is hardly surprising that Sartre decided that nausea is the fundamental truth of human existence, and that all forms of emotion are self-deception.

This is expanded in *Being and Nothingness* (1943), a work that is an undeniably brilliant—but utterly negative—analysis of human relations, in the tradition of Schopenhauer's *World as Will and Idea*. According to Sartre, there are three types of being. Objects exist "in themselves," and Sartre calls objects the "en-soi." Human beings exist as objects of consciousness "for themselves," and Sartre calls them the "pour-soi." But the pour-soi experiences itself as a kind of gap in nature, and is inclined to envy chairs and other solid objects for being wholly themselves. The pour-soi longs to become an en-soi, a being that is certain of its own identity.

But there is another type of being, being-for-others. Other people define how I feel about myself by their attitude towards me. If someone treats me as contemptible, I cannot help feeling contemptible. And in making me feel contemptible, the other person is taking away my freedom. Conversely, if someone I respect assures me that I am wonderful, they increase my freedom.

So Sartre sees the relations between human beings as a kind of war—we try to impose our idea on them, and they try to impose their idea on me. It is like arm wrestling. Human relations are basically a form of conflict. This applies even to love. When a man says, "I love you" to a woman, he really wants her to give herself to him, and so dominate and possess her. But there is a sense in which he can never "possess" her. As soon as he makes love, she ceases to be flesh, and becomes an object. So love is bound to be disappointing. The sadist or the tyrant tries to overcome the problem by treating others with such brutality that he feels himself to be a solid object, a being-in-itself. Yet in fact, the sadist meets with exactly the same kind of frustration as the lover; he cannot "possess" the other. The same applies to the tyrant. When Ivan the Terrible has massacred all the inhabitants of Novgorod, he is merely faced with a pile of corpses, and his own inadequate self, permanently frustrated, tormented, and no better off than before. It is rather like a hungry man eating and remaining as hungry as ever.

So, according to Sartre's analysis, human beings are enmeshed in delusions, and can never escape them. "It is meaningless that we live, and meaningless that we die . . . Man is a useless passion."

But before we accept this gloomy view, we should bear in mind the failure of insight revealed in *Nausea* and the *Sketch of a Theory of the Emotions*. One thing is obvious about Sartre. He goes around in a state of low-pressure consciousness—a kind of permanent "leakage." This is because his assumptions about life and the world are so naturally pessimistic that he seldom feels highly motivated.

In fact, Sartre recognized that the threat of arrest and torture had the effect of closing his inner "leaks" and making life altogether more interesting. Yet he still failed to draw the obvious conclusion: that the fault lay in his own boredom and negativity. It never seemed to strike him that boredom is something that should be regarded as reprehensible. He never seems to notice the obvious fact that when we say something is a "bore," we are merely revealing our own weakness and self-indulgence.

The reason is obvious. Sartre has advanced so far into an intellectual justification of boredom—that reality is basically "nauseating"—that his "energy cistern" is permanently low. He has committed himself to a point of view from which he cannot rise above negativity. Even his memories of the Resistance cannot raise the pressure of his consciousness for any length of time.

All this becomes clear in what has always been his most popular play, *Huis Clos—In Camera*—devoted to his proposition that "Hell is other people." The three characters who find themselves in hell—a Second Empire drawing room—are a pacifist who died a coward, a woman who murdered her baby, and a lesbian. They are selected so they will cause one another maximum torment. The man, Garcin, is sexually interested in the baby killer, Estelle, and left alone, they might lie to one another and admire one another. But Ines, the lesbian, makes this impossible, so they are forced to spend all eternity recognizing that they will always cause one another maximum friction and discomfort. It is virtually a dramatization of *Being and Nothingness*.

One perceptive critic, Philip Thody, has pointed out that Sartre's real weakness is that while he can present a credible picture of hell, he has no compensatory vision of heaven—for according to *Being and Nothingness*, the characters would still be no better off even if they admired one another; human relations lead inevitably to frustration.

In September 1944 Paris was liberated. And Sartre at last came into his own. With *In Camera*, *The Respectful Prostitute*, and *Crime Passionnel* he became France's most successful author. His friend, Albert Camus, another ex-Resistance fighter, shared his success. Like Sartre, Camus had laid the groundwork for being taken seriously with earlier works—the novel, *The Outsider* (*L'Etranger*), and the study of the "human condition," *The Myth of Sisyphus*. Camus' new novel, *The Plague*, became a best-seller largely because the French interpreted the bubonic plague that strikes a small Algerian town as the German invaders. Existentialism became the fashion. When, in October 1945, Sartre gave a lecture called *Is Existentialism a Humanism?*, the crowds were so great that hundreds had to be turned away, and Sartre had to repeat it the next evening. (In this lecture, Sartre described T. E. Lawrence as an existentialist, although this was cut out of the published version, and I was unaware of it when I made Lawrence a central figure in *The Outsider* in 1956.)

For the "existentialists"—Sartre, Camus and Simone de Beauvoir—fame and fortune had arrived; their success was spectacular. Sartre launched a magazine, *Les Temps Modernes*, which quickly became a vehicle for left-wing opinions. Beauvoir dramatized all this in her novel, *The Mandarins*, which contains obvious portraits of Sartre and Camus, and which also became a best-seller.

My own experience of overnight "fame" in 1956 convinces me that, no matter how desirable it sounds, that kind of sensational success is a poisoned chalice. Writers were never intended to swim in a literary maelstrom; all truly significant writing is the result of working alone—for as Yeats said, "Truth flourishes where the scholar's lamp has shone." Anyone who writes with a feeling that his audience is looking over his shoulder is bound to experience a loss of spontaneity.

In Camus' case, the break with Sartre over Camus' book, *The Rebel,* was a deeply depressing experience, and the 1957 Nobel Prize was a kind of final blow. Those who had always thought he had been too successful, but had been intimidated by his reputation for integrity, now began to attack him. By the time of his death in a car accident in 1960, Camus was disillusioned and embittered.

Sartre was, to some extent, protected by his oracular obscurity; but he also found that living in the public spotlight took its toll. He was to write only one more play that compares with his best. *Les Sequestrés D'Altona* (*The Hermits of Altona*, 1959), is a more elaborate version of *In Camera*, in which hell is a mansion in Altona, near Hamburg, owned by a wealthy shipbuilder. His son, who tortured Russians during the war, has locked himself away in a room, tormented by guilt yet refusing to face it—his only consolation being that he believes postwar Germany to be in ruins. One line is utterly typical of Sartre, "Mad people tell the truth, and there is only one truth: the horror of being alive." And at the end of the play, the wealthy shipbuilder and his son both commit suicide. Altona is yet another depressing study in "bad faith," in which there is not a single gleam of hope—or room for further development.

The fascination that Sartre revealed for the homosexual rebel Jean Genet—of whom he wrote a book, *Saint Genet, Actor and Martyr* (1952)—is also based on the notion of self-deception: the fact that after Genet was caught stealing, he accepted that he had been labeled a thief, and was determined to be a thief and a criminal. In his determination to be "evil," he had betrayed fellow criminals, and become a homosexual prostitute. Yet—as we can guess from *Being and Nothingness*—this attempt to turn himself into an en-soi, a fully defined being, is bound to fail. He remains an actor rather than the "real thing."

Oddly enough, Sartre's vast book on Genet aroused Genet's resentment. It bathed him in the same kind of spotlight that had made Camus so unhappy, and made him awkward and self-conscious; he was even less happy in his role as existential saint than in that of criminal and anarchist. He later accused Sartre of destroying his creative impulse.

Sartre's enthusiasm for Genet raises in the reader's mind a suspicion that, in practice, "existentialist morality" is simply muddled and self-contradictory. The truth is that Genet's books, with their shock tactics and sadism, fail to convince the reader that he is making valid use of his creative powers, and most readers will find his anti-authoritarianism childish.

Sartre's attitude to Genet is one of the first signs that something has started to go wrong. He seems to have lost all common sense. How can anyone who claims to be a philosopher, and not just a political agitator, talk about "that Hell of misery and blood known as the Free World," and declare that true progress now lies in the attempt of the colored races to liberate themselves through violence?

The explanation probably lies in the fact that the early Sartre was too cynical and pessimistic to have any political commitment, and that the war convinced him that this was irresponsible—in short, induced a feeling of guilt. The early play *Mort Sans Sepulture*—about the Resistance—shows him obsessed by torture and brutality. Typically, Sartre failed to realize that showing a person being tortured on stage would only alienate the audience, since it would destroy the "suspension of disbelief," and make the torture seem a frivolous attempt to bully the audience into submission. The same kind of miscalculation seems to lie behind his increasingly strident leftism. The early Sartre had been deeply suspicious of communism, and the hero of the novel, *The Age of Reason*, feels simply that he is too intelligent to swallow such crude dogmas. Yet by the 1950s, Sartre has swallowed it, and by the 1960s is embracing Maoism. It all seems to have as little to do with philosophy as Heidegger's brief and disastrous flirtation with Nazism.

It also seems to have been Sartre's guilt about his early cynicism and detachment that drove him to attempt to unite existentialism and

Marxism in the *Critique of Dialectical Reason*. Common sense tells us that existentialism is as incompatible with Marxism as it is with Catholicism. At least Catholicism accepts that man possesses free will, and that he conditions himself by his choice of good or evil. Marxism regards man as a creature entirely conditioned by economic circumstances, and holds the naive belief that sufficient wealth for all would bring the utopian society.

Now, just as Sartre had been forced to revise his views on the impotence of freedom by the war, so now he had somehow to revise his notion that man is a useless passion, and his view that all human relationships are based on hostility. So in the *Critique*, he explains that the hostility of man to man is based on scarcity, lack of enough food to go round. In effect, he has simply surrendered to the Marxist view that the world would become a paradise if all the capitalist were hanged from lampposts. It is hard to understand how a philosopher can indulge in such naiveté.

In fact, Sartre was simply running out of steam. Just as Hemingway's view that all human values are negated by death meant that his work failed to develop after the mid-thirties, so Sartre's early pessimism meant that he had painted himself into a corner. He could continue to make Maoist speeches in defiance of de Gaulle, and invite the police to arrest him, but his development as a thinker and a creative force was at an end. One critic had called volume one of *The Critique of Dialectical Reason* "a mammoth and unreadable book;" but the unfinished volume two is—as the summary by Ronald Aronson in *The Philosophy of Jean Paul Sartre* (in the Library of Living Philosophers series) reveals—so muddled and jargon-ridden as to be incomprehensible.

Sartre's last years were sad—as Simone de Beauvoir's memoir, *Farewell to Sartre*, makes clear. He was still involved in a maelstrom of pointless political activity, drinking too much vodka, and sleeping with enthusiastic groupies. His last major work was his vast book on Flaubert, *The Idiot of the Family*, in which he pays homage to a writer whom he would once have attacked as a bourgeois. The grounds for his enthusiasm are that Flaubert gave his life a sense of purpose by embracing a "project," and recreating himself. It is as though Sartre is aware that his own project has ended in intellectual bankruptcy.

The autobiography, *Words*, is a confession of failure. It is devoted to an astonishingly frank account of his childhood daydreams of fame and glory, and admits, "My retrospective illusions are in pieces.

Martyrdom, salvation, immortality, all are crumbling; the building is falling in ruins . . . I see clearly, I am free from illusions, I know my real tasks, and surely I must deserve a civic prize; for about ten years I have been a man who is waking up, cured of a long, bitter-sweet madness . . . And who no longer has any idea of what to do with his life . . . I have renounced my vocation, but I have not unfrocked myself. I still write. What else can I do?"

Sartre died on Tuesday, April 15, 1980, at the age of 74.

My view of what went wrong with Sartre should have emerged clearly in this essay, but let me restate it briefly. From the moment he tried to create a phenomenology without a transcendental ego, he had condemned himself to self-contradiction. Without some kind of belief in a "permanent self," the whole concept of will and purpose collapses. If it is meaningless that we live and meaningless that we die, then there is no point in making any effort.

Sartre's most important flash of insight came during his period in the Resistance, when he realized that the threat of arrest and torture brought a powerful sense of freedom. Why? Because the threat of crisis arouses us to attention, concentration. This rescues us from our mechanical alter-ego, "the robot," and awakens the will and the imagination. The threat of arrest and death had galvanized Sartre's imagination into recognizing that any form of freedom is preferable to extinction.

Ideally, human beings should be able to develop a form of consciousness in which they are permanently aware of potential disaster, and in which therefore they realize that merely to be alive is a blessing. What is needed, in the last analysis, is a feeling of generalized anticipation, of the kind we experience when we set out on holiday: the sense that although what tomorrow may bring is still unknown, it is sure to be fascinating.

Dostoevsky had faced death on the Semyonovsky Square, and thereafter he never lost his feeling that life is a blessing. But even after his recognition of the value of freedom in the Resistance, Sartre could still write, "Man is a useless passion." From such a foundation, no further development of ideas was possible; instead, he was obliged to content himself with left-wing political agitation, which he would once have condemned as bad faith.

Sartre remains one of the most interesting philosophers of the twentieth century, but his career is a demonstration of the impossibility of long-term development from a foundation of moral nihilism.

22

HUYSMANS:
THE ULTIMATE DECADENT

A few days ago there was a ring at my doorbell, and a man whose face I failed to recognize reminded me that we had been introduced at a science-fiction conference in Ghent many years ago. Now he was taking a girlfriend on a tour of southern England and had decided to include me in his itinerary. When they were installed in my sitting room with glasses of wine, he asked me what I was writing at present; I explained that I had been rereading *A Rébours* as a prelude to writing a chapter about Huysmans. "Ah Huysmans! He is my favorite writer. I have brought *A Rébours* on holiday so I could read it for the tenth time . . ."

It was a double piece of synchronicity, for I had been thinking only that morning, as I reread Brian Banks' *The Image of Huysmans*, that I must begin this chapter by saying that Huysmans remains a "cult figure" who inspires intense devotion in a small group of devotees. Now I had one of them sitting opposite me, and for the next half hour or so—until they had to return to their hotel for dinner—we discussed the strange life of Huysmans and the reason that he continues to exercise such power over a few discerning admirers. My visitor—whose name was Anton—struck me as a typical Huysmans enthusiast—thin, pale, bearded, intensely intellectual, and with a look of one who was not quite "of this world." I could almost hear him quoting that old friend of Huysmans, Villiers de L'Isle Adam, "As for living, our servants can do that for us . . ."

Now the odd thing is that most of Huysmans' admirers would admit that he was probably not a great writer on the scale of Balzac, Hugo, Flaubert, and even Zola; he was too subjective for that. Then what is the source of this fascination which, in my own case, has lasted ever since I discovered *A Rébours* some forty-five years ago, via Wilde's *Picture of Dorian Gray*? It lies, I think, in this: that Huysmans' life and work are inextricably intertwined, and that the life itself is at least as interesting as the work. Moreover, as Brian Banks observes, Huysmans is literally a painter in words, and to read him is to be transported back to the Paris of Manet and Renoir and Toulouse Lautrec. There is no writer, with the possible exception of his friend Maupassant (of whom I shall speak later), who can evoke fin-de-siècle Paris with such vividness and color.

To grasp something of the fascination of Huysmans, it is only necessary to retell the story of how he achieved his early success.

Joris-Karl Huysmans (who preferred to be known as Georges) was born in Paris in 1848, the son of a painter and illustrator who died when his son was eight. His mother remarried, and the remainder of Huysmans' childhood was insecure and affection-starved. He was bullied at the boarding school to which he gained a scholarship, and at the age of seventeen, flatly refused to return there. But the shy, introverted boy had at least one thing in his favor: he lived on the Left Bank, amid the streets described in Henri Murger's *Scenes de la Vie de Bohème*. The book became his bible. Paris did for Huysmans what Dublin did for James Joyce: it provided him with a lifelong subject. Nietzsche remarked, "The great man is the play actor of his own ideals," and Huysmans' ideal was to become a "Bohemian." If he had been born in Marseilles or Lille, it is highly probable that we would never have heard of him. But with the "scenes of Bohemian life" around him every day, he was able to transform boredom with the power of imagination. At sixteen he lost his virginity with a middle-aged prostitute; at nineteen he took a soubrette from a cabaret as his mistress. (He gained access to her by posing as a journalist.) By that time he was studying law and when his stepfather died, he lost no time in abandoning law and moving into a cheap apartment with his mistress. By now he had obtained a post as a sixth-grade clerk of the sixth rank in the Ministry of the Interior, in which he was to remain for the next thirty years—it was so poorly paid that when his mistress gave birth to a baby, Huysmans did not even have enough money for a fire in the room. He was saved from the misery and boredom of living en ménage by the outbreak of the Franco-Prussian war; what became of the mistress and baby is unknown.

Huysmans was conscripted at the end of July, 1870, but he spent most of the short-lived Franco-Prussian war in a hospital with dysentery. He was in Paris during the siege and surrender, but was at his desk—in Versailles—during the bloody Commune and its aftermath. Soon he was back in the Latin Quarter, living the life of la Boheme and deploring what he called the "Americanization" of the Left Bank.

Since he was in his late teens, Huysmans had—following in the footsteps of his father—written the occasional art criticism. Now, under the influence of Baudelaire, he produced a series of prose-poems, which were completed by 1873. It was a late start for a writer—twenty-five—but Huysmans always wrote slowly and meticulously. Through his mother, he obtained an introduction to a publisher (his stepfather had owned a small printing business), but a meeting with M. Hetzel left him shattered. Hetzel told him that he had no talent whatsoever and never would have, and that his style was execrable. It took him some time to recover from this blow to his self-esteem, but he allowed friends to persuade him that Hetzel was an idiot and that he should publish the book at his own expense.

He did so—the *Drageoir à Épices* (translated roughly "Dish—or Cabinet—of Spices") came out in October, 1874. To begin with, it looked as if it was stillborn. But two influential men of letters decided that Huysmans deserved encouragement; one published some extracts from the book in his magazine, while the other wrote letters to critics drawing attention to it. In the following January the poet Theodore de Banville praised the book as a "skillfully cut jewel from the hand of a master goldsmith," and suddenly Huysmans had "arrived." Admittedly, the arrival went almost unnoticed; nevertheless, the book went into a second impression. Huysmans began to meet other artists and writers and a newly-launched periodical opened its columns to him.

Huysmans was certainly fortunate that literary success in Paris depended upon becoming a member of a clique and that his first volume was modest enough to arouse no jealousy. Anatole France, four years Huysmans' senior, was enduring much the same kind of apprenticeship at the time, and was patronized by some of the same people (like Catulle Mendès). Huysmans' early contributions to periodicals revealed his affinity with painting, and his remarkable ability to describe a picture in words. But his attempts to create something on a larger scale ended in failure; by nature, he was a miniaturist. But after abandoning a novel about the war and a volume of short stories, chance again came to his aid. During an evening with friends, Huysmans launched into autobiography, telling them about his liaison with the soubrette, and his anticlimactic war experiences. They pressed him to write about them, and Huysmans decided to try. Part of the war novel was salvaged as a story called *Sac au Dos* (*The Knapsack*), while the soubrette became a girl called Marthe, whose sordid adventures as a lady of loose morals probably inspired Zola's bestseller *Nana*. But Paris was not yet ready for this kind of realism, and Huysmans decided that he would have the book privately printed in Brussels. Even here, luck was against him; most of the copies were impounded by French customs as an offense to public morals.

Yet again he turned defeat into a kind of victory. *Marthe* gained him the friendship of Edmond de Goncourt and Emile Zola. Goncourt and his brother Jules (who had died in 1870) were virtually the founders of the new French "realism" (or naturalism). Zola was at the time (1876) its most controversial champion. He had learned the value of shock tactics in the early novel, *Thérèse Raquin*, with a particularly brutal murder scene. The vast *Rougon-Macquart* cycle, inspired by Balzac's *Comedie Humaine*, was intended to be a demonstration of the laws of heredity, but as the cycle progressed, the shock tactics became increasingly outrageous; every novel contained some scene designed to arouse moral indignation or make the reader feel slightly sick. Zola, a brilliant publicist, had chosen a cunning method of putting critics on the defensive. The pseudo-scientific plan of *Le Rougon-Macquart* meant that if critics accused him of salacity or crude sensationalism, he was able to shout back that they were too squeamish and feeble to endure his brutal honesty. And the critic who really objected to the crudeness and inaccuracy of the "realism" became still more enraged as he saw that he had no hope of escaping his false position.

Posterity has come to agree with Zola's critics: that he was little more than a crude poster artist. But in 1876, the year of the serial publication of *L'Assommoir*, a relentless and melodramatic portrait of a couple sinking into alcoholism, Huysmans was ready to believe that Zola was the greatest of living French novelists. His close friends

Henry Ceard and Ludovic Francmesnil agreed, while another friend, "Professor" Bobin, strongly disagreed. Ceard knocked on Zola's front door, expressing discipleship, and was kindly received. Huysmans soon followed with copies of the *Drageoir* and *Marthe*. Another Zola disciple, Paul Alexis, introduced Huysmans and Ceard to two unknown young writers called Leon Hennique and Guy de Maupassant. The five began to call regularly on the Zolas on Thursdays, and soon Hennique was giving a public lecture in defense of *L'Assommoir*, while Huysmans was publishing a series of articles about it. He declared, "Green pustules and pink flesh are all one to us; we depict both because both exist. . . ." In fact, the association was mutually beneficial; Zola gained an ardent young defender; Huysmans gained notoriety as the philosopher of the new movement called naturalism.

Huysmans' next novel, *Les Soeurs Vatard* (*The Vatard Sisters*), appeared in 1879 and, thanks to his new notoriety, sold fairly well. It is beautifully observed and superbly written. But, like *Marthe*, it is a thoroughly gloomy piece of work—the tale of two working-class sisters, employees in a book bindery (like the one now owned by Huysmans since the death of his mother), who have thoroughly unsatisfactory love affairs with unsuitable men. The lover of the elder of the two, the artist Cyprien Tibaille, is interesting mainly as a foreshadowing of the famous Des Esseintes of *A Rébours*. In a glowing review, Zola said he hoped Huysmans would be "hounded by a pack of envious, impotent fools," for he would then know his own strength. But a hostile critic said with accuracy that it was "bleak, hateful and infinitely sad."

Now Huysmans obtained a job as an art critic, and took a leaf out of Zola's book, determined to cause controversy; his onslaught on the Salon of 1879 created outrage and made him hordes of enemies. And when Leon Hennique suggested that they all produce a war story for a book to be published under Zola's aegis, Huysmans dusted off *Sac au Dos* and made some changes. Zola contributed *The Attack on the Mill*; Hennique, Ceard and Alexis also produced war stories. And the neophyte Maupassant wrote a story called *Boulle de Suif*, which is now the only one in the volume that is remembered. *Les Soirées de Médan* (Medan being Zola's new home in the country) was an immediate success, running through eight editions. It launched the meteoric literary career of Maupassant, and finally made Huysmans something of a household name.

Yet in retrospect, it can clearly be seen that, where Huysmans was concerned, the whole association with Zola was something of a misunderstanding. The truth is that Zola's naturalism had much in common with that of his friends, Manet and Cezanne; he enjoyed transferring the real world onto his own canvas. He was not really a pessimist by temperament, any more than most of the Impressionists were. The gloom and violence of *La Bête Humaine* and *La Terre* were chosen, like striking colors, because they were more effective than lyricism or optimism. If you had asked Zola whether he thought life was tragic, he would have replied that it is certainly intolerable for a large number of people because of poverty and social inequality, but that in essence it is neither tragedy nor triumph.

But Huysmans' pessimism was an integral part of his personality. His miserable schooldays, his unsatisfactory attempt at domesticity, the setbacks of literary life, and the backbiting and envy of the French cultural establishment, had convinced him that life is basically a series of frustrations. He did not believe in happiness. If you had asked Huysmans the same question, he would have replied: not tragic but futile. In fact, he was convinced that the nihilistic Schopenhauer was one of the few philosophers who had seen life clearly and without distortion.

This meant that while Zola's life was a search for success and fame—which he achieved in abundance—Huysmans' was a search for a personal fulfillment which he believed, intellectually speaking, to be beyond his grasp—in fact beyond the grasp of any human being. The result is that although they thought themselves allies in naturalism, he and Zola were really traveling in opposite directions. Zola was successful and satisfied, while Huysmans was like a man groaning with a toothache. Sooner or later, Zola's attitude was bound to strike him as shallow and irritating.

The gulf between Zola and Huysmans can be clearly seen in Huysmans next publication, *Croquis Parisiens* (*Parisian Sketches*), published in 1880, the same year as Zola's *Nana*. Huysmans' book is a series of prose poems, all full of "atmosphere" and of Huysmans' rather lugubrious, "decadent" attitude to life. "Nature is only interesting when she is sickly and desolate. I will not attempt to deny her marvels and her glories, the occasions when the heartiness of her laughter causes her to split her bodice of dark rocks and flaunt her green nippled bosom in the sunlight; but I must admit that I do not experience when faced with the exuberance of her full-flowing sap, anything like the pitying attraction which is aroused in me by a desolate corner in a large town, a ravaged piece of hillside, or a narrow ditch dribbling along between two slender trees." This is not "naturalism." It is the sadness of Verlaine or Ernest Dowson, and of Yeats' "tragic generation"; it has something in common with Balzac but nothing whatever with the coarse vitality of *Nana*.

One particularly significant piece in the *Croquis* was called "The Prose Poem of Roast Meat", and describes a bachelor going for his regular evening meal in a local restaurant where the food is cheap and bad. "The moment has come for the reddish lukewarm damp-smelling meat to turn your stomach." And as he eats his atrocious meal and drinks soda water, he thinks of a girl he almost married, and imagines what it would have been like to be eating at his own table and drinking good burgundy. But then he sees "the other side of the picture": "having to take part in a continual exchange of inane ideas" and play silly games with his children, saddled with a nagging wife who probably sleeps with other men. Then his thoughts turn to a mature mistress "whose appetite for love was at an end," and who would put up with his "little fads" and cook him excellent meals of tender beefsteaks. This, he decides, would be the ideal.

The daydream took root and turned into his next novel, *En Ménage*, his best so far. But the subject is as uninspiring as in *Marthe* and *The Vatard Sisters*: the moderately successful novelist, Andre Jayant, decides to marry to escape the dreariness of bachelor life, but finds his petty-minded, empty-headed wife unbearable. When she is unfaithful, he leaves her to live with a prostitute, but is unable to suppress his jealousy of her clients. He then returns to an earlier mistress, but when she leaves him to go and work in London, finally heaves a sigh and goes back to his wife.

And here, for the first time, the reader is struck forcefully by the reflection that the hero's boredom and dissatisfaction are entirely his own fault. His attitude towards life is negative and self-pitying. He puts little into it, and consequently gets little out of it. All children and teenagers are familiar with the problem. They find it easy to slip into a state of fretful boredom which causes "negative feedback." The feeling that nothing is worth the effort, causing a sinking of the energies (for we summon energy, like summoning the genie out of the lamp, when we are gripped by purpose), which in turn increases the feeling that life is a bore, which increases the sense of fatigue. And so on in a cycle of self-enfeeblement. It seems incredible that a man in his thirties could still be subject to this childhood ailment, and that he should lack the insight to grasp his predicament. But that was clearly Huysmans' problem, and there is no point in pretending otherwise. If he were not such a fascinating word painter, we would lose patience. As it is, we read him for the language and the atmosphere, and wish that he had half the exuberant vitality of his friend Maupassant, whose uproarious collection, *La Maison Tellier* (whose title story is about a crowd of prostitutes on an outing from a provincial brothel), appeared in the same year.

But we can see that, given his negative "premises," Huysmans is going to find it increasingly difficult to find a subject to write about—not to mention the energy to sustain the effort of creation. So we are not surprised to learn that soon after publishing *En Ménage*, he was suffering attacks of neuralgia and becoming increasingly bored with Zola's demands for research into subjects like suburban architecture and the design of rare postage stamps, which Zola was too lazy to do himself.

It seems somehow typical that the next novel, *A Vau L'Eau* (*Drifting Downstream*), is little more than a long short story less than a fifth the size of *En Ménage*. It also reads like a postscript to *En Ménage*, in that the hero, Jean Folantin, is a bored little clerk whose sexual relationships are as disastrous as those of Andre Jayant of the previous novel, and who ends by deciding that since Schopenhauer is right when he says that "life is a pendulum that swings between suffering and boredom," he will now abandon all attempt at controlling his own destiny and "drift downstream." In his biography of Huysmans, Robert Baldick says that Folantin is one of the "great types" in French literature—one who has been succeeded by Duhamel's Salavin and Sartre's Roquentin. In fact, the closest literary relatives of Folantin are Goncharov's Oblomov, the heroes of Samuel Beckett, and those of the Russian nihilist Mikhail Artsybashev (of whom I shall speak later).

And so Huysmans found himself at the end of his tether. What was he to do after deciding to drift downstream? To begin with, he decided that it was time to abandon naturalism. After all, if he found everyday life so boring, what was the point in describing it in detail? The answer had to be a change of scene—from boredom and objectivity to poetry and intense subjectivity. He would create a hero who, like *de L'Isle Adam's* Axel, would regard mere living as an affair for servants. His hero, of course, had to be rich enough to indulge his whims, and intelligent enough to find pleasure in his own company—in other words, the complete opposite of Folantin.

The result, *A Rébours*, became one of the most famous novels of its time. The title is almost untranslatable. *Against the Grain* sounds oddly anonymous; *Against Nature* is closer to the spirit of the book. But since Huysmans explains that his hero, Des Esseintes, occasionally takes his nourishment "à rébours"—through the rear end—when eating bores him, it could equally be translated *Up the Arsehole*—a version that would undoubtedly have pleased the author.

Des Esseintes is a bored aristocrat of feeble constitution who has tried "unnatural loves and perverse pleasures" (in fact Huysmans' own experiments with homosexuality had disgusted him), and now wants only to escape the world and live in a self-created cocoon. This has the charm of a daydream; Huysmans spends chapter after chapter self-indulgently describing the life of someone who wishes to turn his back on the coarseness of reality, and live a life of the mind and the emotions. "Travel struck him as a waste of time, since he believed that the imagination could provide a more-than-adequate substitute for the vulgar reality of actual experience . . ."

This sentence also captures the fundamental appeal of the book, Huysmans' intuition that the evolution of man lies in the imagination. But it also underlines the nature of his problem: his gloomy certainty that "this world" is a bore and that the only solution lies in "escape." In fact, every child knows that imagination is not a substitute for reality but a transcendence of it; they know it because every delightful experience underlines the point. The happiness of Christmas Day, of birthday parties, of visits to the seaside, of drowsy summer picnics by the river, is a happiness based on reality. But happiness stimulates the imagination and transforms reality, like looking at a tree through a prism. The answer is not therefore to turn one's back on reality, but to transform it by a strengthening of the power of imagination, which the French psychologist Pierre Janet rightly identified as "the reality function." Doctor Johnson glimpsed the answer when he commented, "When a man knows he is to be hanged in a fortnight, it concentrates his mind wonderfully." It would be a pity to get ourselves hanged to stimulate the imagination; but there is nothing to prevent us from disciplining the imagination, until it can reproduce the sense of urgency of a man about to be hanged.

I allow myself the indulgence of this commentary because the problem stated so powerfully by Huysmans is the problem at the heart of my first book, *The Outsider* (1956), which is fundamentally a study of the "romantic agony," and of "outsiders" who, like Huysmans, are inclined to feel that life is a tale told by an idiot. Des Esseintes symbolizes the problem so well that he can also be made to illuminate its solution.

The truth is that Des Esseintes has simply allowed himself to collapse like a punctured tire. "During the last months of his residence in Paris . . . sapped by disillusionment, depressed by hypochondria and weighed down by boredom, he had been reduced to such a state of nervous sensitivity that the sight of a disagreeable person or thing was deeply impressed upon his mind, and it took several days even to begin removing the imprint . . ." So he spends his days reading his favorite Latin writers, tasting liqueurs from his "mouth-organ," which will allow a single drop of each to fall on his tongue (an enterprise doomed to failure since a drop of any single liqueur would destroy the taste of all the others), and meditating upon the paintings of Gustave Moreau.

In Chapter Six, an altogether more sinister note is struck. Des Esseintes picks up a poverty-stricken urchin and decides, just for the fun of it, to try and turn him into a murderer by plunging him into a life of luxury and then abandoning him, so that he will become a criminal. The plan goes awry, but the episode suddenly makes the reader aware that Des Esseintes is not merely a harmless aesthete. There would have been no difference in principle in deliberately turning the boy into a drug addict—or committing the murder himself. His philosophy is chillingly close to that of de Sade.

The most amusing—and typical—episode in the novel is the one in which Des Esseintes feels a sudden urge to go to London, but decides to stop on the way for a meal in the English tavern near the Gare St. Lazare—and then, after eating an English meal, reflects that he has now tasted the very essence of London; by comparison, the real thing will be a bore. So he goes home again.

Typically, the novel ends on a note of defeat. Ordered back to Paris by his doctor, Des Esseintes decides that even "the noble pessimism of Schopenhauer" is no answer. So after pronouncing a curse on the corruption of the modern world, and the Americanization of everything he cares about, he prepares to go and rejoin "the servile riff-raff" of Paris. He ends up with a kind of prayer: "Lord, take pity on the

Christian who doubts, on the unbeliever who would fain believe, on the galley slave of life who puts out to sea alone in the night, beneath a firmament no longer lit by the consoling beacon fires of ancient hope." As Brian Banks observes in *The Image of Huysmans*, he is obviously ready to fling himself into the arms of religion.

This, of course, is what he did—although not before exploring the realm of late nineteenth-century occultism and demonology.

But before embarking on this venture into non-naturalism, Huysmans was to write two more "naturalistic" novels. One of these, *A Dilemma*, need not detain us; first, it was actually written before *A Rébours*, and second, it is simply an unpleasant study in the villainy of the bourgeoisie, in which a rascally lawyer, and his politician son, set out to defraud a pregnant girl of the money due to her after the death of her lover. It is Huysmans at his most negative.

En Rade is a different matter. It has been translated as *Becalmed*, but the title actually means "in dry dock," referring to a ship that has been laid up for repair.

Here Huysmans takes the logical next step after *A Rébours*. Des Esseintes wants to turn his back on the real world; Jacques Marles, the hero of *En Rade*, retires to the ruined Chateau de Lourps (where Des Esseintes was born), with its "catarrhal gutter pipes, blotchy plaster, rheumy windows, fistular stonework and leprous bricks," and discovers that he has a strange capacity for floating off into a world of dreams. In effect, Marles is able to achieve what Rimbaud called "an ordered derangement of the senses," or Jung, "active imagination." The first time is when Marles is lying on a bed beside his sleeping wife.

"Suddenly, something strange happened. The green bars of the trellis-work began to undulate, while the salmon-colored wooden surround began to ripple like a running stream."

This is what Huysmans—in common with all his fellow Romantics—really wanted: for the real world to dissolve away, giving way to a world of strange visions.

In this case he seems to float through the ceiling, where he sees an immense palace, "reaching up into the clouds in layers of terraces, esplanades, lakes enclosed by brazen banks, towers crowned with battlements of iron, domes covered with scales, obelisks in groups with their points covered in snow like mountain peaks . . ."

The vision is, in fact, based on a painting of Gustave Moreau, who also inspired Wilde. And, as in Moreau, the centerpiece is a beautiful girl, whose clothes are stripped off by a man with a domelike head. Then she is made to lie down with her thighs open, and subjected to "the transports of an irrevocable union, abusing her skin rendered noble with unguents, crushing her unblemished flesh, desecrating the tight ciborium of her thighs . . ."

Marles has a number of these dream-visions, the most remarkable being one of a kind of moon landscape. But Marles' strange experiences fail to reach any kind of climax, and at the end of the book, he and his wife simply decide to return to Paris. Huysmans must have recognized that Marles' capacity to enter a dream world could lead nowhere, for Marles can never become a permanent inhabitant of the world of dreams—except, perhaps, by dying.

En Rade was a failure; most of its critics, including Zola, pointed out that Huysmans had simply failed to integrate his two worlds. Huysmans commented that he wished he had stuck to his original plan—to alternate a chapter of reality with a chapter of dreams. But this would not have helped. The challenge he failed to meet was to connect the dreamworld and the world of reality, so they bear some meaningful relation to one another. Instead, they remain as disconnected as if they belonged to two different books.

Once again, Huysmans' attempt to solve the problem of idealism and reality had failed. And it was at this point that he began to wonder whether he might not find his solution in "the occult," whose starting point is the existence of another reality.

He chose as his guide an unfrocked Abbé named Boullan, whom he believed to be wronged by the ecclesiastical authorities—only to discover, after Boullan's death, that he had done more horrific things than anyone had accused him of.

Huysmans' excursion into demonology is described in one of his most powerful novels, *Là Bas* (*Down Below*), which brought him even wider notoriety than *A Rébours*. But the student who by now knows his Huysmans can see perfectly well that all this is just one more attempt to solve the problem of his boredom. And, moreover, that as usual, he has failed to solve it because he has failed to grasp that it is his own fault.

When he writes about the sadistic crimes against children committed by Gilles de Rais (of whom the hero is writing a biography), it is obvious that Huysmans is not truly aware of the horror of the subject; his imagination—or what the psychologist Janet would have called his "reality function"—is too feeble to grasp the reality of a man who disembowels children, and he treats it as a bizarre eccentricity. (This is probably true of the majority of people who are fascinated by murder; my collaborator on *An Encyclopedia of Murder*, Pat Pitman, suddenly found the subject nauseating after she had had a baby.)

The enfeeblement of his "reality function" again becomes apparent in a key episode in which the hero, Durtal, receives a letter from an unknown woman declaring her admiration. The reader's curiosity is piqued (for whatever his faults, Huysmans knows how to keep us turning the pages), and Durtal's attempts to establish her identity are amusing and inventive. Inevitably, when Durtal finally meets Hyacinthe Chantelouve, that experienced coquette pretends indifference, and he is soon convinced that he is in love with her. But when she finally comes to his apartment, and vanishes into the bedroom, he suddenly realizes that he no longer desires her. "Disillusion had come even before possession." And after possessing her, "Ah, yes, his disillusion was complete. The satiety following justified the lack of appetite preceding. She revolted and horrified him. Was it possible to have so desired a woman only to come to—that?" In fact, the real Hyacinthe Chantelouve was something of a tart, but it is impossible not to feel that the effete and exhausted Huysmans would have felt the same about the goddess of love herself.

Mme. Chantelouve introduces Durtal to Canon Docre, a Satanist (based on a Belgian priest, Louis van Haecke), and Durtal finally attends a black mass, in which the altar boys are aging poufs, covered in cosmetics; after one of them has fellated Docre, the priest ejaculates on the host, then empties his bowels on the altar. After this, Mme. de Chantelouve takes Durtal to a cheap bar where she insists on having sex among the rubbish on the floor. It is the last straw, and Durtal ends the affair.

Huysmans described the last stage of his journey at some length in the three novels which still arouse most enthusiasm among Catholic readers: *En Route*, *La Cathédrale* and *L'Oblat*. I must confess that although I went to enormous lengths to find secondhand copies of the trilogy, I have never succeeded in finishing it. This is not because the books lack literary merit, but because it was so clear to me that Huysmans had simply chosen the wrong solution, and was wasting his time; under the circumstances, I did not propose to let him waste mine. It is reported that, when Tolstoy was dying, he remarked, "Even on my deathbed, two and two do not make six," and we would respect Huysmans more if he had the courage to face this fact. The decision to abandon reason and swallow the dogmas of Catholicism was no answer to his problems, because it sprang out of weakness and out of the old conviction that the only solution was to turn his back on "the world." Des Esseinte tried it and found it didn't work. Durtal seems unaware that he is merely repeating the mistakes of Des Esseintes in a religious key. But it is perfectly obvious to the reader that while Huysmans' attitude towards himself and towards life remains fundamentally negative, there can be no solution. It seems somehow typical that Huysmans died of cancer of the throat after appalling suffering.

And so, in retrospect, it is impossible not to feel that Huysmans' life was a sad moral fable. He possessed immense talent, even a touch of genius; the only thing he lacked was insight into his own boredom. But then, unlike his contemporary Nietzsche—whose life was in many ways so like his own—he was not a philosopher. In *Zarathustra*—whose essence lies in the comment, "I have made my philosophy out of my will to health"—Nietzsche has left us a masterpiece of optimism of which Huysmans would have been incapable. But then, in his finest prose, Huysmans left us some masterpieces of atmosphere of which Nietzsche would have been incapable. Perhaps that is achievement enough for any man.

23

ZOLA AND MAUPASSANT

I became interested in Emile Zola as a result of my fascination with Jack the Ripper. This had come about, as I have described in an earlier chapter, through a book called *The Fifty Most Amazing Crimes in the Last Hundred Years*, which had been given to my father by someone at the factory where he worked. We children were told that we were not allowed to read it; consequently, we seized every opportunity when our parents were out.

Each chapter had a picture of the murderer at the beginning—Crippen, Seddon, Dr. Pritchard. But the chapter on Jack the Ripper only had a large question mark. Naturally, I found it the most interesting chapter in the book—the mystery of the unknown maniac who had killed and mutilated five women in the autumn of 1888. In due course, my interest in the Ripper would be reflected in my first novel, *Ritual in the Dark*.

When I learned that Zola had written a novel about a "sex maniac"—*La Bête Humaine*—I went to the Reading Room of the British Museum, and ordered it. I was twenty at the time, and driven continually by powerful sexual desires. So I found this story of a young man—Jacques Lantier—who is tormented by a desire to attack girls, obsessively readable. Yet it soon became clear to me that Zola is not a serious novelist in the same sense as Dickens or Dostoevsky. He is out to shock, and the final scene, in which the driverless train rushes on into the night, seemed melodramatic and unconvincing.

Four years later, when *The Outsider* had been accepted by Victor Gollancz, the novelist Angus Wilson—whom I had met in the Reading Room—offered to lend me his country cottage to finish my "Jack the Ripper" novel, *Ritual in the Dark*. The cottage was in the middle of a field, near the village of Bradfield St. George, in Suffolk, and I was impressed by the number of books there. (Many of them were review copies, and it struck me as unutterably glamorous to receive free books from publishers.) Among them were a dozen or so volumes of Zola, in a recently-published edition, and Angus' own small book on Zola.

I read a few novels of Zola, including *La Terre*, *Thérèse Raquin* and *Pot Bouille*. Since I have already commented on Zola in the chapter on Huysmans, I shall not repeat it here; only say that I found his painstaking realism impressive. He made a habit of choosing some typical area of modern life for each novel—coal mines, the railway, the Paris meat market, a department store—and carefully researched it for months before he began writing. As a method, it excited me, but in Zola's case, the results were disappointing. He lacked vision, he lacked true genius—in fact, he was little more than a kind of literary journalist, deliberately spicing his sordid novels with sex as a cook might shake in the red pepper. Great novels, such as *Crime and Punishment* and *War and Peace*, leave behind a sense of satisfaction, such as we feel after listening to great music; Zola's novels always left me slightly shameful, as if I had been masturbating. So although I have read perhaps a dozen of his novels, and read at least two biographies, I no longer feel any urge to return to Zola. And I find Angus Wilson's contention that he is a great novelist, comparable to Dickens or Balzac, absurd and perverse.

On the other hand, it seems to me that there is a great deal to be said for Maupassant. As a teenager, I had read many of his short stories—in a Penguin volume containing *Boule de Suif* and other stories—but had not become an addict. Then, when I was married and living in London, I found a large volume of his stories—a hundred or more—in the local library. This, I found, was the way to read them—one after another, like eating peanuts. It is obvious that Maupassant heard some anecdote, or had some casual thought, that became the germ for a short story. But instead of writing it down in a notebook, as Henry James would, and brooding on how to "dramatize" it, Maupassant probably rushed home and wrote it down in two or three hours—then went off to join his mistress, or some friends sitting outside a cafe on a tree-lined boulevard. The result is usually excellent, like a sketch by a master painter.

For example, the story, "On a Spring Evening," quite clearly sprang from the thought of how sad it must be for women to spend their lives unmarried, to never experience the pleasure of lovemaking. He begins by describing two cousins, Jeanne and Jacques, who have been together since childhood, and who are expected to marry. Neither feels the slightest passion. But one day, Jeanne hears Jacques' mother saying that she is quite certain that the two are about to fall in love. And from that moment, says Maupassant, Jeanne begins to adore Jacques, and blushes whenever he comes into the room. Maupassant's observation of how self-consciousness can create a kind of hothouse of emotion is shrewd and convincing. Her new interest touches Jacques' vanity, and he begins to love her.

Aunt Lison, the sister of their widowed mothers, is a quiet, subdued little woman to whom no one pays any attention.

One spring evening, after they have been walking on the dewy lawn, Jeanne and Jacques come indoors, to find Aunt Lison waiting up for them. Jacques notices that Jeanne's shoes are covered with dew, and asks tenderly, "Aren't your dear little feet cold?" At this, Aunt Lison bursts into floods of tears. When the lovers finally persuade her to speak, she stammers, "No one has ever said that to me."

Yet this story also reveals the basic ambiguity of Maupassant. We might read it as a touching tribute to a poor old lady by a sensitive and compassionate writer. But the reader also suspects that the story sprang out of his own healthy sense of fulfillment, and is really a disguised form of self-congratulation.

This is, in fact, the essence of Maupassant. He seems to write of human misery with the detachment of a Martian psychologist. Dostoevsky was tormented by human misery; Maupassant analyses it clinically.

When we see a title like "The Story of a Farm Girl," we can be quite sure that it will be about a girl's betrayal. This, in fact, is true, but it has an additional twist. Jeanne, the farm girl, lets herself be seduced on a promise of marriage, by a farm laborer; when she becomes pregnant, he renews his promises of marriage, then flees. The baby is born prematurely, but survives. Jeanne leaves it with neighbors and goes back to work. The farmer, a childless widower, proposes to her, and when she refuses, forces himself on her. Finally, they marry. But she fails to become pregnant, and he becomes bitter and dissatisfied. One day, after a quarrel, he begins to beat her; she can stand it no longer, and confesses that she has a child. To her astonishment, her husband is delighted; they will go and fetch the child, and he will adopt it. And so the story ends with the wife making her husband a plate of soup, while he walks up and down and chuckles with satisfaction.

So, for once, a Maupassant story has a happy ending. One feels that Maupassant is indifferent whether it was happy or unhappy; he is simply an observer, a kind of photographer who loves taking snapshots of everyday life.

Tolstoy was deeply impressed by Maupassant's novel, *A Woman's Life*, which again seems to be a compassionate portrait of an innocent, idealistic girl, who longs for life and love. She marries a viscount, who seems to her handsome and noble, then finds out that he is mean and treacherous. He is killed by a cuckolded husband, and she now devotes her life to her son. But he proves to have inherited all his father's worst qualities, and causes her endless pain. Finally, her son's mistress dies soon after giving birth to a daughter; a servant girl goes to fetch the child, and hands it to her mistress. Overcome with emotion, the woman kisses the baby's face. And the servant remarks, "Life, after all, is neither as good or as bad as we think it."

But Tolstoy found Maupassant's later books immoral. *Bel-Ami* is about a handsome but penniless journalist who seduces his way to wealth and position, with the author's obvious approval. Suddenly, it becomes clear that Maupassant, like Zola, is obsessed by sex, and by the male's ability to achieve a sense of power by making women fall in love with him. Maupassant is the archetypal "male chauvinist pig." Sex fascinates him; in fact, he is virtually a sex maniac. Story after story, novel after novel, is about seduction. But he also seems to take a certain pleasure in showing women made miserable by unfaithful men, and one suspects that this increases his sense of male superiority. (Maupassant was a handsome man, a superb athlete, and an incorrigible libertine.)

But the reader has to admit that he is at his best in describing affairs of the heart and the paradoxes of the sexual impulse. A story called "The Unknown" is a classic. Roger des Annettes, a young man-about-town who prides himself on his powers as a seducer, describes how he passed a beautiful girl who filled him with feverish desire. It was a year later before he saw her again, and he followed her until she entered a house. He questioned the concierge, but the man did not know the woman he was talking about.

Eight months later, hurrying round a corner, he cannons into her. Apologizing profusely, he goes on to tell her that he has admired her for two years, and hoped to make her acquaintance. He begs her for the privilege of being allowed to call, and is dumbfounded when she says, "Give me your address. I will call on you."

She keeps her word and arrives a few mornings later. They have hardly exchanged more than a few words when he begins to undress her. As he watches, she completes undressing herself. But when she turns her back, he sees a patch of black hair between her shoulder blades. The thought of enchantresses from the Arabian Nights has the effect of causing his desire to drain away, and "when I came to sing my song of love, I found I had no voice left." And when it is clear to her that des Annettes is temporarily impotent, she says icily, "There was not much point in putting me to so much trouble, was there?" and dresses again. Subsequently, he has seen her twice in the street, but she has ignored his greeting.

What Maupassant has pinpointed here is the essentially aggressive nature of the male sexual impulse. For two years des Annettes has dreamed about "the unknown," who fills him with a purely erotic desire. She is not beautiful, but plump and sturdy, with a helmet of black hair, and the shadow of a moustache on her lip. But when she agrees to call at his house, the dream is already beginning to dissolve; this is too easy. And when, after less than twenty words, she allows him to begin taking her clothes off, it again seems suspiciously easy. At that point, the sight of the patch of black hair between her shoulder blades is enough to undermine the will to power that has fueled his obsession, and he suffers what Stendhal called "le fiasco"—a form of Sartre's "nausea." A whole essay could be written on the implications of this story, but Maupassant, with consummate skill, allows it to speak for itself.

A story called "The Revenge" underlines the absurd nature of the male sexual impulse. M. de Garelle is relaxing in an armchair in a hotel in Cannes, thinking about the wife whom he has recently divorced, when he is intrigued by a glimpse of a woman with a superb figure. Then, as she passes, he recognizes his wife. He engages her in conversation; at first she discourages him, then begins to enjoy the situation. He raises the question that torments him: whether she was unfaithful to him. She admits she was. In that case, he says, she owes him the stolen kisses that she gave to her lover. And when her husband's voice calls to her, he threatens to introduce himself, and tell the husband about her infidelity. (He is certain that her present husband was not her lover; otherwise—he reasons—he would not have married her.) Finally, she agrees to meet him after dinner. And M. de Garelle relaxes in his armchair, and reflects that he greatly prefers his present situation to the previous one—particularly now he has heard her husband summoning her with a proprietary tone.

The absurdity is obvious. He has already possessed her, so becoming her lover will offer no new revelations. She is the same person; he is the same person; it is merely the situation that has changed. And in the new situation, he is the wooer, trying to persuade her to cuckold her husband. Nothing could reveal more clearly that sex exists almost entirely in the mind.

But Maupassant's attitude towards sex is not entirely cynical. The late novel, *Notre Coeur*, although as a whole an artistic failure, contains one pleasantly idyllic episode. A rich bachelor falls in love with a society hostess, in spite of his determination not to do so. She gives herself to him, but he becomes her slave. One day, at a country hotel, he meets a pretty servant girl, and takes a liking to her. The next time he sees her, he notices that she is miserable; she admits that the proprietor is trying to seduce her, and that two young libertines have been treating her like a tart. Impulsively, he suggests that she enter his service, and gives her money. The next day she comes to his home. He finds her presence soothing, and the thought of his unhappy love affair and unfaithful mistress ceases to torment him.

One day, when he is tired and depressed, the girl reads him *Manon Lescaut*, and he begins to feel better. He can see that the girl is in love with him, but has no intention of taking advantage of her—it would cause too many complications. But in the middle of the night, he hears a noise and creeps downstairs. She is lying naked in the bath, and he is so overcome by her beauty that he falls on his knees beside her. She flings her arms round his neck, and his good resolutions evaporate. (In the American edition, this episode has been censored.)

But the idyll ends when his mistress arrives to see him, and he agrees to return to Paris. He tells the servant girl that he will take her with him, and set her up in her own apartment. And as the book ends, the reader knows that she is going to be miserable.

What is quite clear, by the end of *Notre Coeur*, is that Maupassant has lost all sense of direction. He can still tell a good story, but it has no conclusion. His last novel, *As Strong as Death*, is about a successful painter who for years has been having an affair with another man's wife. Then, one day, he realizes he is falling in love with her daughter. It is an interesting situation, and in his younger days, Maupassant might have resolved it by making him seduce the daughter, then showing the consequences. Instead, he shows the painter growing increasingly miserable and distressed, and the reader feels relieved when he is killed in a street accident. The novel seems quite pointless.

One of the basic themes of this book has been the impossibility of artistic development without some kind of a constructive philosophy. It may be possible for a painter to go on painting without any new ideas, for he merely has to observe nature and repeat what he has done in the past. But it is virtually impossible for a writer to mature without new ideas. So a writer like Hemingway, whose philosophy is basically pessimistic, has cut himself off from all possibility of development.

The same is true of Maupassant. He began as an observer, who was so fascinated by life that he made endless vivid sketches of people and events. But it is soon clear that he finds seduction the most fascinating thing in the world—and the chapters in *Notre Coeur* about the servant girl are so well done that he almost convinces us that this is true.

But seduction is merely the manifestation of the sexual illusion. When a man is in love, he feels that possessing the girl will be a foretaste of heaven. But the only real "development" that can follow possession is a satisfying relationship. Maupassant was obsessed by the idea that the male is a kind of sultan, and the whole female species a potential harem. But although promiscuity may be enjoyable, no person in his right mind would want to devote his life to it, any more than any person in his right mind would want to devote his life to cocktail parties or gourmet meals—or even to the pursuit of adventure.

But Maupassant had nothing else to fall back on. He regarded the decadent social world of Paris with a certain approval, and achieved his only sense of adventure from love affairs. In the preface to one of his least interesting novels, *Pierre and Jean*, he explains his theory of literature; he is a naturalist, and the writer's business is simply to observe and record what he sees. But he also confesses that he has no philosophical convictions; he sees life as totally deterministic. So in the last analysis, he is merely a writer, and nothing more. There is nothing in his work to appeal to those who read in order to be stimulated to think.

Fate saved Maupassant from increasing disillusionment by afflicting him with syphilis, picked up in a brothel; he began to go insane when he was forty—his story, "The Horla," is a horrifying account of a man's mental breakdown—and died three years later.

24

LEONID ANDREYEV

I can still read Maupassant's stories with enjoyment. I cannot say the same of another writer I greatly admired in my twenties, Leonid Andreyev. Andreyev was one of the literary heirs of Dostoevsky, but he lacked Dostoevsky's deep religious sense, and substituted a kind of savage pessimism that lends his work a certain gloomy power.

Born in the small Russian town of Oryol in August 1871, Andreyev was the son of a civil servant and a descendant of Polish aristocrats. His mother, although almost illiterate, had a vivid imagination, and told marvelous stories; she took him to the theater and encouraged him to read. He loved Jules Verne, Fenimore Cooper, and Dickens.

Later, among fellow students, he became known as "the duke"—proud, disdainful, but given to bursts of wild, high spirits. (This manic-depressive temperament was reinforced by Schopenhauer, and a tendency—inherited from his father—to alcoholism.) Like so many Russians, he spent a great deal of his time brooding on the meaning of life (which was the reason that I found him so interesting).

At an early stage, he read Schopenhauer, and Schopenhauer's disciple Eduard von Hartmann, author of *Philosophy of the Unconscious* (which I regard as in many ways a greater work than *The World as Will and Illusion*). Gorky remarks, in a preface to Andreyev's only novel, *Sashka Jigoulev*, "A friend of his writes in her reminiscences of him: 'He used to torture us.' 'You only think that the world exists,' he would say, 'when it is only your idea of it—it is possible that you too do not exist in reality—that you only do so in my imagination.'" Certainly, their influence was the worst possible thing Andreyev could have encountered at this stage.

He was only sixteen when he decided to "test his fate" by playing a form of Russian roulette. The story is typical. He describes how, walking along behind a party of friends who were singing and making merry, he was suddenly struck by the thought, "Why are they alive?" At that moment, he caught sight of a passing train. Some local trains had low furnaces, which left only a few inches between the train and the railtrack; Andreyev lay down between the rails, risking the possibility of being crushed or horribly maimed. He reflected, "If I remain alive, it will mean that my life has significance of some kind. If the train crushed me under its wheels, it will mean that providence has wished it so."

Fortunately, the train that passed first was one with a high furnace. But Andreyev failed to live up to his promise; instead of deciding that providence had give him a sign that his life was significant, he quickly relapsed into the old pessimism, and later tried to shoot himself with a revolver, causing permanent heart damage. And at a wild student party, he also stabbed himself.

At the age of eighteen, he fell in love with a fellow student; unfortunately, she had a streak of cruelty, and took pleasure in tormenting him. Andreyev became aware of the tremendous power of sex. But he was inclined—as we shall see—to equate this power with sheer irrationality.

One of the chief obsessions of his early stories is failure of communication between human beings. In *The Lie*, the hero is tormented by the suspicion that his beloved has been unfaithful to him. He tries to persuade her to confess; she insists that she is faithful. Finally, in a frenzy, he kills her—only to realize that he can now never learn the truth. "I killed the woman, but I immortalized the lie."

In *Laughter*, a student who has spent two and a half hours waiting for his beloved in the frost, learns that she has gone to a fancy dress party. A group of students decide to gate-crash, and don masks. But the only mask left for the student is a Chinese mask that is totally expressionless. In this he goes to the party. But when the girl sees him, she bursts into laughter. All his attempts to touch her heart make her laugh even more.

In *Silence*, the daughter of a priest becomes silent and depressed after returning from St. Petersburg, and will not answer questions. Finally, she commits suicide. Her mother is struck with paralysis, and is unable to speak. The priest goes to his daughter's grave and puts his ear to the ground, hoping to hear her voice, but again encounters silence.

The trouble with these stories is that we feel they lack any broader significance. The hero of *The Lie* is obviously a young man consumed by jealousy. This feeling of intense frustration when the craving to know something is denied is typical of the very young; every child knows the feeling when someone refuses to tell him a secret. As he grows up, he learns to shrug and turn his thoughts elsewhere.

The same criticism applies to *Laughter*. We feel that it is an artificial dilemma—all the hero has to do is remove the mask. It is true that the story is supposed to be symbolic, that Andreyev is speaking of the impossibility of real communication. But even that is untrue. We can, with an effort, communicate our deepest thoughts or feelings. Andreyev is simply exaggerating the problem of communication.

And again, the same is true of *Silence*. Apparently this, like most of Andreyev's stories, was based on a real event; the daughter of a priest in Andreyev's local church in Oryol committed suicide. But Andreyev has, in effect, "personalized" the situation, and made it a symbol of his own adolescent sense of noncommunication.

Another group of Andreyev's stories deals with the attempt of individuals to retreat from the miseries and shocks of reality, to a life in which they can feel sheltered—"fugitives from life." In the early story, *By the Window*, the civil servant protagonist has withdrawn from life. He achieves a sense of security by narrowing down his awareness to a state that is not unlike that of patients in a mental home who spend their days staring at the television set, even when it is turned off. He is acutely distressed when builders begin to transform the house opposite his window, for it means that his hypnotic routine is being broken.

The best expression of Andreyev's contempt for these "life deniers" is *The Grand Slam*, about a group of people who meet regularly to play cards. They are not interested in one another as individuals—just as card players. One of them dreams of achieving a grand slam. One day, as he is about to take his bonus card, he has a heart attack and dies. His partner turns up the bonus card and finds it is an ace. But the card player will never know that he was about to achieve his life's ambition.

Here it is clear that Andreyev is attacking people who turn their backs on life, who deliberately narrow their senses "to avoid complications." And clearly, this comprises a large part of the human race. Yet Andreyev seems to have no alternative to recommend.

His best known story, *The Wall*, seems to be totally pessimistic. The scene is a leper hospital—which Andreyev obviously felt to be an appropriate symbol for the world. One leper urges the others to hurl themselves at the high wall that cuts them off from the world. They fling themselves against it, and the bodies pile up. Finally, they give up, although the leper who started the rebellion continues to exhort them to try and break down the wall.

Andreyev apparently felt that the wall was not simply a symbol of the frustrations of human existence, but of the imperfections of human nature. Even so, the story produces an effect of despair. The rebel leper obviously believes that if enough bodies pile up, they will finally be able to climb over the wall. But the realistic reader can see that the idea is absurd—when there are enough bodies at the foot of the wall, it will be unapproachable anyway. They would be more sensible to look for a rope or a ladder.

Andreyev's pessimism is expressed again in one of his most powerful stories, *The Abyss*. Two idealistic students walk in the woods and discuss poetry and philosophy. They are attacked by three ruffians, who knock the male unconscious, then rape the girl. He wakes up to find her unconscious and naked. He tries to cover her up, then is suddenly overcome with lust, and rapes her himself.

D. H. Lawrence would have probably regarded this as a parable of the power of sex, and the strength of male desire; Andreyev regarded it as a proof that all our ideals are false, and that at bottom we are little more than brutes.

Nevertheless, the story, written in 1902, made Andreyev famous. So did another tale, *In the Fog,* about another young student, who rebels against the respectability of his family. He goes to a prostitute, and experiences immense physical satisfaction. But he is infected with syphilis, which fills him with a tormented sense of doom. When he encounters another prostitute, he murders her, then commits suicide. Both these stories created a scandal, and Andreyev was suddenly the most famous young writer in Russia.

Yet we feel that, in both stories, the symbolism is contrived to express something that is not necessarily true. The student of *In the Fog* is stifled by his respectable home, and ventures beyond its comfortable boundaries; the result is ruin. The same applies to *The Abyss*, where the woods symbolize the wild and dangerous world that lies beyond respectability. (An encounter with two prostitutes reinforces the symbolism.) The penalty for venturing into this world is disaster. Yet in *The Grand Slam* and *By the Window*, Andreyev has attacked people who prefer to live within narrow limits. Apparently he was incapable of grasping the implications of his own stories. Zenaida Hippius, the wife of the novelist Merezhkovsky, remarked that "Andreyev is unable to cope with the problems which he raises in his works."

In the decade that followed, Andreyev was to have many more successes, particularly in the theater. His novel about the Russo-Japanese war, *The Red Laugh* (written in nine days), became a best-seller. Plays like *The Life of Man* and *The Black Masks* made a fortune. Both, as the titles suggest, are "symbolic," and the latter returns to his early theme that most people are little more than masks, whose personalities are distorted by contact with the external world and falsified (a version of Sartre's "Hell is other people").

Andreyev was deeply sensitive to the attacks of critics, brought about by his success. He built a villa in Finland, not too far from St. Petersburg, and moved there in the spring of 1908. There he wrote the short novel, *The Seven That Were Hanged*, about the execution of six captured revolutionaries and a murderer. It reads like a parable based on Doctor Johnson's remark that "when a man is to be hanged in a fortnight it concentrates his mind wonderfully," and is the closest that Andreyev ever came to optimism. Facing death, the revolutionaries gradually learn to transcend it. One of them, the intellectual Werner, who has felt a profound contempt for men, experiences a kind of vision in his cell: "On one side he saw life, and on the other he saw death; and they were like two deep seas, sparkling and beautiful." It begins to look as if Andreyev is at last beginning to see life as a whole.

Yet—as we have seen so often—a writer whose vision is fundamentally pessimistic finds it difficult to develop. Andreyev was to write many more successful works—like the play *The Black Masks* and *He Who Gets Slapped*, about a disillusioned intellectual who chooses to become a circus clown, but his work seems to be marking time. There was a sense in which he had nothing more to say.

This is particularly obvious in his only full-length novel, *Sashka Jigoulev* (1911). Andreyev seldom attempted lengthy fictions—partly because, as Gorky remarks, he hated the labor of writing. But in *Sashka*

Jigoulev, he seems to have taken a deep breath and determined to try and do a full-length portrait of a revolutionary—the kind of person he had portrayed in *Darkness*.

Sashka's real name is Sashka (Alexander) Pogodin, and he is the son of a general. His father had destined him for the army, but when the general dies of a heart attack, his mother loses no time in withdrawing him from military school. Together with Sashka's talented younger sister Lina, they go to live in a small Russian town, in a pleasant house which his mother keeps meticulously clean. She is half-Greek, and Andreyev tells us that she has a taste for beautiful things.

Marriage to the general had made her miserable. He was a drunk, and when drunk, was capable of being cruel and stupid. He struck his wife in the stomach when she was seven months pregnant, and she lost the baby. The two separated, and he spent several years getting drunk and having love affairs. Finally, he begged his wife to take him back, promising never to drink again. He kept his promise, and they had Sashka and Lina. But on his deathbed, he admits that he hates her "for what she has done for him"—presumably, in depriving him of alcohol.

All her hopes center on the serious-minded Sashka—who, unlike his sister, seems to have no particular talents. But he has a social conscience, and when the Russo-Japanese war breaks out in 1904, reproaches his mother for aborting his career in the army.

After the defeat, Russia is in ferment, and small-scale revolutions break out in many parts of Russia. These are put down ferociously by the authorities. When Sashka learns that the local governor, Telepnev, who has ordered the execution of many revolutionaries, was a close friend of his father and mother, Sashka conceives the idea of assassinating him. He places his plan before a revolutionary committee, but they turn him down. One of the committee, Kolesnikov, is impressed by him, and the two become friends. Finally, Sashka decides to use up a small legacy left him by his father to buy weapons, and to lead a group of rebel peasants. His only real talent is for idealism and leadership, and he decides to place these at the service of the oppressed.

The second part of the novel deals with Sashka—now Sasha Jigoulev—as a revolutionary leader. Yet from this point—where the action begins—the novel goes to pieces. Sashka shoots a railway clerk in the course of a robbery, and realizes that he has become a murderer. Then we are told, "In the short period of not more than a month,

Sashka's gang carried out a number of successful robberies and attacks; the post office was looted, a diligence driver and two policemen were killed." And we are told that Sashka was soon a legendary robber and murderer—although, since two other gang leaders are using his name, it is not clear what he is responsible for.

They burn the houses of landowners; the peasants loot and get drunk. Various members of the gang are killed. And finally, Sashka realizes that all this murder and destruction is pointless. One by one, his followers desert him. When the few who are left set fire to a field of corn, out of sheer joy of destruction, he seems to awaken from sleep. "For whose good had he sacrificed his purity, the joy of youth, his mother's love and his immortal soul? . . . Who could and would dare to forgive him and his murders . . . ?" And when one of the gang commits suicide—evidently feeling, as he does, that it has all turned futile—he decides to go back to see his mother and sister, hoping that a taste of his old life might fill the void inside him. But they have left the house, and Sashka realizes that there is nowhere to go.

In the next scene, Andreyev kills him off. He does not even describe his death—merely tells us that Sashka is shot when the police attack the cave in which he and several men are hiding. An acquaintance has to point out which is his corpse. Andreyev ends portentously: "Sasha Pogodin, a noble and unhappy youth, died an awful and shameful death, to which he had been predestined by those who had lived before and had burdened Russia with their sins." And in an epilogue, we are shown Sashka's mother and sister living a lonely life, like two old maids, while his mother refuses to believe that he is dead, and fantasizes that he has escaped to America.

The novel is apparently based on the life of a real bandit called Sashka the Seminarian, who became a revolutionary leader. But it seems oddly pointless. Perhaps this is the point—that Sashka's dreams of donating his purity to the revolutionary movement—are based on immaturity and illusion, and that the reality leaves him empty and morally exhausted. Or perhaps, as Gorky suggests, it is about the mistake that one can fight evil with evil. In fact, this could have been the subject of a powerful novel, but Andreyev's failure to interest the reader gives the whole exercise an air of futility. Sashka Jigoulev is a demonstration of Andryev's intellectual and artistic bankruptcy.

In retrospect, it is possible to see that Andreyev's major drawback was an inability to think. He lived a life of the emotions, and seldom read books. He was also, like his father, an alcoholic, and was subject to fits of guilt and depression. Gorky describes how, in his early days in St. Petersburg, Andreyev would drink all night, and take pleasure in picking up the most sluttish prostitutes he could find.

And yet, rereading his stories for the first time in thirty years, I have to admit that they have a certain power. This springs from the fact that he wrote spontaneously, out of intuition, and that they often say more than he was aware that he was saying.

The Abyss is a good example. Andreyev felt that he was speaking simply about "the beast in man," the savage that hides behind the facade of culture and humanism. But the story somehow succeeds in conveying far greater questions. As the student Nemovetsky kneels by the unconscious body of Zinaida, he realizes that he is incapable of comprehending the horror of what has happened. Then, as he shakes her and tries to bring her back to life, he understands why, as the warm naked body begins to excite him. As he kisses her, he gives way to desire, and flings himself on her.

Any male can understand how this is possible. An attractive girl seems to contain the secret of the universe; the male wants to know her in the fullest sense—not merely her body, but what soap and toothpaste she uses, how she dries her hair, what she eats for breakfast. This is what Faust felt when he saw Gretchen for the first time—a sense that she was "the eternal feminine." So when Nemovetsky rapes Zinaida, he is not merely giving way to lust, but trying to seize a dream. Yet another part of us, the analytical mind, tells us that this dream is nonsense. If Nemovetsky had married Zinaida, he would soon realize that she is not an embodiment of the eternal feminine—simply a pretty, ordinary, seventeen-year-old girl. Like Charles Bovary, he will continue to enjoy sex, but as a kind of after-dinner dessert.

In fact, when a lover feels obliged to make love when his energies are low, the female sexual organs cease to be infinitely alluring; a vagina is experienced merely as an orifice, like any other orifice of the body.

Nemovetsky's violent sexual excitement raises the question: which is true? Is sex an illusion? Or does it really offer some promise of coming closer to the mystery of the universe?

Andreyev would undoubtedly have taken the view that it is an illusion. As an admirer of Schopenhauer and Hartmann, he felt that life is always deceiving us.

Now this, it seems to me, is an appalling and dangerous mistake, like the belief of Sartre and William James that "nausea" is more real than happiness.

It is true that sexual excitement is a kind of fever, and that "after coitus, man feels sad." Yet if we examine sexual excitement closely, with the eye of a phenomenologist, we can see that the more we become sexually aroused, the more we seem to be reminded of other things connected with sex. Sex is essentially associative. In a state of intense sexual arousal, we seem to be flooded with memories of everything that has excited us since we first became sexually aware.

Now I recognize in this state precisely the same phenomenon that I experience when my head is full of ideas, and I want to rush to my typewriter and pour them onto paper. I am simultaneously aware of a dozen things I want to say, and I am forced to try and persuade them to get into a queue and wait their turn. And that queue is certainly no illusion.

The same thing happens when we set out on holiday. We are filled with a sense of anticipation that is general rather than particular. We feel that anything that happens will be interesting and exciting. In effect, we are seeing life from a "bird's-eye view" rather than a "worm's-eye view."

Andreyev catches this in *The Seven That Were Hanged*, when Werner has his vision. "His thought became more and more vibrant. It seemed to him that tongues of flame were moving in his head, trying to escape from his brain to lighten the dark distance. Finally, the flame darted forth, and the horizon was brilliantly illuminated."

So it would seem quite clear that there is a vital sense in which sex is not an illusion, but a glimpse of a wider reality. It plays a vital part in arousing our sense of will and purpose.

Now it has always seemed clear to me that we possess two types of will. When I force myself to undertake some routine task, simply because I know it has to be done, I summon a kind of physical will, which has the strength of a carthorse, and seems equally uninspired.

On the other hand, when I am filled with a sense of excitement, I hurl myself into activity with an eagerness that comes from another kind of will; a will that is based on a sense of meaning and purpose. By analogy, with the physical will, this might be called the spiritual will. But I have always preferred a more down-to-earth term. A bullet is fired when a mass of cordite is detonated inside the cartridge. But this cordite is detonated by a small cap of a highly explosive substance called mercuric fulminate, which is struck by the hammer. Cordite, like the physical will, has great power, but is difficult to detonate. If we set light to it with a match, it merely burns.

So I refer to this highly purposive will as the fulminate will, and to the "carthorse" as the cordite will.

Now the problem with human beings is that their sense of meaning and purpose is easily eroded. Everyone knows what it is to feel tired towards the end of a journey, and then, suddenly reminded that we are nearly home, to feel flooded with energy. This is because the "fulminate will" has suddenly been "detonated" by a sense of reality. The same thing happened to Proust's hero in *Swann's Way* as he tasted the cake dipped in herb tea and was flooded with happiness.

If human beings could arouse the fulminate will whenever they felt like it, they would become gods or supermen. And it is precisely because the fulminate will (which we might also label the true will) falls asleep so easily that human beings are so easily bored and defeated.

Now it is perfectly clear that when we experience this "true will," we experience a sense of energy and optimism. It is always associated with optimism. That is why writers whose philosophy is basically pessimistic find it so hard to develop.

Most of the great Russian writers—with a few rare exceptions—are subject to fits of depression and boredom. This would not be important if, like Tolstoy and Dostoevsky, they felt that there is a deeper meaning in human existence. But Andreyev was subject to manic depression—he wrote, "Today, I woke in a carefree, joyous mood, but some two hours later I felt I was the most unhappy man in the world." And, like most manic depressives, he was inclined to believe that the depression told him the truth about life. Which meant that the true will, the fulminate will, had no chance to operate.

Andreyev was filled with hope by the 1914 war; he saw it as a new beginning for civilization. In 1916, he accepted a post on the board of a newly-launched newspaper, the *Russian Will*, which was basically a government organ, financed by German bankers. Andreyev's old friend Maxim Gorky refused to join, and Andreyev's acceptance caused hostility amongst those on the left. Andreyev, on the other hand, was delighted; he felt that his financial worries were at an end, and that in his new position of power, he could hit back at some of his critics.

But the newspaper was overtaken by the first revolution, of February 1917, which again Andreyev welcomed as a new beginning. The Bolshevik revolution of October 1917 destroyed his hopes—and also his reputation. The new masters of Russia had no time for this symbolic pessimist, and no royalties were allowed across the Finnish border, so that he and his family were suddenly poverty-stricken. His new allies were bankers and businessmen who had been driven out of Russia, and who hated the revolution. These people had no understanding of Andreyev, and had probably regarded his work as valueless; now they were glad of him as an ally in their fight against Bolshevism. And Andreyev, feeling lost and out of place, did his best in his totally unsuitable role of anti-Bolshevik propagandist.

But at forty-seven, Andreyev was worn out. His early attempt at suicide had weakened his heart, and his health was failing. Living in a wooden house on a hillside, overlooking a lake, he gave way to melancholy, and died of a heart attack on September 12, 1919. Few Russian newspapers bothered to report his death. The man who had taken Russian literature by storm in the early years of the century was forgotten.

25

MIKHAIL ARTSYBASHEV

Mikhail Artsybashev is an altogether less interesting writer than Andreyev, yet as a case history, his story is even more fascinating. For a brief period—between 1907 and the beginning of the First World War—they were Russia's most famous—and most criticized—writers. Then both plunged into oblivion.

I came upon Artsybashev when, in about 1956, I discovered his novel, *Sanine*, in a secondhand bookshop. I found it a remarkable piece of work—amusing, challenging, full of ideas; it had an iconoclastic flavor that reminded me of Shaw.

Vladimir Sanine, a young man who has been a student, and has also been involved in some revolutionary activity, returns to his hometown—one of these small Russian towns where, as P. G. Wodehouse says, nothing ever happens until page 500, when the moujik commits suicide. His mother is a dull, conventional woman, completely lacking in vitality; in her youth she has had love affairs, but all that is long behind her, and she tries to forget it. But her daughter Lida is beautiful and vital, and has many admirers, including an empty-headed officer named Sarudine and a gentle, good-natured doctor named Novikov. Sanine himself finds his sister sexually attractive.

Rather like Shaw's Captain Bluntshli in *Arms and the Man*, Sanine is a cheerful, practical, down-to-earth character who is impatient with all forms of hypocrisy and romantic idealism.

Within a few chapters, Lida has allowed Sarudine to seduce her, after which, he soon loses interest. When she finds she is pregnant, she contemplates suicide. But her brother, who soon discovers her secret, thinks she is mad. Why should she be ashamed of having a baby? Sanine calls on Novikov, tells him that Lida is pregnant, and is delighted when Novikov responds by offering to marry her. Sanine leaves his sister and Novikov together, and when he returns, they are holding hands.

When Sarudine calls at the house, Sanine is rude to him, and advises him to leave town. Infuriated, Sarudine sends his seconds to challenge Sanine to a duel. Sanine cheerfully declines; he might kill Sarudine, or Sarudine might kill him, and he has no intention of risking either outcome. The officers are shocked and contemptuous, but Sanine is indifferent to their opinion.

When Sarudine approaches him in a park, carrying a whip, Sanine does not wait to be struck; he punches him on the nose with such force that Sarudine collapses on all fours.

Sarudine's world suddenly falls to pieces; he has been publicly humiliated by a man who refuses to behave like an officer and gentleman; mad with humiliation, he blows out his brains.

In another typical scene, Sanine and his friend Ivanov go out for a day on the river. They hear women's voices, and realize that a group of young girls is bathing. When Sanine suggests that they go and spy on them, Ivanov blushes and raises objections. Sanine asks with astonishment, "Do you mean you don't want to see them?" Ivanov asks defensively why they should hide—why not watch them openly. "Because it's more exciting," Sanine replies, entirely without shame.

He goes on to tell Ivanov that if the sight of naked women fails to arouse his desires, then he would undoubtedly deserve to be called chaste. But if he feels these natural desires and tries to suppress them, then he is a hypocrite. (The novel is full of this rather dubious kind of logic.) Whereupon they go and spy on the women, and see a pretty schoolteacher called Sina (with whom their friend Yuri is in love) standing there naked. Their gasps of admiration are overheard, and they make off. Clearly, the whole point of the episode is to demonstrate that when Sanine wants to do something, he does it as naturally as a child or an animal, untroubled by questions about morality. Sanine's animal vitality is underlined later, when they are caught in a storm, and he stretches out his arms and shouts with glee.

In a subsequent chapter, Sanine rows Sina across the river by moonlight. She finds him attractive, and when they stand up to change places, she stumbles into his arms, and deliberately prolongs the contact. Sanine seizes his opportunity, and in spite of her resistance, takes her virginity; she struggles but soon gives up.

The next day she is horrified at what she has done. When Sanine calls on her, she tells him to go away. But Sanine begs her not to bear him any ill will—and adds that if she gives Yuri as much happiness as she has given him, he will be a lucky man. Suddenly, Sina decides to look on the bright side—after all, it is a beautiful day, and they still find one another attractive. For a moment, she sees the world as he sees it—as something simple and beautiful. They kiss "like brother and sister," and when he has gone, she lies down in the grass and reflects that some things are perhaps best forgotten.

The implication is that Sanine's simple, healthy attitude to life can communicate itself to other people.

In fact Yuri is deeply self-divided; he loves Sina and longs to possess her, but is not sure that he wants to settle down and become a husband and father. Tormented by his inner conflicts, he commits suicide. At his funeral, Sanine deeply offends the mourners by remarking, "One fool less in the world."

At the end of the novel, Sanine decides to leave town, but finds the stuffy train unendurable. While he dozes, a bullying tradesman maltreats his wife; Sanine wakes up and calls him a brute, then, in disgust, walks onto the platform of the train. The dawn is rising, and as the train slows down, he jumps off, then walks across the fields to meet the sun.

The reason for the success of *Sanine* is obvious. Unlike so many Russian novels, the book has a healthy, open-air atmosphere. And Artsybashev's advice to "Do what you will" came at exactly the right time, when Russian youth was undergoing its own equivalent of the sexual revolution. It became, according to Mirsky's *History of Russian Literature*, the bible of every Russian teenager, and many a schoolgirl followed Sanine's advice and threw away her inhibitions about sex.

The novel was translated into many languages, including Japanese, and made Artsybashev one of the most celebrated young writers in Russia. He had been twenty-five when he wrote it; it had to wait another three years, until after the revolution of 1905, before the censor would pass it. But even in this delay, Artsybashev was lucky; by 1907 the world was ready for it.

I must admit that, reading *Sanine* thirty or more years after I discovered it, I am no longer so impressed. It is now clear to me that Artsybashev was obsessed by sex, that he had the normal desire of young males to seduce every girl in the world, and that at twenty-five, he could see no good reason not to. He was also profoundly and gloomily Russian, an heir of Dostoevsky, and in spite of *Sanine*, was also prone to the strange Russian proclivity to self-torment. Dostoevsky's Kirilov, in *The Possessed*, commits suicide on the grounds that if God does not exist, then he himself must be God, and must prove it by taking on the ultimate responsibility for his own death. Artsybashev regarded this kind of self-torment as absurd. So he created the Nietzschean Sanine (while taking care to dismiss Nietzsche as unreadable), who declares bourgeois morality to be nonsense.

Compared to most Russian novels, *Sanine* is like a breath of fresh air. But closer examination raises all kinds of doubts. Vladimir Sanine is apparently Artsybashev's attempt to create his ideal hero—strong, healthy, intelligent, clear-sighted. But these qualities only appear in contrast to the shortcomings of the people around him. What will Sanine do when he leaves the small town and faces the world? Will he, like his creator, write books? If so, what will these books advocate, besides sexual freedom? While appearing to know all the answers, Sanine, in fact, leaves most of the questions hanging in the air.

As soon as we begin to question Sanine's simplistic attitude towards life, to ask what he actually stands for, we become aware of his shortcomings as a human being. There is a scene in which his friend Soloveitchik, a pacifist, asks him, "Suppose a man can't see his way clear, but is always thinking and worrying, since everything perplexes and terrifies him—tell me, wouldn't it be better for him to die?" And Sanine replies heartlessly, "You are a dead man, and for a dead man, the best place is the grave. Goodbye." He walks out, and Soloveitchik kills himself. But was Soloveitchik really a "dead man?" Surely all he needed to be told was that a little courage and determination can solve most problems? Sanine's honesty suddenly begins to look more like William James' "certain blindness in human beings."

We feel the same about Sanine's comment at Yuri's funeral, "One fool less in the world." Is he himself such an extraordinary human being that he is justified in taking this ruthless attitude? Perhaps Yuri was a fool. But is Sanine such a superman that he has a right to condemn?

We feel that Artsybashev has loaded the dice in favor of his hero by placing him against a background of mediocrities, so he appears a giant among pygmies. But how would he cope in the wider world? This is a question that could only have been answered by a sequel to *Sanine*. But Artsybashev wrote no such sequel. In fact, his next novel must have struck the enthusiastic groups of young "Saninists" who had formed all over Russia, as intensely disappointing.

The Millionaire (1910) is a curiously nihilistic work whose message is that a millionaire has no friends because everyone wants something from him. Since *Sanine*, Artsybashev seems to have undergone some shattering disillusionment that has destroyed his faith in humanity; success seems to have filled him with a kind of dyspeptic rage.

At the beginning of the novel, its hero Mishuiev sits in a restaurant with the beautiful Maria, whom he has stolen from her husband—a good, decent man who was Mishuiev's friend. But now that he has her, his adoration has changed to "a cold, unaccountable aversion." The tone is not unlike that of Aldous Huxley's *Point Counterpoint*—one feels that the author is choking with bile, and hates everybody he writes about.

The Millionaire is a record of Mishuiev's increasing disillusionment with humanity. He breaks with Maria, and goes back to the factory owned by himself and his brother. The workers, who are badly treated, are threatening to go on strike for a thirty percent wage rise. Mishuiev is flattered to hear that, when his suicide was falsely reported recently, the workers declined to believe it; they love him and trust him. He faces the crowd of strikers, and assures them that he will do everything he can to satisfy their demands. Then he goes into conference with his brother and the factory manager, who assure him that it would be ruinous to give the workers thirty percent, and finally persuade Mishuiev to offer them ten percent. When he does so, the workers boo and jeer, and finally attack him. Suddenly, Mishuiev realizes that he was deceiving himself to imagine that the workers "loved" him. Like everyone else, they are out for what they can get from him.

Battered and bruised, he calls on a man who has always been an honest friend, a famous poet. The poet tells him bluntly that he has no right to expect the workers to love him; he is their natural enemy, because he lives by exploiting them. But when Mishuiev asks whether they would have been justified in killing him, the poet tries to take back his words—he has just remembered that he needs Mishuiev's help to finance a new magazine. Once again, Mishuiev is disillusioned. That night, he commits suicide by jumping overboard from a steamer.

This conclusion leaves the reader feeling baffled. What on earth has happened to the yea-saying Nietzschean of *Sanine*? A few important clues are provided by Artsybashev's earlier work. His two great influences had been Tolstoy and Dostoevsky. And the influence of both of them can be felt in an early short novel, *The Death of Lande*. Ivan Lande (mentioned in *Sanine*) is a naturally saintly man, Artsybashev's own attempt to create a kind of Prince Myshkin. He is so sorry for the local workers that he gives away all his money, thereby enraging his family. A beautiful girl is impressed by his goodness and leaves the artist who loves her to attach herself to Lande; but when Lande realizes she expects "carnal" love, he is shocked and embarrassed, and the girl ends by hating him. Finally, anxious to visit a friend dying of consumption, he asks a priest to lend him money; but the priest regards Lande's friend as blasphemer and an atheist, and refuses. Trusting in God, Lande sets out without money, and on the way, falls ill and dies in a forest.

The moral of the story seems to be that Lande, for all his Myshkin-like saintliness, is a fool. If he had not given away all his money, he would not have died. Artsybashev seems to be saying that true virtue begins with an instinct for self-preservation. And this interpretation seems to be reinforced by the passage in *Sanine*, where Sanine admits that he failed to retaliate when a student struck him because Lande was standing nearby. But he soon decided that it was a "false moral victory," and at the first sneering remark from the student, thrashed him until he became unconscious. This caused, he admits, an estrangement from Lande, but at least Sanine felt that he had turned his back on false moral values—he declares that he has come to feel that Lande's life is "poor and miserable," and that he is a "beggar by choice." (Artsybashev's attitude to saintliness seems to be as skeptical as that of Anatole France in *Thais*.)

So in theory, at least, Artsybashev seems to have advanced from Dostoyevskyan humility to Nietzschean self-reliance. Yet, as we have seen, Vladimir Sanine is very far from being a satisfactory human being—many readers may feel that he suffers from a form of moral blindness. Above all, one wants to know what Sanine intends to do next, how he intends to apply his theories to his future life, and Artsybashev is clearly incapable of answering this question.

It is obvious that, like his contemporary D. H. Lawrence, Artsybashev felt that sex is one of the most important means of human fulfillment. Yet his works do not contain a single example of a genuinely fulfilled sexual relationship. When one of his male characters has persuaded a woman to take off her clothes, he immediately reacts by hating her.

Artsybashev's first story, *Pasha Tumanov* (1901), offers another clue to what went wrong with his work. It is about a schoolboy who fails his exams, contemplates suicide, and instead shoots the headmaster with a revolver. In an autobiographical note, Artsybashev explains that it sprang from "an actual occurrence and my own hatred for the superannuated schools." The story, apparently, was suppressed by the censor, who would only allow works that showed the educational system in a favorable light. But while it is possible to understand how desperate a schoolboy must become to commit suicide or murder the headmaster, it is difficult to feel that the story is making any real point. Speaking about why Pasha has wasted seven years of schooling, the author admits, "It was partly laziness . . ." It is true that Artsybashev is criticizing the rather dreary "cramming" that Russian schoolmasters regarded as the essence of education, but there was nothing to stop Pasha from spending the seven years acquiring his own education. The flat truth is that he is blaming the system for something that is essentially his own fault—and that in doing so, he reveals one of Artsybashev's major weaknesses: a kind of spoiledness, a desire to have his own way.

Now contrary to the opinion of Russian critics, Artsybashev is undoubtedly a serious writer. Like a true disciple of Dostoevsky, he wants to know what life is all about, why human beings suffer, and what we can hope to do about it. But the answer he suggests in *Sanine* is: do what you like, reject all obligations to society and other people. This attitude is strikingly similar to the "Do what you will" that was the motto of the "magician" Aleister Crowley, whose spoiledness and selfishness wrecked many lives. Sanine seems to be embarked on the same path.

So, unsurprisingly, *Sanine* failed to provide Artsybashev with a springboard for further progress. Because its hero is locked up in his own subjectivity, there is nothing for him to do. At about the same time, J. K. Huysmans was sending his hero Durtal on a spiritual journey that began with devil worship in *Là Bàs* and ended with Durtal's acceptance of Christian spirituality in *L'Oblat*. But it is impossible to imagine Sanine taking a similar journey, for he believes he has already solved his problems by embracing an "immoralism" similar to that preached by Andre Gide. The problem is that his solution seems to be a kind of dead end.

Artsybashev wrote *Sanine* in 1903; the next major event was the Revolution of 1905, with its violence and brutality. For Artsybashev, the experience may have been the equivalent of Dostoevsky's near-execution on the Semyonovsky Square. He wrote the *Tales of the Revolution*, which brought him his first taste of fame. These stories were full of violence and horror. But unlike Dostoevsky, Artsybashev was not sent into exile. On the contrary, his next publication, *Sanine*, turned him into a guru. For young Russians, Artsybashev became a kind of combination of the Beat Generation and the Angry Young Men.

Yet he was a guru who had failed to solve his own problems. He was incapable of accepting some kind of religious or mystical, or even practical, solution. That is one reason why *The Millionaire* reflects a new cynicism and weariness. Before Sanine leaps off the train at the end he reflects, "What a vile thing man is." *The Millionaire* is simply an exploration of that utterly negative theme. The settings are still beautiful—Artsybashev had started life as a painter, and this can be seen in his descriptions: "The arrival of the evening steamer was signaled across the bay by lights that, mirrored in the dark water, resembled garlands of bright flowers." But his major characters all seem to feel that life is meaningless and cruel; as to Mishuiev, he seems no more than a spoiled brat suffering from spiritual dyspepsia. The Angry Young Man has turned into something more like a Russian Samuel Becket.

This certainly applies to Artsybashev's last novel, *Breaking Point*, perhaps the most nihilistic novel ever written. It deals with a suicide epidemic in a small town, and the opening paragraph again reveals Artsybashev's spiritual malaise: "This little town lay in the Steppes, and beyond its outskirts, beyond the vibrating air of the distant countryside, lay the intangible depths of the horizon of towering forests and the remote, indifferent sky. It was easy here to realize the vanity and futility of the handful of human beings who lived, suffered and died in this place."

Now Henry James would have told him that this is artistically indefensible. The novelist's business is to present, not to tell the reader what he ought to be feeling. "The little town was parched by the heat; ordinary life went on—quiet, dead and dreary." Or later, "There was no change in this dreary grey landscape all day long. The rain poured down unceasingly; everything—earth and sky and woods and villages and flying crows and the drenched grey peasants at the deserted wayside stations staring blankly after the train—seemed to overflow into a sordid lugubrious melancholy."

What is happening is quite clear. Artsybashev has abandoned even a semblance of objectivity—of being a phenomenologist—and is quite simply allowing his own negative emotions to overflow into the text.

Most of the characters in *Breaking Point* are bored. Near the beginning, we share the thoughts of the little student Tchish:

"The little town was parched by the heat; ordinary life went on—quiet, dead, dreary . . . Already he had been stuck for two years in this hole, an exile from the city, with no idea when he would get away again, and he hated it with the whole force of his being. Somewhere or other, throwing out a million sparks, human lives are being forged, full of the joy of battle, fraught with pain and ecstasy, and ravaged by countless storms—but here! Just as if no one had heard a word spoken aloud, or seen a bright face, since the beginning of the world . . ."

We can see that Artsybashev is bored and miserable, and that, like a child, he feels that his boredom is an absolute truth which applies to the whole world. In this he resembles the Huysmans of *A Rébours*, but his attitude is even more negative and subjective. He is trying to convince us, in the face of obvious logic, that the "worm's-eye view" of human existence is true and that the "bird's-eye view" is false. And clearly, no person with any sense is going to accept this, since a bird's-eye view, by necessity, offers a wider perspective.

Tchish is the underpaid tutor of the children of the merchant Tregulev. After the lesson, their elder sister Lisa, a pretty seventeen-year-old blonde, asks Tchish if he knows the painter Dcheniev, and he tells her that Dcheniev has a reputation of a Don Juan—a schoolgirl has tried to kill herself for him, and he has deserted a mistress he has impregnated. Lisa is fascinated, and one senses that she is to be Dcheniev's next victim. And since Artsybashev loves nothing so much as describing a seduction, we can be fairly sure that he will not disappoint.

We are also introduced to Dr. Arnoldi, a huge, fat man who drinks vodka in the mid-afternoon, but who has deep compassion for human beings—half his patients seems to be on their deathbeds.

Apart from the philandering Dcheniev, there are two other major male characters in the book: the industrialist Arbusov, and his engineer Naumov. Arbusov is in love with a girl called Nina, who allowed herself to be seduced by Dcheniev; now Arbusov is full of Russian melancholy, and seems to be intent on drinking himself to death. Naumov stands apart from the other characters as the author's mouthpiece. Like Schopenhauer, Naumov has come to the conclusion that human life is illusion, and that all effort is futile.

". . . it seems to me unnatural that humanity, after bitter experience has convinced it that life in its deepest essentials is unhappy, has not yet arrived at the conclusion that death is the best remedy to put an end to this endless and useless martyrdom once and for all. Why do you think it's the most natural thing for people to live? . . . the will to live—I don't understand that. Have you ever once seen a happy life?"

His aim, he explains, is to "try to destroy in human beings the illusion of life."

Fairly early in the book, Dcheniev seduces Lisa, and gets her pregnant. The moment he has possessed her, she bores him, and he longs for her to go. The submissive Lisa kisses his hand, looks at him adoringly, and obliges. Dcheniev is already interested in another woman, a beautiful actress who has come to the town to sit by the deathbed of a woman who was once a famous actress. (Artsybashev punctuates the book with deaths to underline his point that life is futile.) She finally gives way to him when he loses patience with her mocking refusal to submit, and hurls her to the ground and horsewhips her. She goes away with him to Moscow. Yet, unlike his other mistresses, she is too sensible to fall in love with him. Her refusal to surrender is the beginning of Dcheniev's disintegration.

Inevitably, Lisa drowns herself. An officer called Krause then blows out his brains in front of a roomful of people. Another officer, Treniev, kills himself because his relations with his wife are an emotional seesaw. A clerk called Ryskov kills himself because his literary aspirations are unfulfilled. Dcheniev kills himself after confessing to Dr. Arnoldi that even his favorite hobby of seduction has failed him. "I have heard the same words, experienced the same caresses, from ten women. The rest was nothing but boredom, misery and repulsion. My soul has grown desolate, I have dissipated my emotion on trivialities." And after persuading Arbusov to go back to Nina, he shoots himself.

What follows is undoubtedly the most unconvincing scene in the book; Nina and Arbusov are reconciled, and he carries her to bed and possesses her. Inevitably, Arbusov experiences the same revulsions as Artsybashev's other males. "It was all over. What he had striven for so long . . . had happened. . . . an insane, incomprehensible repulsion saturated his whole being. He felt neither happiness, nor delight, nor passion—nothing but fatigue and abhorrence, and an invincible desire to leave her . . . It was incomprehensible to him that he should have suffered, hated and loved so keenly only for the sake of this momentary flash of gratification, after which there was nothing left . . ."

Suddenly, we can see quite clearly what is wrong—not simply with Arbusov, but his creator. This is "the sexual illusion" in its most absurd form. Artsybashev reasons that to fall in love with a woman is to want to possess her, and that to possess her means merely to have sexual intercourse. Even Andreyev knew better than this; the narrator in *The Lie* is mad with jealousy because he believes his mistress has given herself to another man; he at least knows that possessing a woman's body is only a small part of possessing her. Artsybashev, like D. H. Lawrence, seems to feel that sex ought to be some ultimate mystical act, and that if it fails to reach this level, then it is a swindle. It seems to be beyond his understanding that being "in love" involves far more than the sexual act, and that two people in love might be perfectly contented after lovemaking.

So the scene between Arbusov and Nina is simply unconvincing; we feel—as with certain scenes in Graham Greene (whom Artsybashev resembles in so many ways)—that it is all contrived to convince the reader of the cruelty of life, and that he is trying to convince us of something that is simply untrue.

Breaking Point ends with the suicide of the little student Tchish:

"Bluish light penetrated the room; timidly, with pale eyes it looked in every corner. Then the snow gradually ceased to fall. Everything was covered; smooth, white and pure, the earth was wrapped in it. The trees stood motionless in the garden, little ridges of snow on every branch. And Tchish's room was equally still and cold. The bare walls, severe and empty, looked down on the anxious silence they enclosed.

"The little student was hanging from a hook on the wall, next to his short overcoat. In front of him, on the floor, stood his galoshes, old and torn."

There is no record of how *Breaking Point* was received, but it is probably fair to assume that the critics greeted it with hostility.

Artsybashev would write no more novels in the remaining sixteen years of his life—indeed, it is impossible to see how he could have written any more. Instead, he devoted himself to the drama, with plays as savagely pessimistic as those of Andreyev. After the 1917 revolution, his books were banned. In 1923, he was exiled by the Bolsheviks, and spent the last years of his life writing splenetic articles against them. He died in 1927, at the age of forty-nine. His work has since been thoroughly and totally forgotten; in his *History of Russian Literature*, Prince Mirsky dismisses him as "a curious and, on the whole, regrettable episode in the history of Russian literature," while Marc Slonim says in *Russian Literature—1900–1917* that "the work of this second-rate writer offered merely historical interest."

I am, however, inclined to take issue with this. It is true that Artsybashev is, in the last analysis, unsatisfactory. But his case is typical of so many writers of the twentieth century, from Andreyev to Beckett, that it is worth closer examination.

As a follower of Tolstoy and Dostoevsky, he was obviously sincere in his desire to understand human life, and the best way to live it. Yet he somehow missed the point. How did this come about?

To begin with, he felt that one of the basic clues to the meaning of life—a clue to which Tolstoy and Dostoevsky had failed to do justice—was sex. Here, as I have already commented, he resembles D. H. Lawrence. For Artsybashev, as for Lawrence, the ecstasy of sexual intercourse seems to offer a vital clue to the intensification of human consciousness. The problem is that it rushes by so fast, like a train rushing through a station, so that we cannot read the name on the sign. Yet no one doubts that a station has a name, and that its sign is not an illusion.

Artsybashev arrived at the illogical conclusion that, in the case of sex, the station has no name. This can be seen in Dcheniev's lengthy description of the delights of falling in love. He insists that the pleasure of sex is far more than possessing a woman. It consists, he says, of the exciting feeling that a woman who was once an untouchable, unattainable stranger, gradually yields herself until she has opened her soul to her lover. Yet in spite of the "magic," he says, the actual consummation is a disappointment.

In other words, sex is about power. When a woman yields, a male feels as if life itself has yielded to his efforts, proving that he is not, after all, a mediocrity, a "creature of circumstance," a sport of destiny. Sex makes us feel that we can win.

Yet mere sexual conquest is eventually unsatisfying. Sex is important, but not that important. Biologically, its purpose is to secure the continuation of the race, and to provide both partners with a mate to share their lives. Artsybashev's characters—from the student Yuri in *Sanine* to Dcheniev in *Breaking Point*—feel that settling down with one woman is an appalling waste of life's possibilities. And in the case of Artsybashev, we sense that the real problem is that he experiences no strong sense of purpose apart from sex. As a writer of ideas, he set out to ask what life was all about, and what we ought to do with our time on earth. But he soon concluded that life is meaningless, which robbed him of artistic purpose and the possibility of development. Like Schopenhauer after *The World as Will and Idea*, he had nothing more to say.

It seems to me that Artsybashev has failed to grasp the essential point. He suffers from "the passive fallacy," the notion that human beings are, as Sartre would say, purely "contingent"—or, as Camus would say, absurd. These writers feel that consciousness is at the mercy of circumstance. They have failed to grasp what Husserl meant when he said that consciousness is intentional.

If I come into a warm room after being out in the cold, the warmth gives me pleasure. So does eating when I am hungry, drinking when I am thirsty, relaxing when I am tired. In fact, discomfort or inconvenience causes us to brace the will. We imagine that the discomfort itself has this "bracing" effect, but this is naive. It merely causes us to make an effort, which in turn summons vitality. So when we go into a warm room, we enjoy it because we have, so to speak, extra vitality to spend, like someone with a pocketful of money. If we sit passively in a warm room all day, our vitality has a tendency to leak away.

What we have to grasp is that we ourselves summon vitality. We can see this if we merely imagine some crisis; we brace ourselves, we focus our attention. Again, Doctor Johnson saw the answer when he said that when a man knows he is to be hanged in a fortnight, it concentrates his mind wonderfully.

Kierkegaard revealed the same insight in *Either/Or*, when he remarks that the human race must have been supremely bored to undertake anything as pointless as building the Tower of Babel, then goes on to point out that every schoolboy knows the answer to this problem when he reacts to a dull lesson by focusing his attention on a fly in his inkwell, or the rain dripping from the eaves. For we exercise our free will in our power to direct our attention. It is true that our attention can be "captured" by some external event; but the very term "to pay attention" reveals that we can bestow it as we like.

In other words, we human beings have a mechanism for summoning vitality. We are inclined to fail to notice this mechanism, because it tends to operate only in times of inconvenience or challenge, and we assume falsely that there is a direct mechanical connection between challenge and response, as if fate had pulled a lever. In fact, fate merely makes us aware that we have to brace ourselves. The will forms the link between the challenge and the response.

When we fail to exercise the will, our minds become slack; our senses droop and grow lazy. Soon we begin to experience the weariness of life failure. This is why "doing what you like," in Sanine's sense, is not good for human beings. As Blake says, damn braces, bless relaxes. And being self-indulgent also relaxes.

We can see that Artsybashev did not possess the insight to recognize this simple fact. Pasha Tumanov blames his headmaster for something that is ninety percent his own fault. This is the typical reaction of the criminal—what Sartre calls "magical thinking"—the tendency to try to escape responsibility by looking around for someone to take the blame. We are all inclined to do this, and insofar as we do so, we are immature. Criminals are permanently immature.

In Artsybashev's defense, it might be said that in *The Death of Lande* he is obscurely aware that mere pacifism, turning the other cheek, is no answer. For Lande, in spite of his compassion, is essentially passive. Artsybashev is groping towards the answer that Nietzsche saw—that human beings must somehow take responsibility for their lives, for their freedom. But Sanine reveals that he is still a long way from grasping this insight. Sanine may have outgrown Victorian morality, but he is still basically a spoiled child who cannot see beyond his own desires.

Admittedly, Sanine does not go as far as Lovelace, the totally selfish hero of Samuel Richardson's *Clarissa*, who declares that the only thing that concerns him is "my own imperial will," and who feels no pangs of conscience about abducting and raping the heroine. Sanine is altogether more good-natured. But he is still a long way from recognizing that the perception of meaning comes through the discipline of consciousness, and that the essence of this discipline lies in attention and concentration. Sanine would regard the self-flagellation of ascetics as futile and pointless, failing to recognize that the aim is to become the controller of consciousness.

In *The Millionaire* we see Artsybashev still looking for someone or something to take the blame. This time he decides that it lies in the hopeless selfishness of human beings. It seems incredible that Mishuiev fails to recognize that he is merely a spoiled child who lacks the self-discipline to be happy—and even stranger that his creator seems to be equally blind to his defects. But in *Breaking Point*, it is obvious that Artsybashev's failure to grasp how his problems are his own fault is due to his fundamentally passive attitude towards his own existence.

Perhaps he should not be condemned too harshly. Thirty years later, Camus and Sartre were still victims of the same fallacy. Camus wrote in *The Myth of Sisyphus*, "Rising, streetcar, four hours in the office or the factory, meal, streetcar, four hours of work, meal, sleep, and Monday, Tuesday, Wednesday, Thursday, Friday and Saturday according to the same rhythm . . . But one day the 'why' arises and everything begins in that weariness tinged with amazement." Camus is failing to see that the problems lies in his boredom, his decision that life is meaningless. It is not life that is absurd; he has decided to release his inner pressure, like letting air out of a tire. And when we let the pressure out of consciousness, when we choose to be mechanical rather than purposive, life seems to become meaningless. In fact, loss of purpose reduces us to a "worm's-eye view," in which we feel trapped in the present—like the characters of *Breaking Point*. Artsybashev might well ask, "But what purpose?" But this would be again to miss the point. Purposes merely trigger the will to raising our inner pressure. This is done by narrowing the attention, as we do when we try to thread a needle. And little self-observation reveals that it is we who allow our energies to drain away by relaxing our vigilance.

The answer seems to lie in developing the imagination to carry us beyond the "worm's-eye view." For example, after spending the whole day writing this piece about Artsybashev, I feel tired, and my attention is flagging. In this state, I could easily allow my sense of vigilance to collapse, so that I experience the sense of meaninglessness experienced by Artsybashev's Naumov. Yet I merely have to imagine what it would be like if I touched the wrong key on this computer (to which I am only just becoming accustomed), and destroyed my day's work, to be shocked back into a sense of values. Human beings differ from animals in that we can use imagination to awaken our sense of values.

There may well have been specific reasons why Artsybashev was inclined to pessimism. *The Columbia Encyclopedia of Modern Literature* states that "he was the son of a district constable from the lesser landed gentry in the Ukraine," and that he began life as a painter—which suggests that his family had the means to send him to art school. It may well be that his inclination to "spoiledness" arose from this background. And it may well be that overwhelming success at the age of twenty-nine reinforced a tendency to want his own way. From Artsybashev's novels, we can have no doubt that he accepted whatever sexual advantages came as a result of this success. We can also probably assume that he was deeply resentful of the critical backlash that came as a result of his huge success, and that, like Dostoevsky after *Poor Folk*, he was incensed to find himself the target of attacks. The "venomous articles" he later wrote against Bolshevism suggest that he was a good hater.

All this may explain Artsybashev's plunge from the life affirmation of *Sanine* to the nihilism of *Breaking Point*, undoubtedly one of the most consistent attempts in world literature to "cover the universe in mud." It is virtually impossible to understand what he hoped to achieve by publishing this hymn to suicide—unless a new reputation as a Russian Schopenhauer. If so, he was unlucky, for *Breaking Point* shows no sign whatsoever of a capacity for sustained thought, or even for honest self-analysis.

What it does show is that he was a genuine novelist, with considerable dramatic power, and a gift for making the reader turn the page. And since Blake said that an error cannot be overturned until it has been fully defined, and no one has demonstrated the paradoxical and futile nature of pessimism better than Artsybashev, he may, after all, have performed a service for modern literature.

26

ANATOLE FRANCE

During my teens, I loved to read volumes of literary criticism, some of it lively, some of it boring and stodgy. I borrowed the *Cambridge History of English Literature* from our local library, volume by volume, and read George Sampson's abridged version several times. When the BBC broadcast Granville Barker's play, *The Secret Life*, I looked it up in Sampson, and was intrigued by his comment that it "shows us the intellectual world reduced to spiritual nihilism." In due course, *The Secret Life* would make its appearance in an early chapter of *The Outsider*.

I also came upon E. M. Forster's *Aspects of the Novel*, and read it many times. It was his comment that *War and Peace* had "an effect like music" that led me to purchase the three-volume Everyman edition when I was sixteen—I read the first volume while I was working for the Collector of Taxes—where, when I had finished my filing, I had plenty of spare time.

It was in Forster that I came across a reference to Anatole France's *Thais*. He mentioned, that, structurally speaking, it had the shape of a cross or hourglass. At the beginning of the novel, Paphnutius, the saintly ascetic, is obsessed by the thought of saving the beautiful courtesan Thais from damnation; by the end of the novel, Thais is a saint, but Paphnutius is damned.

I rushed to the library and borrowed it—it was part of that collected edition bound in orange. It was even more stunning than I expected.

To begin with, it was obvious that France was incredibly erudite. And his intellectual brilliance reminded me of Shaw. I found it hard to understand why I had not discovered him earlier.

Thais is a drama of ideas. When Paphnutius leaves his hermit's cell for Alexandria, he meets a stoic philosopher sitting cross-legged by a river. The man, Timocles, professes to be indifferent to Christ and all other gods. Pressed by Paphnutius, he explains that he is the son of a rich shipowner. One of his brothers conceived a criminal passion for the wife of their elder brother. When they both learned she was being unfaithful with a flute player, they had him whipped to death. She became insane and died, so did the two brothers. Timocles left home and traveled the world, concluding that there is not a single person who is either wise or happy. After seeing a Hindu holyman sitting cross-legged and allowing birds to build their nests in his hair, Timocles decides to imitate him.

When Paphnutius tries to argue, Timocles replies, "Refrain from showing me your doctrines . . . All discussions are useless. My opinion is to have no opinion. My life is devoid of trouble because I have no preferences. Go thy ways and strive not to withdraw me from the benevolent apathy in which I am plunged, as though in a delicious bath . . ." And Paphnutius leaves him, muttering sorrowfully, "Farewell, unhappy Timocles."

In Alexandria, an old woman kisses his hand and asks his blessing. Moments later, children begin to stone him for being "blacker than an ape and more bearded than a goat." He reflects that Timocles is not entirely wrong—the same object or person may be seen quite differently by different people. "Everything in this world is mirage and moving sand. God alone is steadfast."

He calls on his old friend and fellow student Nicias, a wealthy man. At first the doorman tries to turn him away, but when Paphnutius is indifferent to being struck across the face with a stick, begins to tremble, and goes to tell his master. Nicias welcomes him, and expresses the hope that he has renounced his Christian superstitions. Paphnutius indignantly rejects the notion. Nicias is another skeptic, who finds all the classic philosophers unsatisfying. But when Nicias admits that he has once been Thais' lover, Paphnutius expects to see the ground open up and swallow him. And when he tells Nicias that he has come to Alexandria to reclaim Thais' soul for Christ, Nicias warns him, "Beware of offending Venus." And as Paphnutius stalks out of the room, Nicias catches him up and repeats in his ear, "Beware of offending Venus."

In the next scene, Paphnutius falls asleep by the harbor, and dreams that the pagan philosophers are all in hell, being tormented by demons. But the philosophers seem unaware of the demons; they continue their peaceful meditations. A veiled woman tells Paphnutius that before they could be punished, these philosophers would need to be enlightened, and if they were enlightened, then they would know the truth, and would not need to be punished . . . Paphnutius wakes up with a shout of horror.

The underlying purpose of the novel is now clear. France detests bigots, particularly religious bigots, and Thais is fundamentally an attack on all kinds of bigotry and dogma. I shared his feelings. I had listened to Jehovah's Witnesses who came to our door with a gramophone and argued that the world was about to come to an end, and that only the Jehovah's Witnesses would be saved, and I had seen the family of my favorite aunt converted by Mormons, to whom they gave up a tenth (or perhaps a quarter) of their meager income. Ever since I was twelve or thirteen, I had been preoccupied with this problem of truth—that every fool thinks he knows the answer to the riddle of the universe.

We all experience this, of course; even the wisest find it hard not to feel a flash of indignation when someone expresses calmly and with conviction a view that strikes them as outrageous nonsense. By middle age, we have become accustomed to the notion that the world is full of fools. But the young find it far more painful to accept that people can remained fixed in mistaken opinions—for they themselves lack the inner certainty to feel invulnerable. By my mid-teens, the thought of all the religious and political bigotry in the world had already implanted in my mind the notion of writing a book called *The Varieties of Human Self-Delusion*.

So *Thais* had me chortling with delight. France seemed to look down on the world of human stupidity from a great height, and to speak with the voice of true reason. In the theater, where he goes to see Thais act in a Greek drama, Paphnutius enters into discussion with the epicurean philosopher Dorion, who believes that love is a disease of the liver, and whose only pleasure—since he suffers from indigestion—is meditation. At the end of the play, Paphnutius rises to his feet to harangue the audience, but they are already leaving the theater. He reaches the door still prophesying and still ignored by the audience. It made me wish that the same fate had befallen Karl Marx, Adolf Hitler and Billy Graham.

But how could a woman like Thais fall under the spell of a bigoted lunatic like Paphnutius? In the following chapter, in which her biography is summarized, it all becomes credible as we learn that when she was a child, Thais had been baptized a Christian, when a Nubian slave of the family took her to a meeting in a catacomb. Later, the Nubian was crucified—not for being a Christian, but for stealing a salt cellar.

Later, as a successful courtesan, she despises Nicias, who tells her that "there is no knowledge except that of the senses"; "in order to understand the secret of life," she begins to read the works of the philosophers. But she cannot understand them. She attends a Christian service, and is deeply moved to learn that her crucified Nubian slave has now been canonized. When she finds Nicias waiting for her at home, she rejects him with disgust. Then she looks at herself in a mirror, and realizes that her beauty is beginning to fade.

And so when she meets Paphnutius, she is ripe for conversion. He reveals his identity, and speaks of salvation; she flings herself at his feet. After that, he accompanies her to a banquet, where Paphnutius is made welcome, and the guests discuss philosophy. (It is clear that France had Plato's *Symposium* in mind.) But—typically—Paphnutius is less appalled by their pagan blasphemies than by the presence of another Christian, Marcus the Arian, who declines to accept the holy trinity. And at the end of the banquet, as most of the guests lie drunk, the stoic philosopher Eucrites kills himself with a dagger, as a gesture of his own total detachment from life. Paphnutius takes Thais by the hand and leads her quietly out of the house.

The monk returns to his cell, having left Thais in a nunnery. But now Venus begins to take her revenge. The cell seems too small, and he dreams of Thais. At first he believes that the dreams come from God, but when he wakes from one of them to find a young jackal breathing in his face, he knows that they come from the devil. One day, he dreams that Thais has approached his couch with bleeding feet, then slipped in beside him. With typical French delicacy, France implies that he has a wet dream. He wakes up full of self-disgust, and as jackals continue to haunt his cell, he goes into the desert, finds a ruined temple, and sits on top of a column. Soon he is again surrounded by disciples; as pilgrims flock to see him, the temple ruins become the center of a tourist industry, with signs like "Pomegranate wine and genuine Sicilian beer sold here." Paphnutius blesses the sick and they are cured; epileptics fall into convulsions as soon as they see the column, and everyone in the crowd is seized with exaltation. Paphnutius begins to believe that he is saved when a voice tells him that he is to seek out Constans, the brother of the Emperor Constantine, and convert him from his belief in Arianism. As Paphnutius prepares to climb down the ladder, the voice tells him to jump, and he will be supported by angels (one of Christ's temptations in the wilderness). As Paphnutius prepares to obey, he hears a mocking laugh, and realizes that the voice was a demon sent to tempt him.

He flees by night, and finds refuge in a tomb in the ruins of an ancient city. Again, the voice speaks to him, commanding him to look at the paintings on the walls of the tomb, including a dancing girl. The man in whose tomb Paphnutius has taken refuge may be dead, but at least he lived his life fully; Paphnutius will die without having lived. After more hallucinations, including the seductive dancing girl, he feels that he has become polluted by desire.

Monks discover him there; the Abbot Zosimus, a disciple of St. Anthony, tells Paphnutius of his own debauched life before he ruined himself with riotous living, and how, after the death of a friend, he turned to religion. And Paphnutius wonders why God has favored this sinner, while rejecting one as virtuous as himself.

When he hears that Thais of Alexandria, now regarded as a saint, is dying, he hurries to the nunnery where he left her. And as he stands beside her deathbed, he cries out, "Do not die. I love thee . . . God, heaven—all that is nothing. There is nothing true but this worldly life, and the love of human beings . . ." Thais does not hear; she dies, seeing a vision of angels. When Paphnutius seizes her in his arms, the abbess shouts, "Get out, cursed wretch." He raises his head, and the surrounding nuns flee in terror, for Paphnutius' face has become the face of a demon.

Thais overwhelmed me; it seemed to me one of the greatest novels I had ever read. Anatole France joined Bernard Shaw at the head of my pantheon of great writers of the twentieth century. What I found so difficult to understand was why he was so unappreciated. Why had I never heard about him until I read *Aspects of the Novel*? I concluded that the reason was simply that he was a man of exceptionally high intelligence, and most people are stupid—particularly in England, which takes a patronizing and dismissive view of writers of ideas.

In a sense, I felt closer to Anatole France than to Shaw. Like me, he was obviously an obsessive reader. There were, it seemed, two of his novels in Everyman's Library, bound into one volume: *At the Sign of the Reine Pedauque* and *The Revolt of the Angels*. I have my own copy in front of me as I write, and I see that I purchased it in November 1948, when I was seventeen. From its introduction, I learned that Anatole France, born in 1844, was actually named Jacques Antoine Anatole Thibault, and that he was the son of a bookseller whose shop was on the Paris quais. His father, the son of a peasant, had not even learned to read until he was twenty. Anatole made up for it, and devoured everything in his father's bookshop. Yet at the Jesuit school he attended near the Jardins des Luxembourg, he was regarded as lazy and stupid. He disliked the Jesuits—who favored the sons of rich parents—and seems to have had no interest in the lessons. He wanted to direct his attention to what interested him.

Nevertheless, by the age of seventeen he was reading Homer and Virgil in the original, and found them enchanting. All men of intellectual genius experience the need of finding some alternative world, some other reality that they prefer to the world that surrounds them. In fact, it is obviously unnecessary to be an "intellectual" or a genius to experience this need; the workman who has never read a book may satisfy it through an interest in sport, the teenager through an enthusiasm for rock music. But these can hardly be termed "alternative realities," since they coexist comfortably with everyday reality. Intellectual "outsiders" like France need to create a world of the mind, into which they can retreat as if it were their own home. A poet like W. B. Yeats is an extreme case, creating a world of fairies and spirits, and justifying himself with a quotation attributed to Ruskin, "As I go to my work in the British Museum, I see the faces of the people become daily more corrupt."

But France's need to escape was less powerful than Yeats'. His father's shop faced the river; it was a *librairie à chaise*, a bookshop with chairs, so the customers could sit and read and exchange ideas. The teenage Anatole constructed his refuge from the world of the past; he felt more at ease in the streets of ancient Athens or Rome than in modern Paris. He always carried a copy of Virgil in his pocket, and it is not surprising that his first ambition should have been to become a poet, and that his first publication, at the age of twenty-one, should be a little book on the poet Alfred de Vigny.

The fact that he had a stammer and was ugly—that he had a long, equine face and a nose like a snail's shell—also helped to nurture his "outsiderism." A young admirer, Marcel Proust, later asked France how he came to know so much. France replied, "Because, my dear Marcel, when I was your age I was not as good looking as you. People did not ask me out, so I stayed at home reading."

France was lucky. He found a job in a library, and met a young and ambitious publisher of poetry named Lemerre, whose stable of poets were known as "the Parnassians." They were—in the early 1860s—the predecessors of the aesthetes of the 1890s. France was later to write their manifesto, declaring that "since nothing is new under the sun, if art does not wish to immobilize itself by the use of worn-out symbols, it must give up meaning and concentrate exclusively on form." A hostile critic might say that his adherence to this doctrine explains why he never succeeded in achieving true greatness.

Through his literary connections, France began to write reviews in *Le Temps*, and soon became noted for his wit and erudition.

He was not noted as a ladies' man. Something of a mother's boy, the young Thibault was timid with women. He had been in love three times, and been rejected three times, when, at the age of thirty-two, he married a tall, shy girl who was twelve years his junior. Forced to work harder to support a wife, he produced in quick succession three works of fiction: *The Aspirations of Jean Servien*—clearly autobiographical; *Jocasta and the Famished Cat*—two short fictions; and *The Crime of Sylvestre Bonnard*, a novel in two parts. It was this latter that made him famous at the age of thirty-seven, and is still regarded by many as his best work.

I lost no time in reading *Bonnard*, and found it delightful, although not quite as overwhelming as *Thais*. Sylvestre Bonnard is a middle-aged philologist, a Member of the Institute, who lives in a flat over-looking the Seine, cared for by a housekeeper. He is a shy, gentle soul who loves his books. France sets out to create an almost Dickensian atmosphere:

"I had put on my slippers and my dressing gown. I wiped away a tear with which the north wind blowing over the quai had obscured my vision. A bright fire was leaping in the chimney of my study. Ice crystals shaped like fern leaves were sprouting over the window panes, and concealed from me the Seine and the Louvre of the Valois." And after addressing a soothing speech to his cat, Bonnard settles down to reading a catalogue of manuscripts. "I do not know any reading more easy, more fascinating, more delightful, than a catalogue . . ."

A thin, sick-looking young bookseller calls on him; his stock is poor, but Bonnard buys one simply to cheer him up. Then, learning that the bookseller lives in the flat above with his wife and baby, Bonnard sends some logs up to them.

Soon after, the bookseller dies. Bonnard meets the beautiful young widow on the stairs, and she thanks him for the gift of logs.

Ten years later, Bonnard sees in a catalogue a manuscript of the *Golden Legend*, a medieval work on the lives of the saints, which he covets. He learns that it is in the possession of a collector in Sicily, who agrees to allow him to go and see it. Having made the tiring journey, he is infuriated to learn that the collector has meanwhile allowed his son to take the *Legend* to Paris, and that it was all the time within a few doors of his own apartment. Bitterly, he tells the story to a Russian prince and his beautiful wife—he fails to recognize the wife as the young widow to whom he once sent logs.

Back in Paris, he attends an auction and bids for the manuscript; but someone outbids him. Back at home, disappointed but philosophical, he receives a present in the form of a box shaped like a log. Inside is the manuscript of the *Golden Legend*, with a card from the wife of the Russian prince. His housekeeper, who has caught a glimpse of the princess in her carriage, has instantly recognized her as the widow of the bookseller.

It is a charming story, delightfully told. The second half of the book—in which the old bibliophile once again plays the part of the good angel—is even more so. Again, France sets out to conjure up a mood of gentle nostalgia:

"When I left the train at the Melun station, night had already spread its peace over the silent countryside. The soil, heated through all the long day by a strong sun—by a 'gros soleil,' as the harvesters of the Val de Vire say—still exhaled a warm heavy smell. Lush dense odors of grass passed over the level of the fields. I brushed away the dust of the railway carriage and joyfully inhaled the pure air." And he meditates upon the delights of his childhood—a hint that was not lost on his young disciple Marcel Proust.

He is on his way to a country estate to catalogue a library inherited by Paul de Gabry, the son of an old friend, and his charming wife. The atmosphere there is idyllic. One day Bonnard falls asleep at his desk, and dreams of a mischievous fairy. He tells his hostess of his dream, and a few days later, she gives him a wax statuette with an uncanny resemblance to the fairy. It has been made by a young orphan named Jeanne, who is staying in the house. And Bonnard soon discovers that Jeanne is the daughter of a girl with whom he was once in love—Clementine, whose father was a mapmaker.

Jeanne, Bonnard discovers, is not particularly happy. Her guardian is a grasping and rascally lawyer named Mouche, and she is a pupil at the school of a sharp-tongued old maid named Prefere. The latter is at first cool towards Bonnard, but warms to him when she learns that he is a Member of the Institute. She and Jeanne become regular visitors at Bonnard's flat, and Mlle. Prefere finally confides in him that she feels he ought to marry. He smiles and makes polite noises. But when he is invited to dinner at Mlle. Prefere's house, with Mouche as the other guest, he is stupefied when Mlle. Prefere explains to Mouche that she has proposed to him, and that his answer had been a discreet affirmative. Bonnard's terror gives him courage; he loses no time in declaring that he has no intention of getting married, and rushes out of the house.

Next time he calls to see Jeanne at her school, Mlle. Prefere tells him that he will not be allowed to see her any more. "People are talking," she explains, about the middle-aged man and the young girl, and it is her duty to prevent further gossip. Bonnard rushes to the lawyer to complain, but Mouche supports Mlle. Prefere.

When he hears that Jeanne has now been set to work as a servant in Mlle. Prefere's kitchen, Bonnard decides to commit the crime of the title—to abduct her. He manages to whisper to her through her window, then rings the doorbell, and when the servant comes to answer—leaving the coast clear—Jeanne runs out of the other door to meet him, and the two take to their heels.

Bonnard leaves her in the care of Paul de Gabry and his wife. But he is saved from the consequences of his crime when the lawyer M. Mouche is forced to flee the country for embezzling his clients' funds. Bonnard is appointed Jeanne's guardian, and she moves in with him.

By now the reader obviously hopes that Bonnard will marry his young ward. But France was too realistic for such an ending. (To make doubly sure, he later changed Jeanne from Clementine's daughter to her granddaughter.) Jeanne falls in love with one of Bonnard's young students. Bonnard is unhappy, for he has been enjoying having a "daughter." But with his usual generosity, he allows the young couple to marry, and sells his library to provide her with a dowry.

There is more of Dickens in *Sylvestre Bonnard* than the atmosphere. Sylvestre Bonnard belongs to the tradition of Dickens' kindly old gentlemen, like Pickwick, the Cheeryble brothers and Mr. Brownlow. The episode of Mlle. Prefere and Bonnard's "proposal" is straight out of *Pickwick Papers*. The villainous Mouche is like any number of grasping lawyers in Dickens. And, to complete the parallel, France ends the book with a postscript describing the death of Jeanne's first child, who expires as he says, "Godfather, you are not to tell me any more stories." But at the end of the book, when Jeanne and her husband are staying with Bonnard—now retired to a country cottage—she tells him she is pregnant again.

France later came to dislike *Sylvestre Bonnard*, recognizing that it owed its success to sentimentality. That is undoubtedly true. Yet it is one of the few novels where sentimentality is wholly successful.

The enormous success of *Bonnard* would eventually lead to France's election to the Academy (as he had intended it should). But it also made him a distinct literary personality who was quite unlike any of his colleagues. France had established himself in the eyes of the French public as a scholar and bibliophile, one who preferred the world of books to the world of crude everyday reality. From now on, his public were infinitely tolerant of his endless references to classical and medieval authors. For Parisians, France was their great intellectual, their man of learning. He seemed, quite simply, the most intelligent literary man in France. By the mid-1880s, France had achieved the kind of reputation that Shaw would achieve with *Man and Superman* twenty years later.

With his success, France's marriage began to fall apart. It does not seem to have been his fault. He was shy, bookish, and of plebeian origins; Valerie came from an aristocratic background, and preferred horses to books. As they drifted apart, France became a regular visitor at the literary salon of a wealthy and intelligent Jewess, Mme. Arman de Caillavet, and he eventually became her lover. Valerie had been the muse behind *Sylvestre Bonnard*; Mme. Arman was the muse behind *Thais* (1890), *The Sign of the Reine Pedauque*, and the four "political" novels about M. Bergeret, the provincial professor who comes to Paris (and which my favorite critic, Edmund Wilson, regards as France's finest work). One day, after Valerie had called him a maquerau (a cross between a pimp and a gigolo) France strode out of the house in his dressing gown, carrying his inkwell, and never returned.

Surprisingly, *The Sign of the Reine Pedauque* (1893), was also a considerable success—surprisingly, because it is so overladen with classical erudition that it is at times quite unreadable. I read it in the year I bought it—1948—but was not as overwhelmed as I had been by *Thais* and *Sylvestre Bonnard*.

The Reine Pedauque (it means web-footed queen) is the story of the son of a Paris innkeeper, Jacques Tournebroche (his nickname—turnspit), who is a boy of about twelve when the Rabelaisian monk Jerome Coignard comes in to eat. His conversation, laced with classical references, impresses Jacques' father, and he agrees unhesitatingly when the monk offers to become Jacques' tutor in exchange for one good meal a day.

Coignard has had a checkered career. Thrown out of the college at Beauvais, where he taught liberal arts, because of a love affair, he has lived from hand to mouth, becoming in turn a peddler, actor and servant. Discharged from a job as a bishop's librarian because of another love affair, he has written a scurrilous pamphlet about an actress and spent four years in the Bastille. Now he scrapes a living as a public copyist, writing love letters for servant girls, and is glad of some security.

He teaches Jacques Greek and Latin. One day, a mad alchemist named M. D'Astarac comes to the inn, and is so impressed by Coignard and his pupil that he invites them to his home to translate the alchemical manuscript of Zosimus the Panopolitan. They move into a vast, neglected chateau, where M. D'Astarac also supports a Jewish magician, allegedly a hundred years old.

After one of M. D'Astarac's experiments to try and make him see a salamander (or fire spirit), Jacques awakes to find a beautiful girl in the room; he pretends to think her a salamander, and loses no time in pushing her down on the couch and possessing her. In fact, she turns out to be the "niece" of the Jewish mage, who is actually her lover, and to whom the girl, Jael, is glad to be unfaithful with Jacques.

After a brawl with a tax collector, in which a lackey is killed, Jacques, Coignard and a nobleman called D'Anquetil flee from D'Astarac's chateau; Jael accompanies them—as the mistress of D'Anquetil. (France loves to emphasize the infidelity of women.) The Jew follows them, and eventually stabs Coignard, who dies in a travelers' lodging house.

D'Astarac's chateau is eventually burned down, and D'Astarac dies in the fire. The old Jew is drowned in a swamp. And Jacques settles down to tell the story of his "good master" Jerome Coignard.

The Reine Pedauque is an amusing book, full of flashes of brilliance, but it is not a good novel. The alchemist D'Astarac is an absurd invention, and one has the feeling that France invented him on the spur of the moment to revive a sagging plot. The beautiful but faithless women—Jael and Catherine the lacemaker—seem like the sexual fantasies of an adolescent. The Rabelaisian Coignard is amusing but wordy to the point of tiresomeness. (This is an example of his narrative style: "She had been pretty, but could still attract. Her eyes could speak. One day Cicero and Levy, Plato, Aristotle, Thucydides, Polibius and Varro, Epictetus, Seneca, Boethius and Cassiodorus, Homer, Aeschylus, Sophocles, Euripides, Plautus and Terence, Diodorus Siculus, Dionysius of Halicarnassus, St. John Chrysostom and St. Basil, St. Jerome and St. Augustine, Erasmus, Salmasius, Turnebus and Scaliger, St. Thomas Aquinas, St. Bonaventure, Bossuet, Ferri in his train, Lenain Godefroy, Mezeray, Mainbourg, Fabricius, Father Lelong and Father Pitou, all the poets, all the orators, all the historians, all the fathers, all the doctors, all the theologians, all the humanists, all the compilers, assembled on the wall from ceiling to floor, witnessed our embraces. 'You are irresistible,' she said. 'Do not think too badly of me.'")

In spite of which, *Reine Pedauque* was another enormous success. The French liked France's mixture of impropriety and erudition, and his writing finally made him a wealthy man—wealthy enough to buy a villa, and set up his own literary salon in which, naturally, he reigned supreme.

France might easily have become a kind of literary antiquarian, an erudite but sterile escapist, if it had not been for the Dreyfus affair which convulsed France in the 1890s. Dreyfus was a Jewish army officer who was wrongly accused of being a spy because his handwriting resembled that of the true spy, a Hungarian named Esterhazy. Even when the army realized it had made a mistake, it refused to acknowledge it. Emile Zola caused a storm with his famous tract *J'Accuse*, which France signed, and had to flee the country to avoid imprisonment. France fought on with his M. Bergeret novels, denouncing the church and the army as bastions of prejudice, stupidity and ignorance. They turned Anatole France into a major modern novelist.

The Dreyfus scandal had the effect of uniting the French Left, which thereupon gained the power and influence which it has possessed ever since. For a while, France himself was identified with the Left. But after Dreyfus' reinstatement in the army in 1906, he felt the need to reestablish his old position of ironic detachment. The result was *Penguin Island* (1908), the most popular of his books—although one of the least highly regarded by critics. Written after the immense labors of a diffuse and unmemorable life of Joan of Arc, it was regarded by France as a kind of relaxation, and dashed off in a few months. It is a satirical account of French history—disguised as the history of penguins who have been mistakenly baptized by a short-sighted saint and turned into human beings—but is really France's own version of universal history. His account of the Dreyfus affair, in its later pages, satirizes all sides impartially. The book ends by stating France's conviction that history runs in cycles, merely repeating itself (as Spengler was to suggest in *The Decline of the West*) without getting anywhere.

It is, on the whole, a silly and barren exercise, rather like some of Shaw's later plays, that pokes fun at everyone and everything. Its failure to transcend mere satire brings to mind Kenneth Tynan's comment on the magazine *Private Eye*, "Why don't you get yourself a point of view?"

Incredibly, France ended by becoming a supporter of the Communist Party, although he was never actually a member. Yet detachment had become so much a part of his nature that he treats leftists and rightists with the same irony in *Penguin Island*. And in his last major novel, *The Revolt of the Angels* (1914), he returns once again to the theme that the human race is doomed to go round in circles.

This has often been described as one of France's best books, but I have to admit that, even at the age of seventeen, I found it hard to finish. When compared to other writers of the period—D. H. Lawrence, Proust, Joyce and Hamsun—it seems unbearably trivial. The hero is a young aristocrat, Maurice D'Esparvieu, whose guardian angel Arcade gets bored with the inactivity of looking after a lazy young man, and takes to reading philosophy in the D'Esparvieu library. He decides that science has given the church its death blow, and conceives the idea of a rebellion against God. He plots with many other angels, who have decided that they prefer life as human beings.

Finally, as hundreds of thousands of rebel angels are prepared to march on heaven, they ask Satan to lead them. But that night, Satan has a dream in which his legions conquer, and he occupies the throne of God. And in time, Satan becomes exactly like the God he has deposed; he takes pleasure in hearing his praises sung, and loses all sympathy for humanity. As to the former God, he goes to earth, as Satan once did, to aid humanity.

Waking from this dream, Satan tells his followers that he has decided not to lead them after all. It will only initiate yet another cycle of rebellion and slaughter. Instead, he advises them to remain on earth, which they have all come to love, and to devote themselves to helping humanity. They will have overthrown the tyrant God when they have overcome ignorance and fear.

The Revolt of the Angels is irritating and unsatisfying because the meaning is unclear. By "God," France seems to mean someone like Blake's Old Nobodaddy, the tyrant of the early books of the *Old Testament*. France was still fighting the anti-clerical battle of his teens, even though it had become totally irrelevant by 1914. The message is the same as in Leigh Hunt's poem, *Abou Ben Adam*, in which Abou Ben Adam wakes up to find an angel writing in a book of gold the name of those who love God. Ben Adam asks if his name is among them, and the angel replies no. "Then write me down as one that loves his fellow men," says Ben Adam, and the poem concludes, "And lo, Ben Adam's name led all the rest!" But this is simply a failure to understand the true meaning of religion—man's fundamental desire to transcend himself. France's book leaves behind an impression of silliness, superficiality and bad taste.

France had begun *The Revolt of the Angels* while Mme. Arman was still alive. But their love had died a slow and painful death—at least on his side. Although the same age, she grew old more quickly than he did. In her sixties, she wanted France as a husband—or rather, a second husband; he had come to find her too demanding and tiresome, and wanted his freedom. He set off on a lecture tour of South America, ignoring her pleas to go with him, and had an affair with an actress while he was away. They resumed their affair when he returned, but France was experiencing a second youth, and taking advantage of his fame to sleep with female admirers—as well as young girls who were brought to his house by a procurer. When Mme. Arman died suddenly, he was at first upset—but soon consoled himself by getting her maid, thirty years his junior, to move in as his housekeeper; he was eventually to marry her.

When the French Socialists split with the Communists, France decided to remain with the Communist Party. Yet when someone asked him about the future, he replied, "The future? But my poor friend, there is no future—there is nothing. Everything will begin the same again—people will build things and tear them down, and so on forever. So long as men can't get outside themselves, or free themselves from their passions, nothing will ever change." And France had no doubt whatever that men will never get outside themselves or free themselves from their passions.

If he had believed in the general principle of religion, or of evolution, he might have been less nihilistic. But since he had always equated religion with self-deception, there was no hope of this.

By the time France died at the age of eighty, his reputation had suffered a severe decline. His successor in the Academy, Paul Valery, devoted a speech that should have been a eulogy of France to attacking him.

On rereading *Thais*, I can still understand why I once admired it so much. (When I was twenty I told my friend Bill Hopkins that I would give any dozen of my future books to have written *Thais*.) Yet I can also see in it those faults that led to France's decline. The bigoted Paphnutius is too easy a target. And on close examination, none of the other points of view put forward in the book is any more convincing. The hermit Timocles sits "plunged in beneficent apathy like a delicious bath." The monk's friend Nicias is a skeptic and a sensualist who has very little to offer but tolerance. Dorion is not even a sensualist, having a poor digestion; he is merely a cynic.

The story of Paphutius' temptations when he returns to Thebaid is difficult to credit. His longing for Thais is the response of an adolescent rather than an adult. France implies that Paphnutius would have done better if he had slept with a dozen or so courtesans before he became a Christian convert, and no doubt he is right—although it seems highly unlikely that the son of a wealthy family of Alexandria should reach the age of twenty without losing his virginity. But in any case, Paphnutius' downfall is due to bigotry combined with inexperience; that is, he exaggerates the importance of sex like any adolescent.

And what of the saints and ascetics—including Augustine—who have had their full of carnal delights before they were converted—how does France's argument apply to them? The answer, presumably, is that it doesn't—they would have been capable of converting Thais and returning to an undisturbed life of prayer and contemplation. In which case, France's argument, which is meant to apply to Christianity in general, applies only to his own inexperienced hero, and lacks general application.

The real problem, of course, is that France has nothing very convincing to offer in place of the arguments he is rejecting. He himself attached excessive importance to sex and sensual experience—almost certainly because he had remained a virgin so long. So he advises us to reject the delusions of religion and enjoy the kind of life lived by Nicias and his friends. But to judge by the "banquet," this kind of epicurean existence is pleasant but repetitive.

When we compare France with the Shaw of *Man and Superman* or *Back to Methuselah*, we can see that France's major deficiency lies in his lack of evolutionary sense. He was apparently contented to spend his life traveling around Europe with his mistress, eating gourmet meals, and attending literary parties. This regime would have driven Shaw—or any other serious thinker—to suicide.

Which reminds us that, in spite of the breadth of his reading, France never seems to have read any philosophers, with the exception of Plato. It is true that, when France was a young man, his country was sunk in the materialism of August Comte. But France never seems to have experienced any urge to study the philosophical tradition from Descartes, Locke and Hume to Kant and Hegel. For all his brilliance, his mind was oddly passive and incurious.

He was fortunate that the Dreyfus affair aroused him from his classical slumbers and dragged him into the political arena. But by then he was in his fifties, and too old for any real change. His contribution to French literature had been an amusing skepticism, epitomized in his most famous short story, *The Procurator of Judea*, who complains about the fanaticism of the Jews, and cannot recall a man called Jesus of Nazareth, whom he had once condemned to death. But because France had no convictions to replace the convictions he rejected, his work remains as unsatisfying as a meal consisting entirely of cocktails and hors d'oeuvres.

AFTERWORD: THE SEVENTH DEGREE OF CONCENTRATION

What should be clear by now is that, with rare exceptions, the books that have influenced me have been books that made me think. I have, of course, enjoyed many books that simply tell a "good story"—as a child I devoured Rider Haggard and Edgar Rice Burroughs and R. L. Stevenson, but I am easily sated with mere narrative.

In an essay on Lindsay in *The Strange Genius of David Lindsay* I made a distinction between "high fliers" and "low fliers." High fliers are writers like Dostoevsky, Tolstoy, Shaw and Wells, who want to know what we should do with our lives. Low fliers are writers like Jane Austen, Dickens and Thackeray, who may be intelligent, yet never ask the "big question." Lindsay is, of course, a high flier.

Now the basic problem of human existence seems to me quite clear. It is expressed with great clarity in Hermann Hesse's novel *Steppenwolf*. The hero of that novel has enough money to live comfortably, surrounded by books and gramophone records. Yet he finds his life oddly boring. A certain lukewarmness seems to pervade his everyday consciousness. Yet this can vanish quite abruptly, as when he drinks a glass of wine, and feels his spirit soar aloft like a golden bubble. In such a moment he is reminded "of Mozart and the stars"—in other words, he achieves a kind of "bird's-eye view" of his own existence.

Now it is true that our world is full of appalling tragedy—of mass starvation and injustice. Yet the problem for the average person is not deciding between misery and affirmation—what Carlyle called "Everlasting Yes versus Everlasting No"—but rather, the bird's-eye view, which brings a sense of Everlasting Yes, versus that "lukewarmness"—what Heidegger calls "the triviality of everydayness."

This is a fairly new problem for human beings. Our caveman ancestors found life so difficult that they had no time to be bored. But the human intellect has brought order and discovery to the world, and these have transformed civilization, so that a steadily increasing number of people are able to live lives of relative material comfort. But this comfort has brought the curse of "lukewarm" consciousness, and we long for some simple method of being able to summon those moments "of Mozart and the stars" at will.

It seems to me that all this implies is that mankind has a joint purpose, and that therefore no writer is justified in declaring that human existence is meaningless. This is why I have no patience whatsoever with a writer like Samuel Beckett, who seems to me totally worthless. He spent his life declaring that human existence is meaningless; yet if someone had pushed him into a river, he would have struggled to get out.

The problem with Beckett's work is that he does not think—he is an example of what the novelist Ayn Rand calls "the anti-conceptual mentality." His first novel, *Murphy*, begins, "The sun shone, having no alternative, on the nothing new." Beckett fails to see that he is not stating an objective truth—that the world is full of people who open their eyes in the morning and feel that the world is full of "newness." Beckett would dismiss them—as Artsybashev's Naumov dismisses them in *Breaking Point*—as unthinking optimists, who fail to grasp the sheer futility and repetitiveness of human existence. I could respect Beckett if he took the trouble to justify his views, in the manner of Schopenhauer; then we could point out where his arguments cease to be objective. But he will not stay to argue; he declares that existence is so meaningless that reason is a waste of time. Yet the sentence "Reason is a waste of time" is a rational statement that reveals that Beckett has to make use of reason from the moment he wakes up in the morning until he goes to bed at night. Like all pessimists—as I have tried to show in the case of Huysmans, Andreyev and Artsybashev—his views are simply self-contradictory.

But the real objection to Beckett and his fellow pessimists is that they poison our cultural heritage, and in that sense are as culpable as someone who puts poison in a city's water supply. They actively impede the evolution of the human race. For they propagate the "passive fallacy," the notion (fostered also by Cartesian philosophy) that we are merely passive observers looking at a world that we can do little to influence, just as we can do little to influence our own consciousness.

Now I have frequently cited the case of Graham Greene, who plunged into a state of depressive consciousness in his teens, until he decided to play Russian roulette with a revolver and live ammunition. He placed the revolver to his head and pulled the trigger; when the hammer clicked on an empty chamber, he experienced a surge of recognition that the world was full of "infinite possibilities." He also uses the significant phrase, "It was as if a light had been turned on," clearly implying that he felt that he was seeing something, not merely "feeling" it.

What had happened was that shock had blown away his boredom, like the wind blowing away clouds. But it was the sudden convulsion of his own mind that transformed his consciousness, not the revolver.

Abraham Maslow called this kind of convulsion of happiness the "peak experience." But he discovered that "natural peakers" were people whose attitude to life was optimistic and purposive, and who were not inclined to surrender to their own laziness or self-pity. The human mind is like the human hand; it can clench into a fist, or simply hang slack. When Greene pulled the trigger, his mind suddenly "clenched," and it was this clenching action that caused the surge of optimism. Our minds are not passive or paralyzed. Beckett's mind had fallen into a kind of paralysis due to laziness (he admitted that he was inclined to stay in bed all day because he could see no reason for getting up). So the muscles had atrophied until he found it difficult to clench or stretch them.

But the paralysis was due largely to the fact that his intellect had ratified his laziness, convincing him that there was no point in making any effort. And Beckett did his best to spread his paralysis to the rest of the human race. And such was the confusion and irrationality that prevailed in his time, and to a large extent still prevails, that he was awarded the Nobel Prize for his efforts to discourage us all. In Artsybashev's time, the instinct for health and meaning was stronger; no one suggested that Artsybashev deserved the Nobel Prize for *Breaking Point.*

For many years, I sought some method that might produce the same effect as Greene's Russian roulette, inducing an instant peak experience. More recently, I have come to recognize that we already know the basic method.

For example, during the writing of this book, I found that one of the files on my disk had corrupted—it was the one on Huysmans—and I had no copy. My son Rowan spent half a day trying to recover it on his computer (I use an old-fashioned word processor). Finally, he brought me the text on a new disk. But all its words had run together, all its commas had vanished, and meaningless symbols had inserted themselves into the text.

I proceeded to "unscramble" it, and spent most of the day at this unrewarding activity. Yet I experienced no boredom, for I was too relieved to have recovered the chapter. I realized clearly that our boredom is a function of our assumption that something is not worth doing.

The next morning, I still had three pages to "unscramble." And this time, instead of merely working patiently at the text, I concentrated my full attention on it, as if my life depended on it, knitting my eyebrows and scowling like a madman. Almost immediately, I experienced a marvelous sense of control and meaning—I found myself regretting that I only had three pages to unscramble. Then it struck me that it made no difference what I was doing. If I chose to concentrate my attention on blowing my nose, it would have the same effect of creating a sense of control and of potentiality.

Such experiences make us suddenly aware that consciousness can achieve a far higher level of meaning-perception, and can maintain it by a small but continuous effort. The reason that no great effort is required is that once "attention" has closed the usual leaks of mental energy, it is not difficult to maintain it.

The importance of sex lies in its ability to focus the mind, to give us a glimpse of the possibilities of consciousness.

It seems to me that its major possibility can be quite easily expressed. It will be remembered that William James began to recover from his nervous breakdown when he read Renouvier's remark that the proof of free will lies in the fact that we can think one thing rather than another. I can break off this chain of thought to think about my childhood, or what we are having for dinner tonight, or the implications of Gödel's theorem.

But although it is true that I can change the current of my thought, it is not so easy to change the current of my feeling. I can recall what

I felt like on Christmas day as a child, or the first time I saw mountain scenery, or when my first book was accepted. But the glimpse lasts only a split second, then vanishes.

Yet there are moments when I seem to be able to control my feelings as well as my thoughts. If I am lying in bed on a cold winter morning, and I have to get up in ten minutes, I can somehow focus my mind on the warmth of the bed and wallow in contentment until the moment I have to climb out. I can remember the same sensation as a child, listening to the patter of rain on the windows, or sitting inside a "house" made of cardboard boxes, broom handles and an old counterpane. In my teens, I learned to control my moods by reading poetry or listening to music. And on rare occasions of happy relaxation, I seem to be able to control my feelings as easily as I can control a car with power steering. Yet under ordinary circumstances, my feelings respond to my attempt to "steer" them as uncooperatively as one of those dodgem cars at a fairground.

In my childhood, I often lay awake at night, trying hard to get to sleep, feeling thoroughly bored with my thoughts, which insisted on pursuing their own course. In recent years, I have begun to learn the trick of lying awake and enjoying my thoughts, enjoying the warmth of the bed, enjoying the drift into dreams and out again.

It seems to me that this ability to "steer" our feelings, and even our physical states (which closely echo our feelings), is a natural potentiality of consciousness, which human beings will one day take for granted as much as they now take their ability to "steer" the body in any direction they wish to walk.

The simplest way of recognizing that consciousness can be "steered" is to consider the implications of states of crisis.

When we experience any kind of relief from crisis, we catch a glimpse of the possibility of a totally affirmative consciousness. Yet once the relief has passed, we find it virtually impossible to understand what we saw.

The puzzle is this. It is not difficult to understand why Graham Greene experienced a tremendous sense of affirmation when the hammer clicked on an empty chamber, or why Dostoevsky felt that his reprieve was a kind of religious revelation. But then, as he stood in front of the firing squad, Dostoevsky had already recognized what he was about to lose; in other words, he had already achieved a "bird's-eye view" of the world and his own life.

But we glimpse the same insight when the cause is relatively trivial. On my way back from a walk with my dogs, I grope in my pocket for the car keys and find they are missing. And just as I am reconciling myself to the thought of walking a mile to the nearest phone box and ringing my wife, I find that they have slipped through a hole in the lining. Such an "emergency" is hardly life threatening, yet it brings, for a moment, exactly that same sense that life is infinitely valuable. Why?

The glimpse is akin to the "holiday feeling"—that feeling of expansiveness and sheer joy we often experience when setting out on holiday. But that is easy to understand. The combination of relaxation and pleasant anticipation awakens our senses, and enables us to remove the kind of pressure we feel obliged to concentrate upon the present moment. This enables us to stand back and "count our blessings." But why should losing, and then finding, a car key produce the same effect?

The answer, I suspect, lies partly in the experience of Abraham Maslow. Maslow discovered that when his students began to talk to one another about their own peak experiences, they began to have peak experiences all the time. That is because the peak experience reminds us of what Graham Greene glimpsed when the hammer clicked on the chamber: that life is infinitely exciting.

But how is it possible for us to forget this? The answer lies in the nature of the evolution of human consciousness. In order to survive, we have had to learn to focus consciousness narrowly on the problems of the present. Most men spend their lives going back and forth to work; most women spend their lives in household chores. Now our state of cheerfulness depends upon how far we are succeeding with the present task. If it goes badly, we experience a certain depression, a "sinking feeling." This sinking feeling, of course, only applies to the present task; but since the present task occupies our whole internal horizon, then this horizon is darkened by thunderclouds from end to end. If you are staring at the sky through a telescope, then one single cloud can give the impression of an overcast day, although it may be the only cloud in an otherwise blue sky.

Emergency has the effect of causing us to remove the telescope from the eye and take a broader view. And peak experiences remind us that everyday consciousness is a kind of tunnel, and that we only have to remove the telescope to see how much we have to be grateful for.

In other words, we are "trapped" in everyday consciousness. But this is not the fault of everyday consciousness; it is our own fault. Life has taught us to "keep our noses to the grindstone," and we tend to do it from force of habit. If my wife calls me to say my dinner is ready when I am writing a letter, I abandon the letter reluctantly—even though I prefer eating my dinner. My desire to "get things done" is so strong that I have to overcome a certain reluctance to abandon the letter.

As a child, I found it impossible to understand "workaholics" like my father, who had an evening job in addition to his daytime work in a factory. But within a year or two, driven on by ambition, and a desire to escape the kind of life my father led, I spent all my time writing stories and essays that were invariably rejected. Wordsworth had remarked that "shades of the prison house begin to close" around the growing youth; now I had to come to terms with the paradox that we encourage them to close around us.

What can be done about this? This analysis suggests the basic answer. The problem is that consciousness seems to have a compulsive tendency to contract into "tunnel vision." This hardly matters; we need tunnel vision to enable us to work with maximum efficiency. The problem is that when tunnel vision is combined with discouragement, the result is a lowering of inner pressure. And we can become so accustomed to living and working at reduced pressure that it becomes a permanent condition. We begin to live "on the defensive," as it were, and all sense of pleasurable anticipation about the future evaporates. When this happens, trivial worries can plunge the mind into a permanent state of what Kierkegaard called angst. One step beyond that lies mental breakdown. (The novelist William Styron has provided a powerful description of such a breakdown in his book *Darkness Visible*—from which it also emerges that he has no insight whatsoever into the processes that led to the breakdown.)

We can be saved from tunnel vision by being shocked into wakefulness, as in the case of Greene or Dostoevsky. The problem lies in a combination of forgetfulness and laziness. Maslow's students reminded one another of the "bird's-eye view," until perception of the bird's-eye view became a kind of habit. Sartre acquired the same habit during the war, when the threat of arrest and torture kept him in a state of high alertness.

But then Sartre, like Graham Greene, had made it virtually impossible to take any long-term advantage of this insight because his pessimistic philosophy negated it. I have labored in this volume to make the point that long-term artistic development and negative philosophy are incompatible. I have also tried to show that the kind of negative philosophy indulged in by so many writers of the twentieth century is not in accordance with the facts. Pessimistic philosophy is an outcome of the combination of laziness and forgetfulness mentioned above. It has no objective justification. When "the facts" are seen objectively, in a state of "wakefulness," they justify Chesterton's sense of "absurd good news," or Greene's recognition that life is full of infinite possibilities.

The basic answer, as Doctor Johnson recognized, lies in concentration of the mind. I have experienced it perhaps half a dozen times in the past twenty years, most notably as I drove through heavy snow returning from a lecture in Devon, and again on a train journey to Northampton to address a publisher's conference—both are described in a book called *Beyond the Occult*. On both occasions I recognized clearly the truth of Husserl's insight that consciousness is intentional. Our relationship to objects of perception is not passive, like a sponge absorbing water; it is active.

A better analogy might be a game of tennis. When we are lazy and mechanical, we play a purely defensive game; yet we are still forced to hit the ball, for all perception is intentional. But when consciousness achieves something like its proper level of vitality, we play a highly aggressive game, and can feel intentionality in action. In such moments we grasp the true nature of consciousness and the possibilities for human evolution, if we could truly understand this and escape from the fallacy of passive perception.

It seems to me that this leads to an insight which could transform our lives.

We think of consciousness as a mirror, and that what we see in that mirror is "real." This shows a total failure to grasp the nature of human consciousness.

It works by a process of attention and compression, and the faculty called imagination—or "the reality function"—is central to its operation.

Consider Yeats' lines from *Lullaby*:

> *What were all the world's alarms*
> *To mighty Paris when he found*
> *Sleep upon a golden bed*
> *That first dawn in Helen's arms.*

The sheer ecstasy of finally possessing Helen must have transformed his consciousness, so that he felt that no problem could defeat him.

But look more closely at the phenomenology of sexual excitement, and you become aware that it operates through a series of movements of "compression." The first excitement causes us to focus the attention, and to achieve a still higher level of excitement and of focus.

Shaw makes Captain Shotoever say that what he wants to achieve is the "seventh degree of concentration." Imagine seven concentric circles, and that each new level of excitement causes the mind to contract within the next circle, bringing a still higher sense of control.

I am not now speaking simply about sexual excitement, but of every form of conscious intensity: the enjoyment of music, of art, of setting out on holiday, of physical achievement in sport, of the brilliant flash of insight that solves a problem.

When we throw a stone in a pond, concentric rings move outward. Imagine, instead, these same rings moving inward, and you have an image of the basic operation of consciousness.

When you are feeling tired and dull, consciousness is relaxed and passive, and you feel that the physical world is the only reality. As soon as something captures your interest, you move inside that "first circle" of concentration. This is what happens, for example, when you read a newspaper or casually watch television.

If you suddenly see a story that deeply interests you, you focus your attention, and move inside the second circle.

If you become excited—for example, watching your favorite sport on television—you achieve the "third degree of concentration."

Sexual arousal also passes through these three phases—attention, focus, excitement.

Mystics and ascetics recognize the central importance of this process, and deliberately set out to strengthen the "muscle" that aids concentration.

What they have achieved is a certain philosophical recognition. Things are not "as they are." Reality is not what it appears to be. Everyday reality is a mere reflection in a mirror before we achieve the first degree of concentration. It is like looking at a page of print and not "taking it in." This is the state Hemingway described when he said, "You know that's all there is." Sartre called it "nausea."

The first act of concentration brings the print into focus, and causes us to recognize that it has meaning.

The second degree of concentration makes us unaware of the print, as if it has become transparent. We are seeing through it to the events were are reading about.

We should now be able to grasp that, in a perfectly straightforward sense, "everyday reality" is untrue.

Now our notion that everyday reality is "true" is accompanied by another delusion. When you read a newspaper paragraph, you know that the "meanings" have been put there by the journalist who wrote it. When you look at a tree, you feel it has no underlying meaning—apart from what your perception reveals—because no one "wrote" it.

Yet when a poet looks at a tree, in the "third degree of concentration," he is overwhelmed with a sense of its meaning.

When the mystic Jacob Boehme looked at a tree, he seemed to see inside it, to its inner life. He called this vision "the signature of all things." In other words, the tree had ceased to be "merely itself," and was somehow related to everything else. Boehme had achieved the fourth degree of concentration.

We can see that a man who has achieved this fourth degree of concentration would always have a weapon against boredom and tiredness. He would know that everyday perception is partial, incomplete, and that far deeper meanings lie below its surface. All he has to do is to begin that act of concentration.

Maslow's students had achieved this vital insight by discussing peak experiences; this is why they could achieve peak experiences at will.

At the present point in his evolution, man is still trapped in the animal stage. His attitude towards the world is essentially passive.

Yet man has evolved beyond the other animals because his attitude to his own existence is so much less passive than theirs. He is always trying to change things. And this desire to change things has created civilization, and made him the most evolved creature on the surface of the earth.

Yet his conscious attitude towards his perception of the world remains passive. He accepts that "everyday perception" is the truth. This could be compared to a short-sighted man believing that the blurred vision he experiences without his glasses is "truer" than the clearer focus he achieves when he puts them on.

Man is taken in by a confidence trickster; but it is his own fault, because the confidence trickster is his naiveté. It is true that he makes instinctive attempts to control his consciousness—through such simple means as alcohol, sex, sport, holidays—but in a sense, these only make things worse, for he wrongly assumes that the means have changed his state of awareness, failing to realize that they have simply caused him to focus his attention.

Yet he merely has to recognize that the act of focusing attention causes a deeper perception of meaning to stand on the threshold of a new step in human evolution.

This is the purpose of literature—not just great literature, but of all literature: to become so absorbed in an imaginary world that we become suddenly aware that in the battle between the world and the mind, it is the mind that is destined to win.

ABOUT THE AUTHOR

Colin Wilson was born in Leicester, England, June 26, 1931, son of a boot and shoe worker. He became fascinated by chemistry and astronomy at the age of 10, won a scholarship to the Gateway Secondary School at the age of 11, but left at 16, the family not having enough money to think in terms of university. "After a few months of intense misery working in a wool factory," he decided that he wanted to be a writer, not a scientist. "I began writing a vast sequel to Shaw's *Man and Superman*, and a book called *The Quintessence of Shavianism*. At this point, my old school offered me a job as a lab assistant and I remained there a year, until it became obvious to everyone that I had lost interest in science, and they regretfully sacked me."

After a stint in the Civil Service and the RAF, he spent several years wandering around England, taking odd jobs. In 1953, he met his future wife Joy, "whom I persuaded to break her engagement and come to London with me. (We have been together ever since.)"

From spring to autumn 1954, he slept out on Hampstead Heath in a sleeping bag to save rent, while writing during the day in the Reading Room of the British Museum, working on his first novel, *Ritual in the Dark*, and planning a book about existential philosophy, to be called *The Outsider in Literature*.

Wilson says, "I was lucky; *The Outsider* was accepted by the first publisher to whom I sent an outline and some extracts—Victor Gollancz. Published in the last week of May 1956, it received an unprecedented reception from serious critics, and—as journalist Kenneth Allsop wrote—I 'woke up to find myself famous.' The book became a bestseller in England and America, and was translated into a dozen languages. Suddenly, to my bewilderment, I found myself making TV and radio broadcasts, lecturing at universities, and being endlessly written about in the gossip columns."

Fleeing the endless complications of publicity, the Wilsons took the advice of Gollancz and moved to Cornwall, where they still live. There he completed his second book, *Religion and the Rebel*, and went on writing: five more volumes of "the *Outsider* cycle," an *Encyclopedia of Murder*, and a series of novels. Wilson says, "In 'the *Outsider* cycle' it became clear that what I was doing was creating a 'New Existentialism' (summarized in a book of that title) with a positive and evolutionary bias, as contrasted with the nihilistic existentialism of Heidegger, Sartre, and Camus. I still regard this as my major achievement."

In the late '60s he was asked to write a book on "the occult." Initially something of a skeptic, he became convinced of the reality of the paranormal, and produced the quarter-of-a-million-word volume *The Occult* (1971), which achieved the same kind of success as *The Outsider* and sold even more. With the late Dr. Christopher Evans, he edited a series of books, *The Supernatural*, for Aldus Books, and wrote several more volumes on the paranormal, of which the most important are *Mysteries* (1978) and *Beyond the Occult* (1989). Other books on the paranormal include *Poltergeist*, *Afterlife*, and *The Psychic Detectives*.

The Wilsons have three children, Sally, Damon, and Rowan. His sons have coauthored a number of books on crime and unsolved mysteries with him. In thirty-five years he has written more than eighty books, falling mainly into four categories: existential philosophy, criminology, the paranormal, and psychology (including biographies of Wilhelm Reich and Abraham Maslow). He has also produced twenty novels, three plays, and a CD recording, *The Essential Colin Wilson*, consisting of him reading selections from that title.

"I suppose my main departure in the 1990s has been my interest in the problem of ancient civilizations. It began when I was asked to write a film outline on Atlantis for Dino DiLaurentis, and decided to base it on John Anthony West's theory (derived from Schwaller de Lubicz) that the Sphinx was probably built thousands of years earlier than is generally supposed, by survivors from Atlantis. A series of serendipities led to contact with John Anthony West, Graham Hancock, Robert Bauval, Rand Flem-Ath, and others, and led to the writing of *From Atlantis to the Sphinx* (not my title, but my publisher's, alas—I wanted to call it *Before the Sphinx*). It sold well, and Virgin commissioned me to write a book on the possibility of extraterrestrial life, which became *Alien Dawn*, due out here in May and in the United States in October (Fromm)."

In the past five years he has lectured regularly in America, Australia, and Japan.

Hampton Roads Publishing Company

. . .for the evolving human spirit

Hampton Roads Publishing Company
publishes books on a variety of subjects including
metaphysics, health, complementary medicine,
visionary fiction, and other related topics.

For a copy of our latest catalog,
call toll-free, 800-766-8009,
or send your name and address to:

Hampton Roads Publishing Company
134 Burgess Lane
Charlottesville, VA 22902
e-mail: hrpc@hrpub.com